BECOMING

HUMAN

A NEW PERSPECTIVE ON THE ORIGINS OF THE HUMAN MIND

BECOMING
HUMAN

A NEW PERSPECTIVE ON THE ORIGINS OF THE HUMAN MIND

JOSEPH COLLIER, SR.

BECOMING HUMAN
A New Perspective on the Origins of the Human Mind

JOSEPH COLLIER, SR.

GREENBRIAR PUBLISHING
WILLIAMSTOWN, VERMONT

3

BECOMING HUMAN
A New Perspective on the Origins of the Human Mind

Greenbriar Publishing
P. O. Box 751
Williamstown, Vermont 05679

ISBN: 978-0-9767373-1-5
Printed in the United States of America

Please visit online:
www.josephcollier.org

BECOMING HUMAN
A New Perspective on the Origins of the Human Mind

Acknowledgements

I especially want to thank my lovely wife, Andrea M. Levesque, as well as my brother, Durwood C. Collier, for their inestimable assistance in the editing and proofing of "Becoming Human." They have given unstintingly of their time, energy, and judgment, and it is very much appreciated!

As well, I want to thank my children, Hillary, Lauren, and Joseph Jr. for their thoughtful input into my studies over the years, as well as for their support and encouragement! Much love to you guys always!

BECOMING HUMAN
A New Perspective on the Origins of the Human Mind

Table of Contents

BECOMING HUMAN
A New Perspective on the Origins of the Human Mind

Preface

When I was a fourteen-year-old boy growing up in Vermont, I made what to me was an astounding observation that changed the course of my life. It caused me to begin a lifelong interest in the social sciences and related areas.

It all began (as do many things) with a girl, or rather; a small group of them. I was at my first dance. The other boys and I were clustered together as far from the girls as it was possible to get without physically leaving the venue, but close enough so that we could still surveil them with the intensity and fervor only possible in boys of that age. The girls were beautiful, mysterious, and fascinating. We were terrified.

Resplendent in their finery, they clustered around the punch bowl in much the same way as we *supposed* panthers patiently mind a waterhole, knowing that, at some point, the prey would need to drink (or so we imagined). Filled with apprehension and suffering from the dry mouth that invariably attends such a state of undifferentiated anxiety, several of us hesitantly approached the waterhole, our thirst overcoming our trepidation.

The reaction of the girls was unexpected and totally inexplicable to us, as they immediately began to exaggerate their gestures upon our approach. Flourishing their arms in elaborate gesticulations, their voices rose almost as one as they began to giggle incessantly. In my fevered child's psyche, they had ceased acting the way they normally did, and had, as with a single mind, it seemed, commenced behaving like a flock of...birds? Very alluring birds, but birds? I was speechless.

Their curiously beguiling behavior truly appeared to be instinctive, but I knew these girls from school, and they were my friends. I knew them to be smart, capable, and studious. I couldn't understand what had happened. I was totally vexed. It seemed as if they had spontaneously reverted to the instinctive behavior of a bower bird in full courtship display.

We boys were not prepared for that! Rather than entice us with their resplendence as intended, it totally unnerved us. In retrospect, the girls were as unsure as we boys were, in terms of knowing (or not knowing) how to act. We were all equally unsure together, and it was charmingly naive and innocent on all of our parts.

Our mission completed, we (casually) fled the waterhole without further incident; our thirst slaked, our interest piqued, and our confusion complete. What had just happened? We had no idea. It got me thinking, though, and I began to consider other human behaviors in light of this. Armed with this insight, and much to my amazement, I soon began to notice that boys were doing very similarly irrational things, and then, I noticed that adults were. Are humans truly rational, I began to wonder? I still do.

After the "water hole incident," I started to become fascinated by human behavior, but more importantly, what was behind the behavior? What is the nature of human nature? There is a correct answer or answers out there, of course. It hangs just beyond our reach, but perhaps; within our grasp.

I deeply wanted to know how humans became the creatures we are. Toward this end, I earned a degree in psychology, and then, a graduate degree in psychology. I was working on yet another graduate degree before it finally dawned on me that the answers I was seeking weren't in the courses I was taking. I realized that if I was going to understand these things, I was going to have to try to figure it out largely on my own, with the very capable assistance of the myriad of researchers on whom I depend, many who appear in the References/Bibliography section.

I have written this book in an attempt to share my sometimes radical observations, theories, and conclusions with others. I know it can be difficult to diverge from dogma, but if people never departed from doctrinaire views, there would be no progress. All new ideas present this challenge, so prepare to be challenged.

Initially, I simply wanted to satisfy my curiosity, which remains the best reason to do anything. As I work alone, I can indulge myself (it's one of my favorite things to do). If someone reads this book and finds it to be in keeping with what they think, that is wonderful. It is for each of us to make up our own minds as to what we personally believe. There exists a beautiful democracy of the mind in which enlightenment is the ultimate goal, and the most valuable truths are those that we ourselves discover.

In this book, I tell the amazing story of our species' evolutionary rise over a 4 billion year period. What I sought were good explanations as to why humans have developed the way that we have. These explanations needed to apply equally to all people everywhere, and not be based on any particular group, but everyone universally. They needed to not be my own observations of a specific population, extrapolated to include everyone else. Primarily, they needed to answer my questions.

I believe that I have accomplished my task, but there remains much more to do. This has been a complex process and has taken me many years to arrive at a full set of interrelated theories that apply equally to every member of our species. These theories all appear in this book. You will never have seen any of them prior to this, as they've never before been published. Having an open mind and critical thinking abilities are more important than prior exposure to the material. I will say when my theories digress from or agree with those of others. I will also clarify if a theory is mine or not.

Note: I strongly suggest you read the book from front to back to avoid confusion. The first few chapters are necessarily fact-heavy, and much of the rest of the book is based upon them. Most of the other chapters, though, pertain to specific observations, hypotheses, and theories.

It is said that there's nothing new under the sun. In reality, though, every single thing conceived by a human mind was new at some point in time. That which is new is often radical, as radical means very different from the usual or traditional. That which is novel is not necessarily radical, but that which is radical is invariably novel. I also have some radical theories in these pages, and I would like to share them.

How did I determine where to look for such answers as I sought? After trying nearly everything else first, I went back in time. Deep time became my traveling companion, as I journeyed back to the early days of humanity, and kept on going. I went back to the eras of the early mammals, reptiles, amphibians, and kept on going. Eventually, I arrived back at the very beginning of over 4 billion years of life on Earth, and started there. Where I finish will surprise you.

Joseph Collier, Sr.
Morrisville, Vermont

BECOMING HUMAN
A New Perspective on the Origins of the Human Mind
Chapter 1

In the Beginning

Although there is considerable disagreement as to the exact dates when many events from earth's early years occurred, the consensus is that the actual earth formed about 4.54 billion years[1] ago, and the oceans formed several hundred million years later after the Late Heavy Bombardment period[2]. Comets very thoughtfully supplied much of the necessary water.

The story of life's somewhat inauspicious origin commenced about 3.5 to 4.2 billion years[3] ago in earth's oceans, with the first life form to appear, dubbed Archaea. Archaea[4], a single-celled organism lacking a cellular nucleus, formed one of the three 'Domains' of life, as espoused in the 1970s by Dr. Carl Woese and colleagues at the University of Illinois[5]. Bacteria and Eukaryota constitute the other two domains in Woese's theories, and all three are still well-represented in the world of today. Many believe that Bacteria arose at the same time as Archaea. Still others hold that there are more domains than three, but that is beyond the scope of this work. Three domains will suffice quite nicely for our purposes.

The first relatively complex animal life on our planet appeared in the form of organisms referred to as 'comb jelly[6],' of the phylum Ctenophora, as much as 700 million years ago. It should be noted that Ctenophores resemble (but are not) jellyfish, with 8 propulsion cilia arranged similarly to the teeth of a comb; hence, the unusual appellation. Thought to be extinct more than 400 million years ago, species of comb jelly are still in existence. In fact, a NOAA research submersible recently discovered a new species of comb jelly at great depths off the coast of Puerto Rico[7]. Judging from this, it would appear that comb jelly has had a 700 million year run! Now that's longevity!

About 600 million years ago (some would say longer, but I am being conservative), Urmetazoans[8], very primitive creatures closely resembling sponges, evolved Cnidarians, which possessed many novel and important characteristics such as a nervous system and muscles that worked in concert with each other. Cnidarians[9] communicated by means of the first neural net[10], an early conglomeration of neurons spread throughout the body. Not only that, but Cnidarians achieved radial symmetry and a definite body shape. As if that weren't enough, they had eyes!

Cnidarians were very special creatures in that they possessed the evolutionary miracle that was so incredibly difficult to evolve that it took billions of years: the neuron! Neurons[11] are the most complex cells that animals possess, and are the basis for all nervous systems from the crudest neural net through the far more sophisticated central nervous system (CNS) to the most complex human cerebral cortex. The earliest neuron precursors were most probably either choanocytes or mesenchymal cells, depending on who you ask (controversy abounds).

Around 550 million years ago, in the so-called Cambrian Explosion[12], a variety of Deuterostomes[13] developed a very, very crude brain-like structure, as well as bilateral symmetry. Approximately 540 million years ago, one of the very earliest ancestors of our species was a 'bag-like' creature named Saccorhytus Coronarius[14]. Very tiny and unassuming, they were only about a millimeter in diameter. Deuterostomes differ from protosomes like Saccorhytus Coronarius in that the former had both a mouth and anus, while the latter possessed only a mouth.

First discovered as microfossils in China among equally-sized grains of sand, this wriggling mini-monstrosity possessed an enormously outsized mouth and no anus, the mouth serving the role of both orifices. That's a direct ancestor of humans, lest we forget. I think it's always a good thing to inject a bit of humility into any examination of ourselves, lest we remake ourselves into something too god-like. To paraphrase Winston Churchill: If we are humble, perhaps it is because we have much to be humble about.

About 500 million years ago, the first vertebrates[15] appeared in the form of jawless fish with cartilaginous skeletons similar to modern lampreys. A mere 20 million years later (or 480 million years ago), jawed fish[16] with bony skeletons appeared. With the appearance of a bony skeleton, the frames of animals could be much stronger and robust. This made possible many new adaptations. The hinged jaw was one of these sorts of new structures made possible by the increased strength of improved bony material. Even greater improvements were to come as a result of the enormous leap that occurred through the substitution of bone for cartilage. Larger animals with a cartilaginous skeleton can operate fine in water, but they don't fare as well on land due to the greater effects of air not supporting their buoyant bodies as naturally occurs in the water. Larger and stronger animals are now on the horizon, and they are not going to stop when they reach the shore.

Only 10 to 20 million years after that (which is a blink of an eye in geological terms), tetrapods[17] with four limbs evolved to exploit the many delicacies to be found in the shallow water along shorelines. Tetrapods were fish with a flattened skull and a two-lobed brain, making them neuronally somewhat capable. Their front limbs bent backward at the elbow and forward at the knees, which in itself represented a huge evolutionary breakthrough presaging the development of limbs that could flex. With front and back legs that could bend, a tetrapod could take advantage of nearly any coastal environment and tides while remaining wet.

Then, around 375 million years ago, Tiktaalik[18] became one of the earliest fish to (at least partially) come ashore. Possessing many of the bodily structures that humans still possess, such as legs, elbows, wrists, shoulders, and a neck, Tiktaalik could take advantage of the many edible goodies forever beyond the reach of a water-bound fish. One of the best ways to corner the market on a certain type of food is to adapt a capability that only you can exploit. Tetrapods and Tiktaalik both took that approach in much the same way that modern-day giraffes have. Creatures commonly create their own ecological niche in their environment, and it is a constantly repeating theme in the evolution of species in all epochs.

Within about 10 million years, or around 365 million years ago, Acanthostega[18], a primitive amphibian[146], did something nearly unthinkable: it came ashore! It wasn't well-suited to land and its limbs could not completely support its weight for very long, but it did possess both gills and lungs. Luckily for Aconthostega, there was not much competition on terra firma at the time, so it did just fine.

Around 310 to 320 million years ago (there are, of course, numerous beliefs as to exactly when), the first known reptile, Hylonomus[19], evolved from amphibians and moved onto the land. It was a small insectivorous reptile about 8 inches long, and like all amniota, laid its eggs on land. The reptile's nervous system was significantly advanced from that of amphibians, as Hylonomus possessed 12 cranial nerve pairs and a sizable brain for the period, judged by paleontologists to be similar in size to that of modern amphibians. There is, unsurprisingly, no small amount of controversy as to whether Hylonomus was fully reptilian, or if it was still partially amphibian. Either way, Hylonomus was a definite trendsetter for the numerous reptile species that followed.

"By 360 million years ago, our ancestors had colonized the land, eventually giving rise to the first mammals about 200 million years ago. **These creatures already had a small neocortex – extra**

18

layers of neural tissue on the surface of the brain responsible for the complexity and flexibility of mammalian behavior. How and when did this crucial region evolve? That remains a mystery.

Living amphibians and reptiles do not have a direct equivalent, and since their brains do not fill their entire skull cavity, fossils tell us little about the brains of our amphibian and reptilian ancestors".

(Bold is mine.) *Robson, David. (September 2011)NewScientist.https://www.newscientist.com/ article/mg21128311-800-a-brief-history-of-the-brain/#ixzz6x2zdkZwB. Citation #168)*

360 million years ago refers to the initial amphibian incursion onto the land. The first reptile, it is believed, was Hylonomus lyelli, who lived in the Late Carboniferous period. It is, unfortunately, extinct. After Hylonomus, numerous other reptilian species rapidly arose to fill the numerous ecological niches made possible by their many unique adaptations.

Unlike amphibians, Hylonomus was able to complete its breeding cycle terrestrially, and no water need be added. Their eggs were nestled in amniotic fluid much like the ocean water from which their ancestors came, and a durable shell protected the developing embryo even as it allowed it to remain hydrated.

The reptilian evolution of the egg was one of the most monumental developments in the history of life on earth! Suddenly, nearly the entire surface of the earth was open for colonization, and colonize they did. As the reptile invasion of the land proceeded, many new species evolved as the exigencies of varied environments called for a great diversity of different characteristics to burgeon. Soon after the reptiles arrived, they split into two separate branches, the sauropsids, and the synapsids[20]. The sauropsids developed into what we now refer to as dinosaurs, modern birds, and reptiles, while the synapsids became mammals.

The earliest reptiles that were like mammals were the Pelycosaurs[21], which appeared around 260 million years ago. Pelycosaurs were primitive synapsids, characterized by one, rather than two skull openings where the jaw muscles attach, whereas true reptiles have two such openings. Pelycosaurs gave rise to the therapsids[22], who possessed even more mammalian characteristics, including a secondary palate. This adaptation allowed an animal to eat and breathe simultaneously, indicating a creature more capable of vigorous activity than one without a secondary palate.

Inevitably, evolution works its will through large numbers of small adaptations. Slowly and steadily, creatures incrementally assumed a form better suited to the requirements of the specific environments in which they found themselves. The result was that there are often numerous species whose bodies became an admixture of elements usually associated with one type of creature or another, such as a creature that appears to be part reptile and part mammal.

As strange as that may be to consider, it is still far easier than it would be to visualize a mammal springing forth fully formed from the loins of a reptile, which makes absolutely no sense in terms of providing true survival benefits. I mean, is he in an egg? Is his reptilian mother going to attempt to nurse him? There is a reason that evolution favors small and incremental adaptations, even if it might be puzzling to paleontologists. How can we be sure that our distant ancestors were reptilian? Perhaps the fact that human fetuses have distinctly atavistic reptilian musculature at an early period of their development might convince you[169]?

Cynodonts[23] evolved from therapsids. Therapsids were true reptiles, but with many mammalian characteristics. Cynodonts were even more mammalian than therapsids. All mammals, including humans, are cynodonts, but cynodonts are not mammals. They evolved numerous and diverse species beginning around 260 million years ago. Some becoming carnivores, while others became herbivorous. Although cynodonts gave rise to mammals, the non-mammalian Tritylodontid cynodonts themselves became extinct around 100 million years ago, in the Early Cretaceous[24]. Very possibly, they were out-competed by the mammals. We can only hope that cynodonts had a sense of irony, at least, but it's highly doubtful.

Although there is much controversy about exactly when warm-bloodedness enters the picture, it is well established that it began in the Permian[25] period; from around 300 to 250 (more precisely calculated at 251.9 million years ago), when the Triassic[26] period began. The transition between the Permian and the Triassic periods was geologically tumultuous, to say the least. The temperature of the planet rose intensely and abruptly, causing the greatest mass extinctions in the entire history of Earth. With over 90% of all terrestrial species and over 95% of sea life becoming extinct, it is a time known as "The Great Dying."[27] Just to give you an idea of the extent of the devastation that was being wrought, the great majority of what is now Siberia had become a sea of lava!

It is believed that warm-blooded cynodonts evolved a means to regulate body temperatures during the cooler Permian period, as glaciation increased. In the late Permian period, however, the formation of the supercontinent Pangaea[28] caused the temperature to spike. Luckily for cynodonts, the same ability to regulate their internal temperature in cold weather also helped them survive extreme global warming.

Around 220 million years ago (although some say it is closer to 200 million), the first true mammals evolved from cynodonts. Morganucodons[29] are considered to be the first true mammals (that have been discovered at this point in time, anyway). It is entirely possible that new contenders for this particular title may arise. These small, nocturnal, secretive shrew-like creatures are, unfortunately, extinct.

Although there were several distinct mammalian lines at that time, only the Morganucodontids survived, and every mammal in the world is descended from them. Many new features accompanied this evolutionary leap to mammals. They fed their young by lactation and had a regulated body temperature. Most importantly, though, Morganucodons had evolved a more capable neocortex than any other animal, at that point. In comparison with other creatures inhabiting the world of the Triassic, this made them very, very smart. Every mammal's evolutionary trajectory from that point forward was ineluctably altered by this world-shaking neuronal adaptation.

It is very commonly (but incorrectly) believed by some that the neocortex first appeared in mammals. In actuality, though, the first neocortex[30] appeared in fish about 360 million years ago. It had, therefore, been evolving for about 140 million years[31] prior to the appearance of the mammals. The neocortex (which has an analogous structure called the pallium[32] in reptiles, birds, and fish), has evolved more than any other neuronal structure in the 600 million years since the first neuron[33] appeared. Although the exact form of the reptilian brain of 220 million years ago is not entirely understood (as of the writing of this book), it was similar to the more crude brain of the amphibians from which it speciated. Reptiles did have a cortex, but it was a very crude three-layer structure[171].

In mammals, the neocortex took the form of a six-layer neuronal sheet from the onset, but was initially small and nascent. It evolved from the reptilian dorsal pallium. It was a mere vestige of the colossus it would become, and would eventually add the ability to reason to the creature's repertoire. The world would never be the same.

"The neocortex, as the name implies, is the newest addition to our brain and is considered to be the crowning achievement of evolution and the biological substrate of human mental prowess. Although its origin can be traced to reptiles that have emerged during the Carboniferous Period, it first appears as a uniform, six-layered sheet consisting of radially deployed neurons in the early small mammals that emerged from their reptilian ancestors during the transition of the Triassic/Jurassic periods. Increases in size and complexity of the cerebral cortex have culminated in the modern human that had separated from the mouse line between 90 and 100 million years ago and from the Old World monkeys, such as macaque, 25 million years before the present time. If any organ of our body should be substantially different from any other species, it is the cerebral neocortex, the center of extraordinary human cognitive abilities. It is, therefore, surprising how little modern research has been done to elucidate how this human difference emerged." *(Rakic, P. (2009). Evolution of the neocortex: a perspective from developmental biology. Nature reviews. Neuroscience, 10(10), 724–735. https://doi.org /10.1038/nrn2719. Citation #167)*

From this, we can see that the neocortex was initially undersized and underpowered, but that its six-layer sheet had already evolved by the time mammals speciated from reptiles (the author does misstate the time for the initial appearance of the neocortex, I will note). This inherent design is what would make it the game-changer that it became over time; but at first, its effects would have been minimal. Undoubtedly, however, it would have been invaluable to add any extra neuronal assistance to the early mammalian emotional brain, especially as that brain was under tremendous adaptational pressure to evolve novel emotions suitable for the special needs of mammals, as opposed to reptiles. It was a time of great flux and massive evolutionary developments of every kind.

Over the succeeding 100 million years, mammals progressively added greater neocortical brainpower, resulting in animals that were ever-more-capable competitors in all respects. Eventually, it resulted in the modern human brain, which first appeared about 2.5 million years ago with Homo habilis, and which assumed its (more-or-less) final configuration only around 300,000 years ago[34] with Homo sapiens.

In the 20 million years spanning the period from 85 to 65 million years ago, primates evolved from a small arboreal insect-eating mammal known as Euarchonta[35]. From 20 to 16 million years ago, Hominadae[36], the ancestor of great apes, speciated from gibbon's lesser ape ancestors. Hominadae evolved Homininae[37] between 18 to 14 million years ago. As new species emerged, they begin to take on an increasingly more modern appearance by developing such adaptations as flexible wrists, a stiff lower spine, and a flat rib cage. Around 12 million years ago, Danuvius guggenmosi[38] adapted to bipedal locomotion, and 6 million years later, Hominini[39] appeared. Hominini was the last common relative of chimpanzees and humans. Hominini possessed a larynx, making vocalized speech possible.

3.9 million years ago, Australopithicus afarensis[40] was presumably exclusively walking bipedally (based on the fossil record). Living in savannah, their brain was about the size of a modern bonobo, but by approximately 3.6 million years ago, its brain had grown in size by about a third to 400 - 500 cubic centimeters. This is indeed rapid brain growth, as we're only considering a period of about

300,000 years. When changes such as that occur rapidly, it is often a result of evolutionary pressures forcing unusually abrupt adaptational changes.

Consider the comb jelly, unchanged for 700 million years. Why hasn't it changed? Because it hasn't needed to change. It's perfect. Why did Australopithicus' brain grow by a third while the comb jelly's didn't? Obviously, it was because there were pressures for Australopithecus to adapt to have larger brains due to the demands of an environment that comb jelly didn't share.

From 3.5 to 3.3 million years ago, Kenyanthropus platyops[41] speciated from Australopithicus and learned to make improved stone tools. From about 3 to 2 million years ago, humanities ancestor's body hair largely disappeared, indicating that full bipedalism and even running were occurring on a regular basis. The loss of body hair allowed heat to be dissipated through sweating, especially while running long distances.

A modern human, it should be noted, can outrun all other animals on earth over distance, as other animals with fur can only dump extra heat by panting. Human hunters in some parts of Africa still routinely run down gazelle in this way. Yes, although it is hard to believe based on the lifestyle of the average American, the human body really is designed to be able to run down every other animal on earth, and has been doing so for untold millennia.

Homo habilis, Homo rudolfensis, and Homo erectus[42] speciated from one (of several possible species) of Australopithecus approximately 2.4 to 2 million years ago. They made and extensively used highly sophisticated stone tools, and had migrated out of Africa as far as China by

2.12 million years ago. Homo erectus was a trailblazer in the story of humans, even though the species is now extinct. They were the first human species to leave Africa, and lived for about 1.5 to 2 million years altogether, vanishing approximately 250,000 years ago. As humans have only existed as a species for about 300,000 years, Homo erectus managed to achieve many times our longevity (so far). Their body proportions were similar to modern humans, with shorter arms and longer legs than earlier species. They managed to spread far into Western Asia first, then Eastern Asia, and then Indonesia. Except for Homo sapiens, they were the most geographically widespread humans to ever live.

From about 800,000 to 300,000 years ago, Homo heidelbergensis[43] became the last common ancestor between three species: Neanderthals[44], Denisovans[45], and us. As Homo heidelbergensis migrated from Africa into Eurasia, some of the settlers went west into Europe, where they evolved into Neanderthals. Neanderthals subsequently bred with Western European Homo sapiens, with whom they share between 1% and 2% of their DNA.

Other heidelbergensis migrants went east, where they evolved into Denisovans. Modern humans in Southeast Asia, as well as Pacific Islanders, share about 4% to 6% of their DNA with Denisovans, who became extinct only about 15,000 years ago, outliving the Neanderthals by about 25,000 years. Much is still being discovered about Denisovans, and it is very possible that they also evolved other species.

Yet more species (or sub-species) such as Homo floresiensis, Homo luzonensis[46], and Homo naledi[47] have also been identified over the last decade, with more to follow. The Smithsonian National Museum of Natural History lists 21 separate species of humans, although, naturally, there is great controversy about the exact number (which surprises no one in the least). For the sake of peace in our time, therefore, let us stipulate that there is a plurality of human species numbering somewhere between 8 and 21. Very recently, yet another species of ancient human from about 140 thousand years ago has surfaced in China, so the Smithsonian may have to raise that number to 22.

Homo sapiens[48] evolved from those Homo heidelbergensis who did not migrate into Asia Minor and points beyond but remained in Africa. When later Homo sapiens took a similar migratory path out of Africa as their predecessors, they encountered both species, Neanderthal and Denisovans. By this time, Neanderthals had also spread east back through Asia Minor, and on into China and points north.

This rather complex series of migrations has created a number of somewhat confusing dilemmas as to exactly who was where when, as migration paths crossed and re-crossed across the continents. When our species eventually did make their way out of Africa, however, it was quite possibly to the detriment of both other species of humans. The first fossil evidence of our species, Homo sapiens, was discovered in Morocco dating back to about 300,000 years ago[49]. Homo sapiens began to migrate out of Africa approximately 70,000 to 50,000 years ago, where they encountered, competed against, and interbred with both Neanderthals and Denisovans. The three species share some of their DNA[50], and although both Neanderthals and Denisovans are now extinct, the fact that our DNA contains a small portion from both species is proof of cross-breeding. The rest, as they say, is history.

We do know, however, that both of these species flourished and spread for hundreds of thousands of years before the arrival of Homo sapiens; and that they were extinct within several tens of thousands of years after our species' arrival. Perhaps the other two species had a run of incredibly bad luck, or perhaps; they encountered a very aggressive species with whom they could not compete?

In fact, though, Homo sapiens probably did not eradicate (at least) Neanderthals, for a number of reasons. Neanderthals had a nomadic lifestyle which made it hard for them to maintain and grow their population, and this resulted in a restricted gene pool. As well, they widely practiced cannibalism, resulting in the production of misshapen proteins called prions, which cause several fatal neurodegenerative diseases similar to bovine spongiform encephalopathy[51] (BSE), popularly known as 'Mad Cow Disease.'

It is, however, entirely possible that Neanderthals (and possibly also Denisovans) may well have been finished off by the diseases brought by Homo sapiens as they moved into their neighborhoods. Especially in the case of Neanderthals, their small population numbers, restricted gene pool, and propensity to eat other members of their species (thereby producing the prions which led to the neurodegenerative diseases) had very possibly terminated what was already a quite shaky existence.

Is it possible that Homo sapiens killed them off in history's first (but tragically, not last) holocaust? Thankfully, that is thought to be very unlikely, as humans were still about 25,000 years away from developing the complex social organizations necessary to practice the systematic ability to murder our fellows that we know as war. For that, I for one am extremely grateful, as our species has quite enough to feel guilty for already. Given that our DNA was approximately 98.5% the same as that of Neanderthals anyway, there is much evidence that our two interbred species shared not only our beds, but our social organizations, cultures, and technologies, making it far more likely that we were allies, rather than adversaries. The genetic variations introduced by both Neanderthals and Denisovans have contributed many positive attributes to our human genome, and it is fair to say that both species live on in us to this very day.

I must concede, though, that I sometimes consider the way in which some humans behave even toward members of different races (and racial differences are so minor as to make such superficial differences the smallest possible distinction in classification), I wonder how they would react to an 'other' so physically distinct from Homo sapiens as were Neanderthal and Denisovans? Insofar as both species were noticeably quite different physically from humans, I truly have difficulty imagining Homo sapiens getting along amicably with, for instance, Neanderthals, who could fairly effortlessly tear their arms off as if they were a rag doll. It is impossible to have any insight into the natural state of mind of a Neanderthal, but each of us has had plenty of experience with how poorly humans tend to deal with the threat of more powerful competitors.

The consensus of most paleoanthropologists and paleontologists (for the sake of simplicity, I will be using the term paleontologist to refer to both, no offense intended) is that humans were not socially advanced enough to wage war of even the crudest variety that long ago in our pre-history. Human social organizations, they argue, were far away from having the capability to wage war.

I do not agree with that entirely too-glib and facile generality about war. It doesn't take into account how creative humans can be in plotting the destruction of others. There are myriad manners in which humans have disposed of competitors over their long, sad history, and paleontologists could perhaps gain from reading more history, especially as it relates to havoc and destruction (come to think of it, that pretty much *is* our history). So, of course, early Homo sapiens were not forming their brethren into phalanx formations, and prosecuting a war against the Neanderthals, as that would be totally impossible. A *pogrom*, on the other hand, is a human institution with a long and storied history that has never seemed to require a high level of social organization, any more than does a lynch mob. Sometimes, perhaps, mysteries are better remaining mysteries?

BECOMING HUMAN
A New Perspective on the Origins of the Human Mind
Chapter 2

Brain Development

Isn't it amazing how life is perpetually inventing new animals while improving old ones? Evolutionary forces are entirely based on hard science, but they often appear to display the soul and elegance of an artist. We're accustomed to thinking of the very term 'evolution' as nearly synonymous with a set of immutable rules by which life operates, and yet; there is no specific physical force in the universe called evolution.

Rather, it is a combination of physical laws, specific conditions, unique environments, and just plain luck which frequently results in success...and failure. When evolutionary forces are trying out new approaches, it's impossible to say what might result. Who would have supposed that the knees and elbows that Tiktaalik adapted to improve his lakeshore dining experience would make possible a world full of gymnastic species of all types? Once something has begun, it's impossible to know how it will develop.

In the last chapter, we examined a few of the more important evolutionary changes that occurred in our deep past. Actually, though, there is a myriad of unique creatures with incredible developments that arose in this timeframe. I have tried to choose epochs and organisms representative of these developments, but that is not to say that these were the only ones pivotal or essential to modern human development. We must remember that they all represented steps on the path to where we are now and are all in our direct lineage.

Although I talk about specific evolutionary traits, we must remember that there have been millions of evolutions in our past that have brought us to where we are today. Urmetazoans from 650 million years ago differed in innumerable ways from even relatively close relatives like Saccorhytus Coronarius living 100 million years later. Evolution sometimes happens slowly and sometimes happens (relatively) quickly, depending on many factors. Geological changes, extinction events, competition from other species, as well as creatures struggling to survive in a new environment are going to have to adapt and evolve to survive life's inevitable changes. Evolution is the mechanism by which creatures can survive by adapting.

The Cnidaria (from Chapter 1) accomplished this by evolving a very simple 'neural net' which consisted of connected sensory neurons that afforded them a sense of touch with their environment. The neural net eventually evolved into a very crude brain. Deuterostomes possessed a 'brain' at the front end of a neural cord about 550 million years ago, but it appeared more like a 'swelling' of the neural cord and was capable of supporting only the most basic of functions. In time, Deuterostomes gave rise to the vertebrates[52], which possessed a more capable central nervous system and highly organized brain.

As brains adapted to be more powerful, ever higher degrees of organization became critical to keep pace with the new capabilities that were being created as a result of constant evolutionary pressures. The vertebrates evolved to fill a huge gamut of ecological niches, and although their brains are generally organized along similar lines, they are not of similar capacity or capability. Reptile brains[172], for instance, are about a tenth the size of a mammalian brain from a similarly-sized creature[53].

The brains of early aquatic vertebrates began to produce specialized areas that grew forth from the brainstem, the oldest and innermost region of the brain. The brainstem was primarily concerned with basic functions such as breathing, motor responses, and related maintenance duties. In some species, a specialized hindbrain might emerge as an additional adaptation to control swimming actions, for example, so that the forebrain could become more involved in vision and other sensory apparatus.

Since the early aquatic days of the vertebrates, mutations have not only caused changes in the genome but also; the entire genome itself to become duplicated more than once[54]. In this way, numerous spare genes were available which could themselves mutate and evolve in yet more potential directions to fulfill different purposes. Partially from these 'spare materials,' new structures still present in the brains of vertebrates emerged.

The basal ganglia[55] first appeared in aquatic vertebrates and comprised an essential component of the forebrain that remains present in all vertebrates to this day. As well, the optic tecum[56], essential for eyes that can track

34

movement, was a precursor structure to the emotional system that constructs memories and feelings. Even a crude amygdyla[57], a part of the brain associated with an organism's survival responses, developed in fish. The amygdala is a critical neural structure. Over deep time, the amygdala and other crude structures evolved into major components of what became known in later reptiles and early mammals as the 'emotional brain[58].'

A very crude emotional brain evolved as the tetrapod's descendants emerged onto the land. Reptiles (such as Hylonomus, mentioned in chapter 1) evolved from amphibians around 300 million years ago and were soon scooting about the globe depositing eggs and progeny in all directions. Hylonomus, with its elaborate central nervous system and crude emotional brain, was the brainiac of the period, in that some intelligence is far superior to none. Many of the neuronal adaptations were going toward the development of ever more capable emotional structures. Contrary to the beliefs of many, most of what evolved into the emotional system had incredibly ancient roots whose earlier-than-expected existence must cause us to reconsider many of our hitherto incorrect beliefs[59] regarding the early neural evolution of our precursors.

According to the European Molecular Biology Laboratory (EMBL), the hypothalamus and the hormones it produces are *not* even vertebrate inventions! They first evolved in worm-like marine animals whose last common ancestors to vertebrates were flies! Many of our most basic assumptions have been proven so stupendously incorrect in the last 5 or 6 decades so as to necessitate a complete re-thinking of some of our most cherished, incorrect, and wrong-headed presumptions. In 2007, researchers at the EMBL conclusively proved the existence of a multifunctional hypothalamus producing hormones for secretion while also possessing sensory properties[60]. They further hypothesized that very ancient autonomous neurons might have clustered together and become specialized, forming the embryonic hypothalamus.

> "These findings revolutionize the way we see the brain," says Tessmar-Raible. "So far we have always understood it as a processing unit, a bit like a computer that integrates and interprets incoming sensory information. **Now we know that the brain is itself a sensory organ and has been so since very ancient times.**" (Bold is mine). *(Tessmar-Raible, K., Raible, F., Christodoulou, F., Guy, K., Rembold, M., Hausen, H. and Arendt, D. Evolution of the vertebrate hypothalamus: An ancient set of sensory–neurosecretory cell types in the annelid and vertebrate brain, Cell, 29 June 2007. Citation #60)*

I cannot imagine how much else of such an astonishing nature as this has inevitably been missed or misunderstood in the course of human inquiry into the origins of life on earth. Neuronal structures, particularly, are so innately ephemeral as to comprise an especially delicate class unto themselves. This very significant misunderstanding about the development of the hypothalamus just proves yet again that we should not be overconfident in accepting the unquestioned veracity of our own beliefs. Given that modern science often possesses only a fraction of the information necessary to make certitudes, we should more often settle for *probabilities*.

This one finding alone changes the entire picture of how and when this (and other) emotional structures developed and casts significant doubt that we understand these structures nearly as well as we'd like to think we do. This and similar studies have appeared with regularity over the last several decades, and many of them suggest to me that all approaches to such matters should remain flexible enough to allow for such earth-shattering epiphanies as these findings caused when they dropped. There will undoubtedly be many more cherished beliefs that will be sacrificed on the altar of progress. We must welcome the progress it represents.

Reptiles had a crude cortex before speciating mammals that they passed on to us along with the embryonic neocortex. It has to be assumed that the reptilian cortex, whether in a reptile or an early mammal, would have been capable of a certain amount of influence vis-à-vis the feelings-based brain. The cortex, of course, was an interconnected part of that brain.

Let's consider the cortex of a reptile from 220 million years ago. Speciated from amphibians, it was crude but serviceable. It was basic and unsophisticated. It was primarily concerned with maintaining the various systems of its body and mind. It was very effective at doing this, and what it was doing was necessary to ensure a creature's survival. At the same time, it was the emotional, feelings-based component that would've made the great majority of the decisions, taken actions, and motivated behaviors. Don't look now, but it is still trying to do that with us humans every day. The only difference is the power differential between our cerebral cortex and our emotional system.

What would a crude cortex truly be able to do as the amniota ventured forth onto dry land? They were in a completely new environment, with completely new challenges than that to which their forbears had evolved. In such an environment, it would benefit a creature greatly if it could employ its emotions to provide the feelings, direction, and motivation to accomplish necessary tasks. This spontaneously-arising, internally generated force was a tremendously powerful advantage for a creature to possess.

It is nearly impossible to imagine that a very crude cortex such as is presumed to have existed in reptiles at that time could've had a very powerful influence on how the creature reacted to those challenges in its environment. The under-powered cortex was obviously already having problems keeping up, or why would it have evolved a brand new six-layer neocortex in the first place?

Species do not generally evolve superfluous neuronal structures when they are already in a dire need of usable ones. This is simply a point of logic. I think it's fair to assume that the cortex was not up to the challenges of novel terrestrial environments, especially given the climate upheavals of the Permian-Triassic period. It might have worked fine in the amphibians from which reptiles arose, but the life of amphibian was far less challenging than was that of reptiles attempting to expand their range.

While the cortex was certainly doing its best, it is fair to assume that the reason it was evolving new structures was that the structures it had were inadequate to the task at hand. Although it was, at that time, extremely crude, the feelings brain component would have been certainly been dominant over it. The dominance established over the cortex, though, couldn't easily continue as the neocortex evolved to become more powerful and useful, but that story still lay millions of years forward in time.

Modern mammals, with the primary exception of humans, have highly capable neocortexes which have been evolving in the 200 million years since the period we are describing. Yet, despite all the time and adaptations that have occurred, it certainly appears that the average mammalian brain is still largely ruled by feelings. It certainly isn't ruled by reason. Yet, taken as a whole, they have respectable reasoning capabilities, and they use them to solve problems of all sorts. Unlike humans, though, their reasoning capabilities never grew strong enough to overpower their emotional component.

A mammal's reasoning ability of problem-solving frequently shows itself, whereas their emotional system is always on display, with the reason in the background. From this, we can conclude that the balance of capability and the power that results from greater capability is far different than in humans. This is patently intentional on the part of evolutionary adaptations. There has been more than adequate time for mammals (other than humans) to overpower their emotional systems, but yet; they haven't. Mammals have, for whatever reason, found a balance between these two components in which the emotions (except in artificially-selected animals) still determine the majority of their actions and reactions. An ever-increasing intellectual ability is far from an inevitable adaptation in mammals. Humans are the exception that makes the rule (although several other mammalian species are perhaps craftier than we might suppose). This begs the question: if modern mammal's neocortexes are not ascendant over their feelings-based brain components, what chance is there that the incredibly cruder reptilian cortexes from 200 million years ago were? *This* is the decisive question in this debate.

Although I often refer to the feelings-based brain as being dominant over its cortex, I don't wish to simply ignore the presence of the effective and basic processes that the cortex was dependably controlling within what was unquestionably a brain dominated by emotion. It is just that it is difficult to conceive of how such a crude structure as that could have exerted very much influence, compared to what a feelings-based component could muster.

That is because emotions are inherently powerful spurs to action, and they cause the entire creature to react in various ways that are essential to ensuring its continued existence. Emotions, however basic, motivate all creatures who have them. Fear, rage, aggression, and other such emotions allowed them to successfully interact with their environment, and it is highly doubtful that they would have survived without them. Let us remember that this is why emotions evolved in the first place. Metaphorically, if the aforementioned ancient reptile was a car, the emotions were the spark plugs that made it go whenever they fired. Given the time in deep history when they were the decisive factors between life and death, I am pretty they would have been firing virtually constantly.

The radical and rapid increase in brainpower provided terrestrial vertebrates with a very distinct survival advantage over their competitors in this new environment. The land, after all, rests at the bottom of an ocean of air. Water is also a fluid (something that flows) like air, and that provides *some* similarity, but that's where the comparisons end. For one thing, a flying insect can move, attack, and withdraw much more quickly in the relatively thin air because it is not subject to the hydrodynamic density and 'drag' of the aqueous realm.

Things go really fast in the air, and nearly as fast on the ground. The inevitable price of not being able to keep up with the high velocity of terrestrial life was extinction. As the number of species adapting to the land grew, the sheer variety of ways to become another creature's lunch increased exponentially. The key to success for our distant relatives was found in the development of greater mental abilities.

The species that would become human had humble beginnings. Our distant reptilian ancestors left the water for the land and managed to flourish and multiply. In a very real way, that reptilian brain became integrated into our present-day brain[61]. What is referred to as the *lizard* or *reptilian brain* was (more or less) already part of the aquatic vertebrate's brain before it left the water for the land. Its 3 main components were the basal ganglia, brainstem, and cerebellum[62]. It was quite limited, comparatively, but the proof of the success of its design is demonstrated by the multitudes of species that share this humble origin story with both mammals and humans.

A characteristic of the reptilian brain is that it tends to be quite rigid and inflexible. It is more primitive than that of a mammal, but it's effective. It does a fine job of managing drives such as thirst, hunger, sexuality, as well as basic memories and habits. Although reptiles developed feelings brain structures, they are viewed as neither very emotional nor intellectual. This is for the reason that they simply do not possess all of the components in their brains for displaying either trait very deeply.

To be capable of true emotion, a creature must have a highly capable feelings brain composed of an amygdala, thalamus, hypothalamus, hippocampus, and cingulate cortex. There is no universal agreement among experts, I should add, as to which brain components should even be included in the term *feelings brain*.

All of these structures were originally crude and inefficient in conception and operation. Like all neuronal structures, though, they possessed the ability to make major adaptations over time through tiny incremental changes that assisted the creature to survive so that it could pass on its genes to the next generation. In all creatures throughout time, that is the be-all and end-all of life: to survive and procreate.

Brainpower was life, and by 220 million years ago, Cynodonts had evolved the first true paleomammalians[63] with a brain containing a vestigial neocortex in addition to a well-developed feeling brain ready, willing, and very capable. As reptiles had an even less well-developed neocortex than did the paleomammals, their behavior was primarily based on their emotions as expressed through their feelings brain[64].

There is more than one way in which a brain can function, as has been related. In the deep time history of our human story of evolution, our distant ancestors were once directed by a feelings brain before evolving a reasoning brain[65]. Feeling brains are based on emotions rather than abstract thinking, and provide quite a serviceable brain of the sort that was successful for eons. Neuronal structures that can produce feelings are far easier to physically evolve in a brain than are the sorts of incredibly complex neuronal assemblages capable of creating abstract thoughts of the type the neocortex employs.

That is presumed to be why the different emotional structures adapted to become interconnected with each other in the creation of this emotional, feelings-based brain. Interconnecting was necessary to ensure a single coordinated response, action, and purpose determined by that brain. By interconnecting, these structures together provided the capability for a coherent unified response in any given situation[66]. Not only did these limbic structures interconnect for maximum effect; it was so successful that feeling systems are still very similarly constructed. When something is that successful, it should not be interfered with, is Mother Nature's inference.

Between around 600 to 420 million years ago, then, extremely crude versions of what has become associated with primitive brain structures began to emerge, including most of the limbic structures[67]. Like most primitive neuronal components, these structures evolved over deep time, changing to become ever-more-helpful to the creatures that possessed them. The one thing they all shared was the ability to continually adapt to become more capable; and therefore, more helpful in the struggle for survival.

When you consider that these aforementioned structures are sometimes presented as having almost spontaneously appeared in reptiles in the form of a complete feelings brain, those who espouse this belief need to consider that some of these structures *had first appeared more than a hundred million years before* the appearance of reptiles. The feelings-based brain that the reptiles gifted to the early mammals was so very capable *because* its constituent structures had been evolving for a very, very long time.

In the same general period marked by the Permian/Triassic Boundary, reptilian brains had evolved a crude neocortex, which increased their raw brainpower somewhat. Modern mammals have well-developed emotional systems, in addition to reasoning capabilities made possible by their more highly evolved neocortexes that they inherited from their reptilian forebears.

"Human neocortex evolved in a series of ancestors with less neocortex and fewer cortical areas. Thus, **early mammals had little neocortex and roughly 20 cortical areas**, while early primates had much more cortex and around 50 cortical areas. Humans have the largest of primate brains that are 80% neocortex with about 200 areas. Other changes include more and more complex cortical networks, such as those for language, and modular and cellular specializations within areas.

These and other changes allow the impressive mental abilities of humans". (Bold is mine.) *(Jon H. Kaas, The Origin and Evolution of Neocortex: From early mammals to modern humans, Editor: Hofman, Michel A. Progress in Brain Research, Volume 250, 2019, Pages 61-81, ISBN 9780444643179, https://doi.org/10.1016/bs.pbr. 2019.03.017. Citation #166)*

This rather astounding adaptation that was the neocortex was not an evident great leap forward when it first appeared. It is only by looking back hundreds of millions of years later that we truly understand the significance of this embryonic structure that would eventually result in the human brain as we know it. Over the succeeding millions of years, however, the neocortex grew and developed to allow mammals to solve problems that arose in their environment far better than an emotion-based feelings brain could by itself.

For such tricks as that, a reasoning brain is especially effective, even if it only had about 10% of the cortical areas as does a modern human. Again, we see that the fledgling neocortex of the early mammals was indeed "little" and had "roughly 20 cortical areas". It was a start, though, and what made it revolutionary was its future potential. Six cortical layers were twice what most reptilian neuronal structures such as the cortex and hippocampus had. We can't expect the low efficiency of an ancient structure such as a hippocampus to be able to match the high efficiency of a neocortex evolved to have six-layers packed with highly evolved neurons. Luckily for reptiles and early mammals, they were still highly advanced from their contemporaries, so they did all right.

Reasoning capabilities vary widely and have adapted to fit the specific survival requirements of a given species. Usually, but not always, the raw number of neurons available to a creature equates *fairly* closely with its intelligence. There are some relatively smart mammals and some that are not. What a golden hamster, with its 90 million neuron brain may require is not necessarily what a gray squirrel needs, with five times as many neurons as the hamster possesses. If you have ever witnessed the mental gymnastics of which a hungry squirrel in search of a meal is capable, however, you have seen direct evidence of what a highly capable intellect at work can accomplish.

Acceptable terms for structures within a feelings-type brain are well-established in the literature, as well as historically. The term *limbic* was coined by French anatomist Paul Broca[68] in the 1860s to describe subcortical structures (including the amygdala, hypothalamus, and hippocampus) that are concerned with motivation and emotion. Although each structure does far more than just provide for motivational and emotional components of the mind, this explanation is adequate for our purposes, as a further examination of the full capabilities of each structure is well beyond the scope of this book.

The word *limbic* derives from the Latin word for *border*, which describes their general location in the brain between the cerebral hemispheres and the brainstem. *I make extensive use of the terms "emotions," "emotional," "emotional brain," and "emotional system,"* and employ them fairly synonymously with *"feelings," "feelings brain," "feelings-based brain," "limbic," and "limbic brain."* I qualify these terms to be synonymous (unless I specifically point out that I intend a modified meaning in a certain instance, or if the intended meaning is made obvious by contextual use).

I want to make it perfectly clear that I am using the term *limbic* to pertain to the identified structures termed as such by specialists in the relevant pertinent fields. The term is in disfavor by many for numerous reasons, and I have no interest in becoming embroiled in this particular "tempest in a teapot." Allow me to clarify these and related terms to avoid misunderstandings as we proceed through the chapters. As there is great disagreement about the use of the term limbic, limbic system, and limbic brain, I feel the need to mention my use of these terms. They have primarily fallen into disfavor; it would seem, due to several newer theories regarding how human emotional networks operate within the human brain.

As this is not my field or area of interest, I gladly defer to the consensus of opinion within the general fields of brain science, neuroanatomy, neurobiology, and related. Quite frankly, the existences of such emotional networks within the human brain are irrelevant to that which I am writing about in this book. Although the observations of researchers in these areas are very interesting, they don't relate to my theories of the mind in any way that I have been able to decipher.

I am not in any way suggesting that the work of these dedicated researchers is misplaced; but rather, that we are simply talking about two entirely separate concepts. They are referring to the fact, for example, that emotions and their reactions in the modern human brain are not necessarily consigned to being processed only within the limbic structures, but sometimes, elsewhere in our brains. While this is very interesting, I am referring to periods of deep time hundreds of millions of years ago, before many of the evolutionary adaptations which created modern brains even existed.

The biggest difference between what they are doing and what I am doing is that they are concerning themselves with the brain; whereas I, as might be expected for a person with an education in psychology, am focusing on the subjective and internal processes by which our *minds* operate. The brain is what creates the mind, but still; they will forever remain two entirely distinct entities.

The brain is composed of numerous physical structures. The mind is a non-physical entity produced by the physical structures of the brain and body. As such, I don't necessarily feel constrained to employ concepts and theories developed to apply to the brain in what is, after all, a book about the mind. Here is a way to visualize the difference: If the brain is the movie projector and the body is the screen, then the mind is the image that appears on the screen. The image is produced by physical devices but is not itself physical (except for the light bombarding the screen with photons, for you purist physicists out there...yes, I'm aware that a photon is a particle without mass, but this isn't a physics book).

In the current understanding of the brain, the work of processing emotions isn't confined to what has traditionally been termed the *limbic system*, but is understood in terms of *emotion processing networks,* as well as other equivalent terms, but it is beyond the scope of this book to enumerate them, as they are irrelevant in this instance. The very word *limbic* has fallen into disfavor by some, even though it is still broadly used by innumerable experts in the general field, including in the very titles of many of my cited references in the back of the book. If I was writing a book exclusively about brains, this would be very significant. Except for deep time historical references, however, I am writing a book about the mind, not the brain, so my terminology is reflective of this. That is why I have chosen to present it this way.

Whether an emotional reaction is primarily occurring in a limbic structure or the cerebral cortex has no bearing whatsoever on any of my theories. It doesn't matter if the actual physical location of a particular emotional reaction has changed from its original location in the brain. It doesn't affect emotions that evolved over deep time long before there *was* a cerebral cortex to which to shunt the extra emotional workload.

At any rate, I am not interested in the where. I am interested in the what, as in; what happened? Changing the "scene of the crime" in a modern brain doesn't change what occurred back then, what the creature I am describing in a given instance was going through at the time it happened, or the result. That's what I mean when I say such information is extraneous and irrelevant. Not every person who should understand this enormous distinction does understand it. The same thing is true as it applies to humans in the present day. If I am describing the way an emotion can demand the attention of your conscious mind, what difference does it make what part of the brain is processing the emotion, as long as the result remains the same? The answer, quite simply, is that it doesn't.

The simple fact of the matter is that, based on everything I've read, our knowledge of how the brain truly operates is in its early infancy. I have no doubt but that any brain researcher anywhere who is worth their salt would have to concur with this established truth. This is certainly not meant to be a criticism. I am constantly astonished by the remarkable advancements in this area. I am simply stating a fact. When a person creates a theory at any point in time, it nevertheless exists in a milieu of dynamic change as new knowledge is discovered. It was true in Freud's time, and it is just as true now. Over time, our understanding of many things increases. This is the natural order of things, and it isn't about to change anytime soon.

All theories must be considered on their merits unless the factual bases on which they are built becomes untenable. This was the case with, for example, Gestalt psychology. The proponents of Gestalt psychology made some fatally incorrect assumptions about the construction of the brain that invalidated their entire school of thought.

The fact that Fritz Perls later developed Gestalt therapy from the metaphorical ashes of Gestalt psychology, however, doesn't change the fact that the assumptions underpinning this school of psychology were wrong. I use this example for the reason that I had the experience (while in my undergrad studies) of studying with a therapist who had been an acolyte of Perls while he was at Esalen Institute. Perhaps Gestalt psychology was a flop, but the therapy inspired by this scientific *dead-end* has created deep insights into everyone I know who has become intimately acquainted with its teachings, myself included. Sometimes, great results can accrue even from inaccuracy.

In referring to the cortical, reasoning brain, I qualify the words *"reason,"* *"reasoning,"* *"intellect,"* and *"intellectual"* as general blanket terms referring to the thinking brain's capacity to reason, employ logic, deduce meanings, reach conclusions, use abstract concepts, solve problems, and anticipate outcomes. In other words, my intentions in using the terms are to indicate that the reason or intellect is a product of neocortical structures. I qualify the terms to have this broad and generalized meaning, much like the qualifiers I employed in discussing the feelings brain. Mostly, I do this to provide a general definition that best fits the nature of my theories as I envision and propound them; but also, because it pains the literary side of me to use the same word seven times in the same paragraph.

The emotional system, primarily composed of interconnected structures deep within the brain, is responsible for emotional and behavioral responses, while the neocortex is concerned with thought, memory, perception, problem-solving, self-awareness, and abstraction, among other capabilities. Together, these emotional and reasoning brain components greatly increased the inherent capabilities of mammals in innumerable ways[69].

These qualities of mind have enabled them to be incredibly successful and adaptable nearly everywhere on earth, as well as in the water. Mammals are capable of complex social organizations largely because of the presence of both emotional and intellectual abilities that reinforce and enhance the other's capabilities. To exist in any mammalian social order requires both of these qualities, in lesser or greater part, to be successful.

It is widely established that a main reason for evolving a larger neocortex was to make more complex social interactions and organizations possible[70]. It is unquestionably true that it is more complicated to manage many social interactions rather than a few, and mammals with larger brains tend to form larger social groups. Some contend that the size of human communities is directly related to the number of individuals with which one's brain allows you to become familiar.

Through much trial and travail, the primitive neocortex that the early mammals possessed so long ago has evolved into the primary structure of the modern human reasoning brain. Through its many adaptations, it has become something far more complex and powerful than that of any other creature, possessing about *86 billion neurons*[71]! It is a marvel of organized, integrated efficiency, constantly attempting to maintain order on numerous levels. As a brain goes about its work, for instance, a type of specialized glial cells called "microglia" engulf not only synapses but entire neurons, which they nibble away to sculpt neural brain circuitry in a process known as "phagocytosis"[72] (*phagos* being Late Latin for eat).

Weighing only about 3 pounds, the human brain nevertheless consumes nearly a quarter of the body's energy and is powered by pure glucose[73]. A chimpanzee manages to function quite well on about 28 billion neurons, and chimpanzees are our closest relative! A mouse flourishes on only about 75 *million*. Lest we get carried away with our own lofty neuron count, though, let's bring our swelled heads back down to earth by considering that elephant's brains[74] contain over 250 billion neurons; and, may I add, they never forget...and now you know why.

At the pinnacle of the higher creatures are we humans, with neurons dripping out of our ears, while spiders can create perfectly geometrical webs with a mere 100,000. The more neurons in the brain, the more connections they can make to other neurons. The human brain accomplishes its many miracles using only 3 classes of neurons (sensory, motor, and interneurons), and 4 types of neurons (unipolar, bipolar, multipolar, and pseudounipolar[165]). The neurons are assisted in their various operations by non-neuronal support cells called glia. In the human brain, a single neuron can connect up to over 10,000 other neurons[75]. In an entire human brain, it is supposed, there are about *100 trillion synapses*[76] in all! That is a breathtakingly large number, but it gives one an idea of the magnificent complexity of this incredible object.

It also goes a long way to explaining our comparative ignorance of how most parts of it actually operate. The reasons for this are manifold. Part of it is because the tools of investigation, such as the MRI, CT scan, and many genetic tests didn't even exist until recent decades. The other complicating circumstance is the human brain's sheer complexity, as compared to most other brains on earth. It could easily be argued that the most complex creation that has ever existed on this planet is the human brain (although that is the sort of thing a human would say).

In many of the 100 trillion synapses, which are minuscule gaps between the axons and dendrites (both of which are components of neurons), neurotransmitters[77] such as dopamine and serotonin are excreted. Some neurotransmitters improve the electrical conductivity from one neuron to another, while other neurotransmitters inhibit the conductivity between neurons, thus modulating the speed of the electrical signals traveling the neuronal circuitry. This creates another whole level on which to comprehend the complexity of the human brain.

Not only do we have 100 trillion synapses, but they are subject to either being slowed or sped up in their response time, thus complicating the entire synaptic arrangement even more. Some brain researchers even contend that there are over 200 distinct neuronal forms in our brains! The human race, I believe, seriously needs to consider setting aside several centuries in which to *begin* to gain a basic understanding of this brain of ours. The next few hundred years are going to be pretty busy for brain researchers. I am a big fan of their work, but I don't intend to change my terminology every time they change theirs; brain researchers and mind researchers need to stay in their respective lanes, as a general rule, methinks.

It is in humans that higher intelligence has reached its zenith on our planet, at least as far as we know. Some other mammals (like elephants) have evolved *larger* brains, but none more capable of which we are aware. We will be discussing many and varied aspects of the human mind in later chapters in much greater detail, so I will avoid delving any deeper at this time.

Evolving from primitive aquatic forms, our ancestors came out of the water, conquered the land, and spread to all corners of the globe. In that time, innumerable species evolved ever-more-capable bodies and minds in order to increase their odds for survival. Hundreds of millions of years later, mammals appeared, and then, primates[78]. From the line of primates, humans evolved, and became masters of the earth, at least, for this brief moment in time and space.

If almost all mammals (except for humans) are seemingly still primarily under the direction of their feelings brain, it is obviously because their neocortex is not under the same adaptive pressures to grow, flourish, and ultimately dominate the mind as has occurred with human beings. After all, human brains continued to grow and develop to an extreme degree, only reaching their maximum development from between 100,000 to 300,000 years ago with the rise of Homo sapiens. It would seem that, in the case of most other mammals, their original (precursor) feelings brain now has become a powerful emotional system not unlike ours. It appears to have mostly remained in the ascendancy over their reason, even while their neocortical abilities have substantially sharpened from their early days. Most mammals, while being quite clever in many ways, and *especially* as they interact with the specific environment in which they developed, do not seem to be able to usually operate against the mandates of the feelings brain (now in modern mammals, an emotional system).

It is as if evolution decided that mammals seemed to function best when the neocortical component filled the role of vizier to the feelings brain's Caliph. If, on the other hand, the feelings brain had been adjudged to be so inherently inferior, wouldn't it have adaptatively been discarded in favor of an already developed neocortex? I find that to be one of the biggest mysteries in all of creation.

Evolution has had nearly 220 million years in which to devolve the feelings brain, but it hasn't. It stills shines on brightly, supported and strengthened by its neocortex. Only in humans did the neocortex balloon to this outlandish size, resulting in a unique creature simultaneously capable of the greatest accomplishments and most vile acts ever committed by any creature of Earth. As the old saying goes, humans are the only animals that pray...or need to.

While the neocortex was slowly becoming more important in the overall existence of mammals in general, the original feelings brain, in which emotions literally sufficed to assist the creature to make decisions (as opposed to reason making intellectual decisions), was still the only established brain that was powerful enough to serve the actual needs of reptiles and early mammals, assisted as much as possible by its cortex. By this time in the evolution of the feelings brain (composed of interconnected structures such as the hypothalamus, amygdala, and hippocampus) had already established their critical nature[79].

These individual structures, over a very long period, evolved to become better connected to each other with yet more neuronal circuitry. The result was that these structures, assisted by the cortex (and partly, the neocortex) were capable of operating as an entire brain. Unlike our

56

modern human brain, however, this brain was principally driven by feelings and emotions[80]. They acted to motivate the creature to interact with its environment in such a way as to safeguard the creature and promote its interests.

While the reptilian feelings brain was in the executive, a very small but growing neocortex was continuously adapting more neuronal circuitry to increase its reasoning capabilities. Consider, if you will, that the sort of feelings-based brain (and the attendant emotions themselves) that a reptile would evolve would necessarily be far different than that which a mammal would evolve. Much of this has to do with the specific needs of a reptile, which is not nearly as involved in parenting as is a mammal that gestates a baby before it is born, and nurses it for extended periods afterwards[81].

As well, mammals, having a more developed neocortex than their reptilian ancestors, needed a longer period of neotency than did reptiles. Many reptiles come out of the egg with a plethora of instincts allowing them to make decisions that are almost of an adult nature[82]. This is an intentional device commonly practiced by Mother Nature to essentially nullify the need to learn many things that can only be learned in a mammal by teaching imparted from parent to offspring.

It was not a smooth transition by any means from reptile to mammal. Very often, many species were eradicated by the frequent disasters visited upon our earth throughout deep time. Such things provided a tremendous step-up...for the survivors. In many cases, we will probably never be entirely sure how certain situations and events were resolved. We can only say with certainty that things worked out in a way that we can now observe. That means that while we aren't sure what transpired, it concluded thusly. In such a situation, we are forced to make certain speculations that seem to fit the facts of which we are in possession, and seem to be generally in keeping with what we do know about our ancient ancestors.

As creatures with highly developed reasoning capabilities, it is only natural that it is very hard for us to imagine, much less visualize, what it must be like to have a feelings brain, especially in the absence of an accompanying reasoning brain. It is a true exercise in imagination for a person to try to visualize a world in which your actions would directly proceed from an emotional sensation, rather than an intellectual decision.

That is part of the inherent challenge in considering the sorts of brain structures that existed in creatures from so long ago. Thank god for fossils. Most of those ancient species are long since extinct, and the ones that have survived have mutated and evolved into creatures different from their reptilian ancestors of so very long ago.

In the final analysis, though, most reptiles don't need the sort of emotional range or depth required by a mammal, if only because of the enormous differences between reptiles and mammals in how they care for their young. There are many holes in our knowledge that are unlikely to be paved over anytime soon. All that interested people can do, then, is to speculate, hypothesize, and theorize plausible explanations of the world from whence our species came.

In the fullness of time, nearly all manner of creatures has evolved various neuronal structures that serve much the same purpose as a neocortex. Birds and reptiles have developed pallial structures[83] which provide much of the same reason-based decision making that mammals employ. We are not constructed so differently from these other creatures as some would have you believe, and we will all be seeing far more evidence to support this contention in the following years, from what I've seen.

Some birds have far more neurons in their pallial structures than many mammals have in their neocortexes. Some macaques have considerably more neurons in their brains than a German Shepard. Such is the pre-eminent power of reasoning capabilities that many other creatures besides mammals have developed these neuronal structures[84] to allow them to better survive in their respective environments.

What creature does not benefit from a reasoning ability? Especially in a world in which other creatures are developing reasoning structures in *their* brains, not having a similar ability would inevitably result in a species being outperformed by others that are more capable in this regard. The more capable a creature becomes, the greater the evolutionary pressures on less capable creatures (assuming that these animals compete).

If two species are not in direct competition for food, water, territory, or the other essentials of survival, they are not so apt to need to develop improved neuronal brain structures to keep up. If an avian species competed with an arboreal mammalian species, there would likely be evolutionary pressures on the lesser well-endowed to improve their reasoning capabilities

Many species have produced few if any, significant evolutionary adaptations for hundreds of millions of years for the reason that there is no pressure on them to do so. Both in the water and on land, there are multitudes of creatures that do not seem to need to evolve any further than they already have. Necessity is not only the Mother of Invention; but also, the Mother of Evolutionary Adaptations.

In most cases, creatures do not evolve rapidly in the absence of pressures in their environment requiring them to do so. If they are doing fine without the necessity to evolve new attributes or improve older ones, they tend to do neither. Evolution is not something that is necessarily occurring on an even and ongoing basis with every animal on the planet. It is something that is universally *available* to every animal. It serves an essential purpose in the existence of all species, even when it is not actively being exercised.

We are fortunate to be living in a time of great scientific research and curiosity about our origins as a species. It sometimes seems as if the very boundaries of our understanding of the world, as well as our place in it, are being continually redefined to conform to new insights. As our species better understands our own unique story, we can better comprehend the world into which we have evolved; but here we are, world. Ecce homo (Behold the man). Only took us 4.2 billion years. Our species has many faults, it is true, but a lack of persistence isn't one of them.

BECOMING HUMAN
A New Perspective on the Origins of the Human Mind
Chapter 3

Instincts

An instinct is an inborn, unlearned reaction or response to a specific stimulus in an organism's environment that operates automatically, and without involving intellect or reason. The word *instinct* comes from the Latin word *instinctus*, meaning impulse[85]. The American Psychological Association defines an instinct as "an innate, species-specific biological force that impels an organism to do something, particularly to perform a certain act or respond in a certain manner to specific stimuli". Let's agree to use that definition, and let us also qualify our definition of an *instinctive reaction* as an innate, unlearned response to a (usually) external stimulus.

Instincts spring forth *seemingly* spontaneously to satisfy a specific objective. An instinct's objective is determined by a creature's senses and neuronal apparatus as something that needs to be addressed within the creature's environment. Instincts are very primitive in lower creatures, and unsurprisingly, less so in higher creatures. In lower creatures, instincts tend to be extremely reactive. This is because primitive creatures can only instinctively react in a sort of blind way. Higher creatures such as mammals have developed other brain structures such as a neocortex to exert and extend control over certain instinctive reactions.

Fixed Action Patterns (or FAPs)[86] are a term coined by Konrad Lorenz. They are instinctive sequences of highly stereotyped behavior. They tend to be very species-specific. They are very hardwired, and once triggered, always run to the completion of the pattern. There are 6 characteristics of a FAP. They are always stereotyped, complex, species-specific, released, triggered, and unlearned. Because they are rigid and predictable, they tend to make the animal employing them somewhat vulnerable, but as they are unlearned, a FAP can be of use to the animal immediately. For the sake of simplicity, as FAPs are a class of instinctive sequences, I'm just going to call them *instincts*, unless the context makes the more exact term necessary.

All instincts spontaneously arise when an animal reacts to certain well-defined stimuli such as fear, startlement, or aggression. These reactionary instincts appear to be universal in all creatures and are generally very primitive and predictable. They are easily observable in less intelligent creatures such as insects or most fish, less observable in mammals, and even less so in human beings.

Jean Henri Fabre[87] was a French entomologist of the 19th Century. Born in 1823, his observations of insect behavior focused on those not requiring a brain to perform. Actually, though, most insects do have brains, but they are quite tiny. They might contain as few as 100,000 neurons in the case of a fruit fly or 1 million if you were a cockroach. Either way, that is a pretty limiting number.

It is hard not to think of insects as if they were (almost) organic robots, but I find it even harder to imagine that they have no internal life. It is certainly far different and more circumscribed than our lives, but that doesn't mean that they don't exist. Recent studies of insects have revealed under brain scans that apparently, they do have the capacity to show "egocentric behavior" and, according to the study, the results of the scans also indicate that *they are conscious*[88].

William Wundt[89] coined the term *instinct* in the 1870s to describe unlearned, innate behaviors that spontaneously arise in certain situations, and appear to be largely outside of the realm of emotion or intellect. Examples of this include the protective behavior a mother extends toward her offspring when she perceives they are threatened, the *pack* behaviors exhibited by predators intent on securing food, and the defensive *herd* behaviors of their prey. All these behaviors share the common purpose of better equipping members of a species to survive, so that they may pass on their genes to the next generation.

The entire purpose of an instinct is to arise *seemingly* spontaneously to help achieve a certain beneficial objective for an organism. Like a vector, it has magnitude and direction. An instinct is always outwardly directed from an organism into the environment (in the fullest sense of the word). An instinctive reaction is not a single thing, but rather; the sum total of all the specific neuronal circuits and chemicals of the body that creates it. Simply having an instinct does not mean that it will be employed, in the same way that having a ball does not necessarily mean it will be thrown, but rather; that it can be thrown if necessary.

All instincts could ultimately be said to be stored in one's DNA. Most instinct's neuronal circuitry resides in the brain, much of it in the emotional system[90]. Reflexes, on the other hand, tend to be distributed in the brain stem and along the spine. Some refer to the brain stem and medulla as the primal brain, as it is responsible for very basic instincts and drives oriented towards survival. The frontal cortex[91], on the other hand, is involved with much loftier things such as abstract reasoning, memory, problem-solving, and the control of impulses.

When the latter is in control (which is most of the time), the former seems satisfied to be going about the mundane tasks associated with survival. In an emergency or exigent situation, though, the primal brain can exert itself in such a manner as to appear that it has essentially over-mastered the reason. We have all experienced this many times in our lives, for better or for worse (usually worse). As a rule, most of us have learned not to associate high degrees of rationality with our primal brains or emotional systems.

I am not in any way suggesting, of course, that we actually have two brains. We do not. I am, however, suggesting that we have one brain which frequently behaves as if there are two, independently-deciding, usually cooperative, but occasionally adversarial components with distinctly different agendas simultaneously at work to further their own ends. I will be writing about this in considerable detail in later chapters of the book, so I will defer discussion of this in greater depth until that point.

Approach a hornet or scorpion too intimately, and it will sting you as an instinctive reaction. Do the same to a mammal and it may growl, snap, or flee, as it has a broader repertoire of reactions than do its cold-blooded relatives. Even humans have reactionary instincts which can generally be relied upon to show themselves in certain situations. Human infants, for example, instinctively react with fear to loud noises or a perception of falling.

The sudden appearance of a snake can cause some humans to instantly and instinctively react in all sorts of atavistic manners[92]. Like it or not, inside the most complex minds on this planet are many of the most coldly basic instinctive reactions of our far distant progenitors. If they yet remain as part of our repertoire after untold millions of years in which they could easily have been disfavored if they were unhelpful, they obviously still retain value.

Let's endeavor to not make the same mistake as most of our revered precursors. They began by assuming that humans are, essentially, so unlike all other animals as to form a distinctly different creature from all others. If so, it was a creature raised up by the lofty aspirations of its own arrogance and motivated by a need to be like the gods that we humans create and destroy.

All animals have instincts, and we are animals. Therefore, we have instincts. See how simple that is? A century or two ago, when the human sciences were gaining true credibility as things worthy of consideration, such concepts as this would be abhorrent to most people for religious reasons alone. Nowadays, at least, the concept of human instincts can be discussed without the need for supporting liturgical references. If two things should never be combined, it is religion and science.

Some instincts are highly specific to a given species, and others seem to be universally shared by all. A marine turtle crawling up onto a beach to dig a hole in which to deposit her eggs is displaying an instinctive action specific to her species. The survival instinct, by comparison, is universal to all species, from lower to higher creatures; from ant to human. Yes, fellow humans, we do indeed have a survival instinct which most of us employ regularly; and it is a very good thing that we have it.

Not everyone agrees with me, lord knows. The brilliant Abraham Maslow believed that humans have *no* instincts, in that instincts cannot generally be over-ridden, and humans routinely override seemingly instinctive behaviors that in other creatures would not be possible. Maslow[108] believed that we had overcome our instincts, and abandoned them to the higher reasoning powers of our mind. Should we believe that Maslow lacked an instinct for self-preservation? That his higher reasoning powers had allowed him to simply obviate his survival instinct? If so; wow, those are very puissant reasoning powers.

Instincts and instinctive proclivities are still very much present in humans, but most of them are in a much-altered form from their original for good reason. Our species evolved to a point at which many (but not all) instincts in their original state became a hindrance rather than an asset in the game of survival, so they changed into something else, or were, when necessary, *short-circuited* into oblivion. Undeniably, reason and instinct can often be in direct conflict; and with humans, reason generally wins.

Creatures that eventually evolved into humans began as far more primitive organisms with quite rudimentary neural structures. Over many hundreds of millions of years, these structures evolved significantly. Early on, though, instincts were as crude as the creatures that exhibited them. Very primitive creatures were capable of projecting only basic instincts into their environment as a means and method of getting what they wanted, due to their not having a brain. In most cases, lower animals possessed neural nets, very rudimentary structures constructed of neurons that preceded the evolution of true brains by many millions of years[93].

The lower animal was father to the higher animal, and of course, it did not have the sophistication of what its descendants achieved over innumerable generations, as that is the entire point behind evolution. Simple things become more complex as they better adapt to a constantly changing environment. Also, creatures tend to evolve when there is an advantage to evolutionary change. Some creatures have remained virtually unchanged for many hundreds of millions of years. The horseshoe crab[107] and sponges have remained pretty much the same creatures they have always been since time immemorial. Sponges have never seen the need to evolve a brain, and they possess a total of zero neurons.

In lower creatures such as insects, the brain is simple, so the instincts must be commensurately simple. It logically follows that their objectives must also be simple. An instinct cannot be stronger than the neural structures that produce it, after all. Ants in a colony will follow instinctive impulses blindly, while higher animals have the capacity to resist a raw impulsive demand if carrying out such a demand unduly imperils them.

Ants, possessing a brain containing about 250,000 neurons, will attack anything that threatens the colony, while creatures with more capable brains will use their additional capabilities to better inform their actions. Higher creatures such as mammals are no less aggressive than lower creatures but have added capabilities afforded them by merit of the increased emotional control and intelligence provided by their more advanced brain. They can resist and withstand demands for immediate impulsive action if that is what is required to accomplish their ultimate objective of self-preservation. A hungry predatory mammal may restrain itself from attacking prey as it waits for other members of the pack to arrive and assist in the kill, but ants will never show such restraint.

What this example depicts are some of the higher powers at work in a mammal that the ant is unable to access. I would not profess to understand the intellect of an ant, but I can say with certainty that there is a great deal of difference between an ant's brain and that of a mammal that goes far beyond the billions of extra neurons possessed by the mammal. To put it another way, lower animals *must* act on instinct, while higher animals are not forced to act on instinct alone. They have options.

Higher animals exhibiting instinctive reactions similar to those of an ant would not be successful. Such reactions would be, as they are in the ant, extremely predictable. This would put the creature at the mercy of more intelligent animals who are less predictable, and who would then turn such predictable reactions against the creature exhibiting them in short order.

In other words, what gives the ant an advantage would be a tremendous disadvantage to a mammal. How this would play out in the real world can be easily imagined if a colony of rabbits was to mindlessly protect their burrow with the same ferocity as ants defending their colony. That would be a great day to be a fox, but a bad day to be an about-to-be-extinct bunny.

No species with any semblance of a nervous system is going to survive long if it doesn't vigorously react to a predator taking bites out of it. Even a reflex could conceivably evolve the ability to not simply react blindly, but with a bit of purpose. Perhaps it evolves to thrash about when it is attacked, making it a harder-to-consume moving target. That is a common adaptational response.

In time, instead of a mere blind reflex lashing out at a tormentor, a neuronal circuit could evolve to not only help the creature avoid being bitten but to actually bite back at an antagonist. In all likelihood, such a complex series of adaptations would result from a huge number of mutations over numerous generations, with each mutation intensifying in its aggressive proclivities until a true instinct emerged which justified its existence by providing a positive survival benefit to the organism. *Let the word go forth: if you bite me, I will bite you back! Be warned!*

Earlier, when the hornets were attacking, it would have appeared that they were not merely intent on fulfilling their instinctual duty; they were behaving as if they were *tweaked!* Even simple creatures such as hornets can at least emulate an intense, seemingly emotional reaction, and they do it very effectively and successfully. They are very convincing, as well as being very willing to follow up their displays with actions. What do the enraged hornets prove to us? They prove that they are capable of modulating these displays with a range of undeniable, *seemingly* intense emotional levels ranging from "stay back" on the lower end to "run for your lives" on the upper.

Is this angry hornet's display truly emotional? No, as a hornet isn't capable of emotion because it lacks the necessary brain structures. It is certainly not what humans or higher mammals would ever consider emotion, but we have an entire system within our brains that largely bears the emotional burden, whereas the wasp is incredibly constrained in this regard. It is not true emotion, then, but it is definitely *an excellent impersonation of murderous rage*, and that is precisely what makes it effective. Instincts are not emotional, of course, but some displays, especially those of aggression, would lack all power to be helpful to the organism if they weren't imbued with quasi-emotional intent.

If a dog half-heartedly growled at you as you passed by, you would react much differently than if he snapped at you and then chased you down the street with a piece of your pants in his mouth. An instinctive display devoid of intensity may work for some insects and lower animals but would effectively render a mammal unable to care for itself.

Every instinctive reaction or display has two possible perspectives, both of which are worthy of consideration. There is the obvious perspective of a creature such as a human observing another animal behaving in a seemingly instinctive way. The other perspective, naturally, would be that of the creature exhibiting the instinct. We, the observer, know what we *think* is occurring when we see an instinctive display by a creature, but we really know nothing about the inner feelings of that animal. We can therefore state little about the creature other than that which we observe.

We can only infer what the creature is experiencing internally as it projects an innate behavior outward towards its environment, and we are part of that environment. If a dog snaps at us when we walk by, for example, we may conclude that it is a vicious animal. In fact, the poor canine may be afraid and panicking, which is a state of mind that is quite the opposite of our rather hasty conclusion. What I mean to indicate is that our observations, while being all we have to go on, are generally not reliable indicators of anything beyond the actual observational act. The rest is pure inference, and who are we to think that our inferences are as sound as our observations?

Before the dog snapped, perhaps it exhibited other instinctive reactions such as growling or snarling, but again; this gives us no insight into the dog's internal process. Until that far-off day when the dog finally decides to discuss it with us directly, we will remain ignorant of the internal process of this canine of dubious character, as well as every other creature on earth. By a process of elimination, then, we can only have a direct understanding of the internal process of one creature, and that is human beings. Even then, it is doubtful that we have nearly as much insight into our internal processes as we would like to think.

As humans, most of us tend to view instincts as things that animals have, although it is true that some people also believe that humans possess instincts. There are many, many opinions on the matter. Humans are the ones writing the books, however, so we get to make the final determination, either rightly or wrongly (but promoting mistaken assumptions has never stopped us before). We humans tend to anthropomorphize the intents of non-human creatures, often to the detriment of making sound conclusions. We can thereby become victims of our own prejudices, and all prejudices generally run contrary to uncovering the truth of any matter.

To better explain instinctive reactions, I will first differentiate lower creatures from higher creatures in a somewhat arbitrary manner to qualify my terms. Lower creatures are those that blindly follow their instincts for the simple reason that they do not have the mental capability of doing anything else, while higher creatures have developed neuronal structures that allow them more flexibility in their instinctive displays. I would include *most* insects in the lower category, as their instinctive reactions are extremely blind, as well as being numerically limited. No matter how powerfully an insect reacts, the instinctive reaction tends to primarily vary only in terms of intensity, with the reaction itself remaining very predictable.

There are, of course, exceptions to this rule, such as is shown by honeybees[94]. Their incredibly complex instinctive behaviors involve ritualistic dance-like movements that convey such things as the location of nectar-bearing flowers or the presence of predators to their hive mates. How do they perform such an amazing accomplishment? Simple. Their brains contain nearly a million neurons, about 4 times as many as a fruit fly, and 10 times as many as a lobster!

Excepting honeybees and several other species, insect instincts are basic and extremely predictable. They are unlikely to diverge from a rote instinctive expression because they can't do so. One cannot give what one doesn't have, after all, and an insect doesn't have enough brainpower to improvise a new behavior on the fly, nor does it possess an emotional system to add a feelings element to its reaction.

There is, however, a certain power in predictability. If an antagonist can be certain that a hornet and a hundred of its closest friends will gladly sting the hell out of it with little or no provocation or remorse, it is using predictability as an extremely effective tool. With such a predictable menace, you at least know exactly what to expect, so you can act accordingly.

Nearly all insects have only a basic, limited repertoire of possible instinctive reactions in *any* given situation. As its reactions are fixed, the insect can only endlessly project them outward into the world until the event or circumstance which triggered the instinctive reaction is assuaged. When that occurs, it stops. Something that anyone who has ever been attacked by angry hornets can attest to, however, is that insect mentalities are quite capable of turning up the intensity of their reactions to a very high degree. Like, to 11 on a scale of 1 to 10!

This ability to vary the intensity of an instinctive reaction is at least as important to the creature's survival as is the instinct itself. If a hornet is languidly describing lazy figure eights 10 feet above your head, it is conveying a sort of message. If the same hornet, on the other hand, is crawling into your ears and bouncing itself off your forehead, it is conveying a completely different message, and you had better listen!

An instinct is likely to remain active in higher creatures only if it serves an essential function such as to place the creature in peril if it were without it, as is the case with a survival instinct. If an instinct were to lose the benefit to a creature that it originally bestowed, then mutation and natural selection would eventually ensure that it vanished from the instinctive repertoire. The more problematic the instinct, the faster it would be likely to disappear.

As humans, we tend to believe that our awareness of a thing *is* the thing. As we are not aware of our own instincts, we immediately jump to the conclusion that we have none. It would be interesting if, by some miracle, we were able to divine how much a dog or cat is aware of its instincts. I would conjecture that all animals are as fully aware of their instincts as are humans, which is to say, not at all.

In our humanocentric world, instincts tend to be those things that every other animal but we possess. Our fascination with ourselves seemingly knows no bounds. We have even created an epoch of geologic time based on our human impact on our environment and climate, which we have named the *Anthropocene*[109], after ourselves (our human hubris may not be our best feature as a species).

Humans are as unaware of their instincts as are all animals for the express reason that instincts long preceded the appearance of any reasoning abilities such as the neocortex provides. In this case, the human brain (similar to some computers) is not always backwardly compatible. We have no direct insight into our instincts because they reside entirely outside of the conscious realm of our minds.

Instincts are forever beyond the conscious experience of all creatures for that same reason. To a higher animal, they must seem to *just happen*. They spring forth in response to quite specific actions or situations in the environment to which the organism must respond. Instinctive responses are especially essential for the continued existence of creatures with minimal or no brainpower. Basic instincts require only a minimal number of neurons, and when you are a pond snail with only about 11,000, each one is precious.

Instincts are what you require when you *don't* have a feeling or reasoning mind. The crude instincts of lower animals can be counted on to achieve only crude results, but that is precisely what is required to achieve success for most lower animals. Far more sophisticated creatures such as certain birds, on the other hand, can compose incredibly complex instinctive mating dances that verge on displays of kinetic art. How is this possible? Neurons, and lots of them. Many bird species have twice the neurons of the average house cat, which has about 760 million. Ravens have about 2.1 billion neurons, and the average dog has about 2.3 billion (except, of course, for your and my dog, who are, I am sure, canine geniuses)!

Instincts proceed from the unconscious and are themselves unconscious. In lower animals, the requisite neuronal structures to even experience true consciousness do not always exist. In higher animals such as mammals, the conscious mind can react not only to the instinct but also; to the full ramifications of the expression of the instinct. In this way, the conscious mind can intercede (and often circumvent an instinctive expression) when necessary to protect the animal from the potential harm which could accrue from the disparate impulses, drives, and physiological stimuli that can accompany such a display.

What occurs when a higher creature feels threatened? A powerful instinctive display will probably occur, but it will be accompanied by other helpful resources. A rush of biochemicals will be instantly released into the brain and bloodstream, preparing the organism for an optimal physical and mental reaction to the perceived threat. Simultaneously, strong feelings spontaneously encourage an aggressive display and/or action[95]. Rage and hatred, love and the need to protect the beloved inspire and support these feelings, constantly reinforced by the creature's own biochemistry. The creature may snarl and bare its teeth. If that does not have the desired result, the creature acts.

Very possibly, instincts evolved from simple reflex-like reactions to external stimuli, as reflexes are not that dissimilar from crude instincts that occur in creatures possessing only the simplest neural apparatus conceivable. When a crayfish is tapped on its carapace, it will spontaneously execute a dramatic "tail flip response"[96] that completely somersaults itself out of the way of that which touched it. It is similar to the "startle response" of fish, as well as the *literal* jet propulsion response that squid employ to move out of harm's way. All three examples are similar to both reflexes and instincts but are also more than a simple reflex. Biologist Donald Edwards puts it this way:

> "More complex than simple reflexes, these responses result from a 'decision' reached by the animal in response to a specific sort of stimulus. Once triggered, the responses orchestrate the behavior of the animal's entire body. Finally, these escape behaviors are often found to be subject to simple forms of learning, including habituation, dishabituation and sensitization. For the physiologists, an additional attraction was that, in several animals, a 'giant' interneuron was key to the release of the escape behavior. In squid, investigation of the giant neuron and giant synapses led to the discovery of the basic mechanisms of the action potential." (Edwards, Donald H*., Excitation and Habituation of Crayfish Escape, 2009. Journal of Experimental Biology 2009 212: 749-751; doi: 10.1242/jeb.021972. Citation #170)*

As I am not an animal physiologist, I would not claim to understand the intricacies of "giant interneurons" or other such arcane (and lethal-sounding) terms. Habituation, dishabituation, and sensitization, though, are familiar psychological terms that pertain to learned responses. One of the contentions of Edwards' article was that the neural basis of habituation could account for specific patterns of behavior, providing the possibility that "Learning resided in special circuits that could interact with circuits controlling behavior." (ibid.)

What is interesting in this account is that an animal's neural learning mechanisms apparently *can* affect a reflex or instinct in such a way as to encourage or discourage its continued use. It establishes a link between learning and instinct on the neuronal level that has broad implications in the story of the development of instincts in other ancient creatures similar to crayfish; which, like earlier lower creatures, have neither a brain nor a central nervous system.

Reflexes are similar in some ways to instincts, except that instincts are processed in the brain. Reflexes, on the other hand, do not generally require intervention by the brain. J. Gschwend, the German researcher, wrote in 1977:

"On the basis of characteristics of the exteroceptive reflexes and of the instinct it was shown that instinct behavior developed from reflex characteristics (local characteristic of the stimuli, positive and negative taxis, habituation, conditioning). Most similarities are found between reflex and avoidance instinct behavior (instincts for excretion, thermoregulation, body care, pain avoidance and safety.)" And "The neural systems of most reflexes lie distributed in the spinal cord and brainstem, the ones of the instincts in the limbic part of the brain, the nutrition and sex instinct with a hypothalamic pacemaker. Simultaneous activation of two of many instinct motivation systems result, not comparable with the direct reflex interaction, in interactions on the level of the global interaction, and interactions on the level of the global integration which projects the activity patterns via the motor cortex to the peripheral neurons. There it is completed by the reflexes." (Gschwend, J., *Disturbances of the Human Instinct Behavior in Hypothalamic Lesions* (author's translation), *1977. Fortschr Neeurol Psychiatr Grenzgeb. Mar;45(3) :187-93.Citation #144)*

Thus, we see that there are connections between reflexes and instincts, with responses also perhaps being an even greater bridge between the two, such as with our flipped-out crayfish. It isn't hard to imagine how a reflexive neural circuit could be integrated into an instinct (or a part of an instinct) as numerous tiny adaptations over a great amount of time.

In crude creatures, especially, many or most of their interactions are likely to be dramatic, sometimes desperate, and frequently involving life-and-death situations. For such a creature to be taken seriously in such dire circumstances, it must be able to convey its willingness to go to extremes in order to create a convincing display which a rival or antagonist will take the hint from, and go away. Could such "complex" responses adapt to become ever more intricate until they appear very similar to crude instincts?

Basic reflexes employ the simplest kind of neural circuit termed "monosynaptic[97]," meaning that they have a single connection. Edwards intentionally differentiated his tail flip response from a reflex in terms of its greater complexity. There are incredible advantages to be garnered by creatures capable of accomplishing such monumental adaptations, and if a large amount of time in which to allow such a thing to occur is not necessarily a limiting factor, nearly anything becomes possible. Reflexes operate automatically when a sensory nerve is perturbed, *similar* to some responses, such as the startle response of fish. In the case of vertebrate reflexes, sensory nerves send a signal to the spine of the creature, and motor neurons signal muscles to actuate in response.

Humans seem to find instincts a bit confusing. Instincts (and the belief in instincts in higher creatures) come into style and then go out again as old theories die, and new ones inevitably arise to take their place. B. F. Skinner[98], who did most of his work in the 1920s, helped to form a school of thought in psychology called *Behaviorism*, which taught that most behaviors were learned.

In the 1930s, William McDougall[99] recognized that there was a natural "union of instinct and emotion." McDougall believed that a given instinct is naturally connected to an equally specific emotion. I completely agree with him, as I have repeatedly pointed out that instinctive displays tend to be fraught with feelings and quasi-emotional intensity. The connection between the two seems as undeniable to me as it did to William McDougall.

In the 1950s, Conrad Lorenz[100] conclusively proved that goslings instinctively "imprint" on the first object they encounter after hatching (in this case, his boots). This was, obviously, a completely instinctive response on the part of the goslings, equating the boots with their mother. In this respect, Lorenz depicted a distinct difference between learned behaviors and instincts that could not be ignored, and this caused instincts to be considered again in a more serious fashion.

One of the most interesting things about instincts is their universality among all the creatures of the earth, including people. Instincts are not all the same, of course, but come in a huge variety ranging from simple reactions to an elaborate display such as might be demonstrated by an elk during mating season. Certainly, in the case of the elk, it is far from a mere blind instinctive display. Rather, it is a blend of learned behaviors combined with a basic procreation instinct in which the melding of the two becomes an intricate combination of both instinct and learning.

At the core of an instinct is a neuronal circuit, let us recall, and a simple mutation can easily remove a few neurons that would figuratively and literally short it out. Conversely, maintaining an instinct's neuronal circuitry despite inevitable mutations would suggest that an instinct persisting in a creature would probably have evolved redundant circuitry to guard against short circuits, thereby proving its value.

The actual neural circuitry for a crude instinct is quite specific, and will not tolerate much (if any) deviation in the response that the instinct provides. Visualize a basic neuronal instinctive circuit much as you would an electrical circuit, with yet more neuronal connections that can cause it to "activate" upon receipt of an external signal from the creature's neuronal command center in reaction to sensory information that it deems concerning, and you won't be far off.

All lower creatures are purely instinct-driven, and their instincts are usually crude. Insect instincts have nevertheless been perfectly adequate to make them exceedingly successful organisms for hundreds of millions of years. As insects are so successful operating solely on instincts, there would be no evolutionary pressure toward them becoming more intelligent. They are doing just fine as they are.

In human existence, our behavior is fairly often the polar opposite of the sort of preset rigidity which an instinct provides. Humans generally employ inherently flexible learned behaviors, but the rigidity of a basic instinct in a creature has certain advantages that aren't immediately obvious at first glance. When you learn a behavior, it takes time to follow the learning curve that leads to proficiency. Learning behaviors takes time, effort, and millions more neurons than basic creatures possess.

For them, it is a tremendous advantage to have these innate, inborn behaviors ready to spring forth to do their bidding without any training whatsoever. In this respect, they come out of the factory ready to go to work. That is a tremendous advantage for a basic creature; but would, of course, be a catastrophic development for a higher creature.

Creatures that are primarily driven by instincts are coded at the DNA level to be born with "adult" synapses[101] that do not allow variety in their neurotransmitter diet. There is no synaptic modulation such as was described earlier. In a creature whose behavior is dominated by instinct, this provides a positive benefit. In a more intellectually capable creature, however, it would impede learning. That appears to be its exact purpose in instinctive displays; i.e., to reduce variability of response over the pre-programmed instinct. The spider we referenced earlier needs to be able to come out of its egg ready to begin constructing complex webs exactly like grandma used to make. It doesn't need variation in its neurotransmitters. It needs to not have such variations.

Nevertheless, variations occur in all life. In plants, every seed represents a unique phenotype, reflecting a never-precisely-exact version of the combined DNA of the parents. All animals are subject to the same genetic variation as plants. There are no two animals (that aren't clones or otherwise asexually reproduced) that are exactly alike.

The genetic variation inherent in mixing DNA during reproduction ensures a certain amount of variety in every species, and mutations are also frequent occurrences for a multitude of reasons. These differences can translate into variations in even the most hardwired instinct. They are also very important in that they provide variations in individual creatures. Otherwise, every creature would resemble nothing more than cookie-cutter-created life, with each an identical image of the other coming off the assembly line.

The conscious mind of a higher animal simply reacts to what it perceives *might* be the outcome of following instinctive dictates, and acts accordingly. A higher animal can try to restrain or defer instinctive impulses through its interactions with its emotional system or neocortex, but it cannot call them up. Instincts live on a one-way street that leads from the unconscious realm to the outside world, and traffic never reverses.

Even a very crude nervous system permits sensations to be communicated to and from various senses and bodily areas. Creatures as simple as planaria react to being injured in obvious ways. Life always finds a way to ensure that communications happen because it is so essential to the survival of all animals. Even before the evolution of neurons, primitive aquatic organisms communicated critical information essential for survival by deploying "messenger" chemicals into the water to communicate various data, and some sponges still operate this way[102]. The ability to communicate critical internal information is of such preeminent importance so as to encourage creatures to go to *extreme* adaptations to make it happen. This fact alone informs us as to the utterly essential nature of good communications to best promote the interests of all animals.

It is not just animals that go to extreme lengths to communicate, either. Nearly all life forms on the planet appear to have a need to share pertinent information with others of their kind, as long as there is a benefit to be derived by doing so. Many trees and plants can communicate information such as the presence of pests on their leaves and areas where the soil is especially fertile. They do this by such extraordinary means as dispersing chemicals they create on the winds, or through extensive underground systems of roots that transport messenger chemicals from plant to plant, conveying essential information. Our world is stunningly more complex than we sometimes realize, and it is often those things that appear to be the simplest that are actually the most profound.

Positive survival benefits are the engines driving nearly all evolutionary changes. If a mutation isn't beneficial to a creature, it would not assist them in their quest to survive, and they could not pass their mutated genes on to the next generation for the simple reason that they would be another's lunch. Mutations are generally very random changes made inevitable due to how our genetic material is replicated, damaged, and generally messed with by the uncaring environment which constitutes this physical universe that we call home.

As is often the case in life, a seemingly small or insignificant change can have far-reaching consequences. Cnidarians developed eyes 650 million years ago, which was over 3 billion years after Archaea first appeared. It is *theorized* that this occurred when certain cells mutated to be sensitive to light. This sensation informed the creature as to where the sun was positioned. Perhaps food or warmth was also where the sun was, and this adaptation by itself provided a tremendously powerful sense to assist the creature's survival. Further evolutions over eons have resulted in the aqueous orbs we flutter at each other to this very day.

It all began with a neuron[103]. Presumably, the reason it took so long to evolve the neuron was that it must be a very hard thing to do. It was, in fact, the kind of incredibly difficult evolutionary task that took hundreds of millions of years to accomplish, and that's why the neuron itself only appeared around 600 million years ago.

These first neurons were soon diffused over the body and formed what we earlier referred to as neural nets, loops of neural circuitry providing basic sensations. The neural net still exists in jellyfish and anemones, but other animals evolved ever-increasing groupings of neurons to form a true nervous system[104], enabling them to respond to their environments in far more sophisticated ways. A neural net allowed for basic communication of signals within the body, but a nervous system permitted the actual processing of information, which is an enormous improvement in capability for any organism.

The one element that the human brain seems to have the greatest difficulty coping with in all this is the concept of deep time. Many seemingly simple processes in the story of life on earth occurred over hundreds of millions or even billions of years. When one considers that Archaea appeared 3.5 to 4.2 billion years ago, and Deuterostomes, with a very crude brain, didn't appear for over 3 billion more years, it suggests that the hard evolutionary lifting occurred in the *billions* of years it took evolution to create the neuron.

Once the basic working model was there, however, life employed its typically harsh methods of suggesting that it improve. Groups of neurons conglomerated, and, through multiple adaptations, grew ever larger and more powerful. They evolved into neural nets which evolved into nervous systems which eventually evolved into brains, and the same adaptational processes exist to this very day. Evolution isn't just about then; it is also about now. Electro-chemical neuronal circuits evolved to provide for the transmission of nervous signals that allow sensory neurons to sense and motor neurons to actuate muscles. They could now be better coordinated by increasingly capable neuronal structures[104] to improve the animal's odds for survival.

Primitive creatures usually had extra room in their heads not taken up by neurons. Larger modern mammalian brains tend to make a slight "imprint" on the inside of their skulls[105] over time, which can leave clues as to specific brain structures, sizes, etc., but even modern reptiles still tend to have skulls *not* packed to overflowing with brains. In the final analysis, it seems likely that we may never know *exactly* when and to what extent many early primitive neural nets, nervous systems, and brain structures emerged in our ancient ancestors, only that they were present in some form at certain points.

After the neuron appeared, it spurred great evolutionary changes resulting in creatures with far greater capabilities to survive the incessant trials of their various environments. Creatures with improved neural apparatuses were able to both attack and defend better in numerous ways due to these adaptations. As a species evolved to create brains with more capabilities, it simultaneously put additional pressure on competitors to do the same or face extinction.

It is in this sort of milieu that what began as a simple instinct could conceivably evolve into a sophisticated instinct over time. Once the vestigial instinct was initially developed, the primary impediment to its further development in service to the organism would be time...lots and lots of time. The other factors in the equation would be the need for evolutionary change to assure survival, environmental pressures, and the sheer number of creatures contributing to the genetic potpourri. I think that any future adaptations creating a yet more sophisticated instinct would pale in comparison to the original, in that the original is so essential to the basic survival of the species.

Consider the case of Pakicetus[106], a vaguely dog-like carnivorous mammal that lived about 50 million years ago along the shores of the Tethys Sea[110]. In a mere 10 million years, it left the land to return to the sea, creating as it did all of the requisite adaptations necessary to cause it to evolve into the whale! It did this in 10 million years! How complex would a critically essential evolution have to be to require a billion years? When the only obstacle is time, nearly anything is possible.

Positive evolutionary mutations are extremely rare. Given time, though, they will occur. When they do, they can literally be world-changing. A radical series of adaptations of an instinctive nature can change a creature from a mere victim into a creature that can strike back aggressively in self-protection against threats, with the result that the world it inhabits will never be the same again.

Let us suppose that an unnamed reptilian species became wildly successful based on a newly evolved instinct that encouraged aggressive responses. Let us further suppose that it bred and multiplied outrageously as a result, creating hordes of progeny. Each additional member of the species increases the odds of random mutations being even more frequent. Let us further add another 50 million years in which the species evolved several other beneficial instincts. Now, you could be describing a creature successful enough to be one of our early ancestors.

We mammals evolved ever-improving neocortical brain structures that absolutely could not peacefully co-exist with the raw dictates of purely instinctive imperatives. I believe this to be a study in obviousness. The very idea that we could have a feelings-based neural structure, a reason-based neural structure, and unrestrained instincts *operating simultaneously* is simply untenable at every level. I cannot conceive of any situation in which such an unlikely arrangement could be successful. It invites a predictably avoidable consequence not unlike what occurs when we mistakenly invite Uncle Pete and his political opinions to Thanksgiving dinner. We know that people make regrettable decisions regularly, but evolution? It knows better.

There are deep and powerful instinctive currents that flow through all creatures. Instincts are generally unconscious by nature, but they should be heeded even when we become aware of them. Don't try to simply dismiss them, as they yet exist for a reason that is so essential that evolution has tattooed the neural circuitry into our brains, and it's not going to rub off. When a snake slithers out onto the path ahead of you, and you instinctively jump 3 feet straight up, use the experience as a reminder of the ancient parts of you that have given birth to the modern parts, as they are *both* you.

They are also a very real reminder to all humans that although we are extremely unique animals, we remain animals. Instincts should also be heeded for the reason that they have proven themselves to be advantageous over hundreds of millions of years of evolutionary trials and tribulations. When an instinct exists in a higher creature such as a human, it is because it continues to provide a positive survival benefit. It also helps us remember our roots.

BECOMING HUMAN
A New Perspective on the Origins of the Human Mind
Chapter 4

Feelings and Emotions

The fish brain preceded the amphibian brain which preceded the reptilian brain which preceded the mammalian brain. The reptilian complex (as it's also known) is incredibly ancient, but many later versions contained interconnected structures which provided it with a brain primarily directed by the creature's feelings. Feelings motivated the decisions that the creature took in a similar way that reasoning directs the actions we humans take (theoretically, anyway).

Given that reptiles tend to be basic sorts of creatures whose lives are inherently crude and often violent, the most prevalent emotions reptiles display are variants of rage, fear, and aggression (although *some* reptiles can also show positive emotions). Reptiles originally descended from amphibians and had been evolving for about a hundred million years before speciating mammals. Reptiles are our immediate ancestors, but they definitely took a different course to get to where they are today than did we.

The first true brain capable of assuming executive authority over most aspects of a creature's life was a feelings brain, assisted by, at best, a feeble cortex. *Primitive* versions of such components as the amygdala, thalamus, and hippocampus appeared scarcely 100 million years after the initial evolution of the neuron, and the hypothalamus first appeared in ancient marine worms before vertebrates had even evolved. The hypothalamus is especially essential to emotions[111]. The medial parts are associated with displeasure and aversion, while the lateral parts are associated with pleasure and rage (interesting how those two would be together).

Other neuronal structures such as the basal nuclei, brainstem, and cerebellum also first appeared in fish long before amphibians evolved[112]. When you consider how long some of these structures (which would eventually interconnect to form the feelings brain) had been around, you realize that they were already performing many valuable functions as independent structures.

Their continued evolution and interconnection indicate that they were indeed helpful in furthering the interests and ensuring the survival of the organism. In time, the feelings brain became well-interconnected with all other component structures. It was especially effective in creatures up to and including early mammals, with assistance from their still-developing neocortical reasoning abilities. Over deep time, though, the neocortex evolved through the addition of more neurons, and new purposes in which to employ them. The primary way that all neuronal structures gain power is through adaptations that encourage the production of more neurons[113].

In those early days when the reptiles with their three neuronal layers were evolving the first mammals, the emotional centers did actually reside in the physical structures of the limbic system. In more modern brains, and especially in humans, such things as may have historically occurred in limbic structures may now be taking place in areas that we would not traditionally associate them with, such as the cortex.

Why? Because humans have adapted to use our brains as efficiently as possible, and neocortical areas tend to be better organized and more efficient for many functions when compared to the less efficient ancient structures. In more contemporary understanding, neuroscientists refer to "emotion networks" and "emotion processing" to better describe how and where in the brain emotions are processed. As we are primarily concerned with the mind, rather than the brain, however, we are allowing a more generalized understanding of these terms as I have qualified them in an earlier chapter.

Evolution had no great interest in developing several successive brains over hundreds of millions of years. I don't think that's how evolution works. Evolution is incessantly trying to get individual creatures to be their most capable, and to be able to pass on those capabilities to their progeny, and that's it.

There is no great long-term plan. Long-term plans are human constructs. They certainly do not apply to forces of nature made apparent only by the world we live in combined with chemistry and physics which provide the laws of the universe in which we dwell. With evolution, goals are plentiful and ultimately short-term. Getting the creature to survive to make new creatures that are ever-better adapted to their environment is the first rule and the last rule, the Alpha and the Omega, of evolution.

All mammals are emotional. Emotions often appear spontaneously, and seemingly, on their own terms. We think thoughts, but we feel emotions. Often, an emotion will combine with other emotions, creating a virtually infinite number of possible emotional states. Some emotions are perceived as pleasurable, and others are not, but they are all incredibly powerful motivators. To fulfill emotional imperatives, animals will willingly suffer and die, such as when they are defending their young. All mammals will willingly sacrifice their lives toward this end, including people. There are few motivators more insistent and persistent than those which the emotions provide, and that is what makes them so powerful, especially before the development of neocortical reasoning abilities.

Emotions were precursors to reason as being the basis for decision-making by the only two brains that have existed in our entire mammalian history. A feelings brain feels a certain way, and acts on it, whereas a reasoning brain thinks through a course of action and follows it. Both systems produce outcomes that have proven themselves successful over hundreds of millions of years. They have, though, each differentiated themselves from the other by the respective tasks Mother Nature has asked them to perform.

The paleomammalian (or early mammalian) brain is a good example of a feelings brain without a lot of intellectual capability. Although the neocortex was present in an early form in the early mammals, their feelings brain was still driven by emotions that substituted feelings for abstract intelligence and reason.

That is not to say that the early mammals were not able to reason in a primitive way, because they did have the equipment to do that. It is simply that the influence of the feelings brain was far stronger than that of the early cortex and neocortex, and the feelings brain ruled as the chief executive of the organism at that time[168]. Neocortical abilities would have been able to advise and even warn the emotional brain against taking a certain path or making a certain decision, but they were not powerful enough in early mammals to overrule emotional decisions...yet.

The emotions, arising in unconscious processes then as they do now, can be inherently confusing. Emotions arise from the unconscious because that is how they evolved in the feelings brain (beneath the area of the brain that would later become the cortex long before there *was* a cortex). Emotions instantly inform us about how they feel about something, but cannot tell us why. They can't explain themselves because they developed in a part of the brain that preceded the sorts of explanations that only reason affords.

This phenomenon explains why we're always attempting (usually unsuccessfully) to understand our feelings based on the scant and unreliable clues the emotions drop along the way like bread crumbs. In this respect, the emotions are like a one-way mirror for the reason. Emotions inform us as to how we should feel without telling us why we should feel that way. The reason, on the other hand, operates in a precisely *reasonable* but opposite way, with inevitably confusing side-effects and consequences that can make you laugh and cry...mostly cry.

Some parts of our emotions definitely do exist in the conscious mind, like those that keep you awake all night as you strive to find an intellectual solution to an emotional quandary. Is there anyone who wouldn't agree with that last sentence? Sometimes, it seems as if feelings and reasoning components in humans are more *frenemies* than allies. Emotions are capable of rising up and briefly wresting control from the conscious reasoning mind[114]. This happens to humans, and I am quite confident that it also occurs in most mammals far more often than it does with humans, as they have far less reasoning ability than humans. Emotions and the feelings they produce sometimes have completely different goals than reason, and they will make that known in no uncertain terms.

The tension that is thereby created is obviously intended by evolutionary forces. It is a feature, and not a bug. It is as if adaptive forces have conspired to create this evolutionary odd couple simply to vex us humans. Most other mammals generally seem to follow their feelings, unless they're wholly inappropriate, or endanger them.

We humans, though, make reasoning decisions that sometimes incur the wrath of our own emotions as they seek to reverse those decisions. Usually, the reason accedes to the demands of emotions, because they can excoriate us as long as they want until we comply. It's a good deal, especially if you're an emotion.

I can think of some good reasons why nature would favor us with both capabilities. First off, we have to consider that the *feelings brain was already in place* before the neocortex substantially developed. In a manner of speaking, this put the feelings brain in the catbird's seat over the initially feeble neocortex, for a good long while, at least. The obvious reason for the development of the neocortex was to assist the emotional system to use reason to make better decisions. Reason is a very powerful tool for a creature to have in their toolbox, especially at a time in which other creatures were becoming more intelligent.

Unlike feelings of the type produced by the emotional system, reasoning tends to be objective and dispassionate. In some respects, rather than being opposed to feelings, reason actually complements them. Feelings, on the other hand, tend to lead, on occasion, to bad outcomes based on badly conceived initial decisions. The painfully obvious purpose behind the development of the neocortex was to restrain these possible negative tendencies in the area of decision-making.

The neocortex in its early stages was certainly not a powerful or controlling structure in the feelings brain, but we can assume that its reasoning powers would have been very useful in helping to curtail some of the hastier decisions that the feelings brain would've been far more likely to make without its guiding influence. In humans, both the aspects of feeling and reason are afforded a place in our conscious minds. Usually, reason informed by feelings holds sway. On the other hand, an unreasoning person overcome by their emotions is also common.

We humans are a strange admixture of these two aspects of mind, and both are variable in the intensity range of their actions. That makes for a lot of possible combinations of possible states of mind. As unlikely as these two aspects of mind are, to visualize us bereft of either feeling or reasoning is hard to do, because we are creatures who use both faculties *together* to each inform the other, so as to produce a unique blend of both perspectives. What an incredible strength! In a very real way, humans could be correctly described as creatures of high intelligence who also feel deeply or deeply passionate creatures that are really smart.

We have all known people in our lives who typify both extremes of each capacity. Such people, whether suffering from a malady or simply being that way by disposition, are conspicuous among their fellows. What we think of as a normal human being is an amalgam of both qualities. In our daily lives, we unconsciously and effortlessly glide between the realms of reason and feeling, unaware that we are even doing so. That's how effortless the transition is for us. We have literally evolved this way. Partly for reasons we understand, and partly for reasons that only god and evolution understand (and perhaps they are both the same entity). Whatever the case, this is the way that evolution has decided that human beings function best in their environment.

At times, these two aspects appear to be opposed. Feeling and thinking are not really opposite at all; as is, for instance, up and down. Feeling and thinking are simply different. Except for the historical circumstances of 220 million years ago which caused us to derive both capabilities within our minds, we would not view them as opposites, either. The way we view them in this diametrically opposed way is because the emotional force desires a different outcome than does the reason. That is why we view these two as opposites, even while intellectually realizing that something which might be in opposition is not truly opposite.

It is in the nature of our brains to consolidate information for maximum efficiency[115]. When you consider that a human brain is regularly making trillions of synaptic connections at any given moment, you can appreciate the power of such a term as efficiency in a whole new way. The fact remains, however, that we have one brain composed of many structures. Each of these is connected to many other structures in such a way that human consciousness as we apprehend the experience is made manifest on such a constant basis that we humans simply accept it as our norm.

In the main, we don't realize what an enormous series of adaptations had to occur to create this masterpiece of capability and efficacy. Although we do of course have a single, highly unified brain, we all experience a distinct duality to our feelings and reason at times, and this is as it should be. There are many different ways to consider the seeming duality that exists in the normal human brain.

Interactions between the reasoning and emotional components preceded our early mammalian roots. As reptiles had both a feelings brain and a basic cortex, the cortex must have been quite sufficiently interconnected with the feelings brain's neuronal circuitry to effectively do its job. Evolution is not going to create a structure, and then neglect to connect it up.

For very good reasons which we have enumerated, we are the beneficiaries of an adaptation that almost seems to have intentionally both gifted and cursed our species with two distinct aspects of mind, a thinking and a feeling aspect. They are *not* separate minds in any way, shape, or form. Sometimes, though, they can *feel* like they are, such as when our feelings and reasoning capabilities conflict. What we really have, then, is a single mind that *innately considers things from two perspectives.* It operates this way because it evolved this way. Our human mind is perfectly capable of doing this, and there are good reasons why it would do so which we will consider at greater length in later chapters.

I think folks should take time in their existences to consider things such as this, given that the circumstances that arise from this reality of what goes on behind our eyes affects who we are, and how we live our lives. In the final analysis, who we are as creatures is sometimes a good thing, and sometimes a bad thing. It all depends on what it is that we are doing.

In all cases, though, our feelings can be as important as our reasoning capabilities, because we are not merely organic computers with legs. We are creatures of this wild planet who have only recently, in the great scheme of things, come forth to claim dominance over all other creatures with whom we share this world.

For whatever reason, it would appear that evolution has decided that human beings function best with two principle aspects to their mind. If either had been disfavored, they would have disappeared. In nature, things don't always evolve; sometimes they devolve if that's in the best interest of the organism.

In the case of humans, though, we have been evolutionarily selected to *naturally* entertain two outlooks on the same situation. Much of the time, through a long-established understanding between the two, both components seem to be able to do their jobs without interfering overmuch with the other. It is only at certain times that one, the other, or both are suddenly in a situation in which they shift into overdrive. It could be occasioned by an emergency of some kind, or some other distressing event that is inherently very stressful or disconcerting that causes the entire apple cart which is the human conscious mind to temporarily overturn.

At such times, it's sometimes the emotional system that snatches control[117]. Some might call this the primal brain exerting itself, and there may be an *element* of truth to that. The emotions in humans (and all mammals) are very strong all by themselves. This is partly because there are many other brain components to reinforce such an "amygdala hijacking." The hijacking is a transitory process, and the much-chastised reason is usually soon returned to the driver's seat.

At the same time, though, emotions are so incredibly strong in human beings that when they combine forces with their reasoning abilities, they together form something far stronger than either alone could produce. When the two are in accord, you have pure reasoning power partially melded with (and partially always apart from) the feeling component. When these two aspects are in balance, they make a team that is immensely powerful and creates the modern world as we know it, with all its beauties and faults.

Because our ancestors evolved with a feelings brain before the advent of the thinking brain, feelings will always factor into all our decisions, formulations, and outlooks. A feeling brain has limitations, although it is far easier to construct the neural circuitry, which is why it evolved so long before the reasoning brain. Emotions are also very important and powerful components in our minds as motivators of actions.

Powerful feelings on their own can establish and evoke purpose, direction, and the energy needed to complete what is deemed to be essential tasks. The greater the importance that the emotions attach to a specific goal or desire, the greater the energy and motivation that they will apply to ensure that it is satisfactorily completed.

The later reptilian feelings brain packed a great deal of power in what was *relatively* simple neuronal wiring. Because of that quality, it was the best brain to evolve until the rise of the mammals. As we know that the early mammals were *primarily* directed by their feelings brain, the early neocortex would have been in a subservient capacity of advising without controlling the feelings-based decisions that resulted.

When the neocortex appeared on the scene, it was not, of course, immediately pushed to the head of the line. Like everything else, it began as a relatively inconsequential grouping of neurons that must've been of some basic value, or they presumably would have vanished. We know that they did not vanish, though; but that they grew both in numbers of neurons and capabilities. It is indisputable that the neocortex was initially not powerful, and wouldn't have been capable of taking over the operation of an entire brain. That would have been millions of years down the road. That, naturally, would've been catastrophic. That did not happen for that very reason.

It makes the most sense to suppose that the neocortex back in the early times was in a situation not dissimilar to that which the emotional system is in now. That when the neocortex perceived that the emotional brain was acting hastily because it was incapable of thinking things through, the neocortex could rise up and assail the hasty feelings brain.

Presumably, in a way very similar to the way our emotional system is capable of making our conscious mind's existence difficult, the less powerful component *seems to have the capability to assert itself* at all times, in the case of emotions. Perhaps, and this is a speculation on my part, the neocortex developed a similar ability. It is hard to imagine it wouldn't have such a capability, in greater or lesser part. What would be the point of having it if it wasn't capable of asserting itself?

I find it incredibly odd that evolutionary adaptations would create an apparent duality in our conscious mind *because* it appears that best serves the needs of our species, but it certainly appears that it did precisely that. Of course, it is not simply humans who live in this sort of balance between the neocortex and the emotional system. There is an entire world of other mammals out there that are far more similar to us than we might like to believe.

Unlike us, though, most of them have far more difficulty successfully asserting their reason against their emotional system. If you watch them closely, though, you see that they confront their realities in ways very similar to us. That's not to say that they are our intellectual equals. Rather, it is to say that they are also creatures of both feeling and reason. The main difference is that, in their case, the emotions are still in the ascendant over their reasoning capabilities, or so it certainly appears.

Over time, the crude feelings brains of reptiles evolved into the complex emotional systems of mammals. All of this happened over many millions of years, undoubtedly irregularly, depending upon the demands of the environments in which these evolutions occurred. One has to always remember that evolution doesn't just happen over epochs. Rather, evolution is happening every moment of every day and seeks to create ever greater efficacy without any conscious thought involved in the process.

In the final analysis, the feelings brain served a similar purpose as a primitive intellect, with feelings instead of reasoning making the decisions, and acting as motivating spurs to action. Why did the brains of our ancestors develop this way, with an initial feelings brain appearing so long before a reasoning brain? Simply because the three neuronal layers of some limbic structures and the simplified construction of reptilian neural components are far more primitive and easier to evolve than those of a neocortex. Evolving a six-layer neocortex? Now *that's* hard!

We should imagine emotions as arising from a very primitive origin because those who evolved emotions were themselves crude, primitive creatures. If some emotions seem somewhat refined now, it is because they have had a long time in which to refine themselves. A refined emotion is a more capable emotion, but it nevertheless has to have undergone innumerable evolutions so that it is always of use to the creature. Hopefully, it also serves a long-term positive benefit which may or may not be immediately obvious. We don't grow as species by huge leaps, but by minute adaptations to better suit ourselves to our environments.

Emotions form a continuous part of a feedback loop of feelings and thoughts. Emotions inform and edify all creatures that possess them, and are especially necessary for social creatures, for numerous reasons that we will consider in later chapters. Emotions make us feel. They also inform us when to act, spontaneously offer possible actions, and suggest what to do in that action.

Emotions are a necessary tool for the survival of all mammals, including humans, but only people have an advanced capability for abstract thought in addition to them. Evolutionary adaptations are capable of quashing the emotional system by making it a disfavored adaptation, and the intellectual part of the brain would certainly be able to complete its tasks without emotional input. It would, however, be a far different creature than are humans now.

We could have easily evolved a purely reasoning mind, but we have not done that. Rather, what has resulted from the metaphorical collision of the feelings brain and the neocortex is a single mind composed of two primary aspects. Somehow, they have each learned to contribute to the ongoing conversation that is human existence, and in that union, create something greater than the sum of their parts.

We are not simply thinking creatures who feel, any more than we are feeling creatures who think. We are a true synthesis of both. That can be both a strength and weakness, it is true, but it is also what makes us who and what we are. Having one capability without the other would make us a poor compromise lacking either the passion needed to motivate us or the wit necessary to harness that passion.

BECOMING HUMAN
A New Perspective on the Origins of the Human Mind
Chapter 5

Reason and the Neocortex

Fortune may favor the bold, but evolution definitely favors intelligence. "Becoming Human" is a book about the human mind, rather than the human brain. A mind, though, is not possible without a brain to nurture and support its activities. I am intentionally avoiding references to brain anatomy and physiology except where it is necessary in order to explain some components. Further information about the brain is easily obtainable for those so inclined but is far outside the scope of this work.

In this book, I'm trying to better understand my species. I feel that some theories of human personality and behavior that I've encountered have been too limited to adequately explain why humans behave the way they do. It seems to me that many theories are dealing with only a limited perspective on life and living, but do not put those theories into a fuller and more relevant outlook by which to judge such things in a broader context.

That does not mean that I think such theories are necessarily incorrect. It means that I find it difficult to try to understand *anything* without an appropriately broad perspective of the factors undergirding it. If there are critically important realities of which one is unaware in their study of *any* given thing, they can't be expected to create an accurate theory of that thing, as they lack essential information pertinent to the formulation of their theory. Ancient people regularly theorized that the sun was at the center of the universe based on their observations that it certainly *appeared* to occupy that position based on the available data.

Human knowledge accumulates over time and is directly proportional to the effort of a myriad of dedicated researchers, scientists, experimenters, observers, and theoreticians. Information that is available to a researcher now substantially differs from that which was known a century ago, when psychology was in its infancy. As many early theories still form the cornerstones of current beliefs, however, it is only proper that they be considered anew in light of the massive amounts of additional accumulated knowledge obtained over the last hundred-plus years; information that is accumulating at an ever-increasing rate. It is a fascinating time for lovers of knowledge.

Restraining a powerful impulse to act is one of the hardest things that any mammal can attempt. Consider the plight of your poor pup as she silently regards the roast provocatively perched on the edge of the counter. If you look deeply into her eyes, you can see that the strain is very evident. Every fiber of her being is telling her to bury her teeth in the succulent goodness of the roast. At the same time, her reason is in overdrive as it attempts with all its might to restrain such impulses. If you then place the roast far beyond her reach so that it can no longer torment her, she will visibly relax as her intellectual load is diminished.

This is not unlike how human minds can resist the innumerable impulsive emotional pressures constantly exhorting them to act. The reason mediates between the raw impulses and the possible consequences of heeding those impulses. If following an impulse would result in negative consequences, the reason can overrule the impulse. In other words, the reason engages in a risk-to-benefit analysis and consciously decides a course of action that will yield the greatest benefits while diminishing negative consequences. In this, humans are behaving similarly to our anxiety-ridden pooch. The only difference is in the complexity of the thoughts of which our minds are capable, and the ability of the reason to be a decisive factor.

A feature of being human that does not exist in any other animal is the incredibly powerful nature of our minds to think abstractly, and to retain these abstractions as permanent objects. That is the true game-changer in the story of how we became human. Without this ability, we would be just another social animal. With this ability, we became masters of the world.

While human and higher animal's minds can both mitigate against the negative consequences of blindly following impulses and feelings, we differ greatly in the *degree of control* that we can exert in this manner when compared to other animals. As our species developed ever-increasing reasoning abilities, we also developed greater control over impulses and emotions.

When our mind's conscious control of impulses and feelings increased to the point that we could resist the exhortations and siren's calls of our emotion's fondest desires, we became capable of the sort of intellectual control necessary for beginning to develop social orders. It then became inevitable that every change in the mind's raw intelligence level created the opportunity to make greater social orders possible. These new orders required an ever-increasing level of intelligence that was necessary to order and sustain such societies[152].

As our social organizations grew in complexity and our minds grew in intelligence and capability, a point of equilibrium occurred in which there was no longer any further benefit to be obtained by increasing social complexity. Without an ever-increasing need to become more intelligent in order to properly serve that social order, we essentially stopped increasing in native intelligence. I have seen no compelling evidence to support the premise that present-day humans are any more intelligent than our prehistoric ancestors (Indeed, if smart is as smart does, an argument could be made that we are backsliding). Primitive Homo sapiens first appeared around 300,000[118] years ago, had become modern Homo sapiens by around 200,000 years ago, and some have hypothesized that the brain has not appreciably evolved in the last 100,000[119] years.

Like most evolutionary changes, then, our brains increased in intelligence to the extent that increased intelligence was necessary. Higher intelligence helped us to accomplish the task of being able to create and maintain social orders necessary for the survival and success of the species. When that had been achieved, there was no need for ever-greater intelligence; and there was, therefore, no adaptive pressure to change.

When the giraffe evolved its long neck, by way of comparison, it was to feed on tree leaves above the reach of

110

other animals, thus providing an ecological niche in which it could thrive. The giraffe didn't continue to grow an ever-increasingly longer neck beyond what was necessary to ensure survival, nor did humans grow ever-increasing intelligence levels beyond that which was necessary to ensure survival. As a rule, that's how evolution tends to work.

Although other higher creatures, especially mammals, have *some* ability to restrain themselves when under threat, only humans have true executive control over their actions when their reason asserts itself as the dominant and deciding factor. We are creatures whose behavior is *ultimately* determined by our reasoning abilities. We have emotions that make us feel and act in certain ways. We have impulses that appear to be the motive forces behind some of our (usually more memorable) behaviors.

Blocking a powerful emotional impulse (and most impulses are emotional in origin) is so difficult that it takes a very large amount of psychic energy to accomplish. Most people go to great lengths to avoid such occasions simply because of the stress that results from the internal confrontation that must occur to resist and block such things. If a person were in a situation in which such stresses occurred frequently, it would take all of their limited psychic energy to resist taking such impulsive actions, leaving precious little to perform the other essential tasks required of the reasoning mind.

Unlike animals, though, we do not appear to be *very* instinctively motivated. As we observe animals around us, we can't help but note that there appear to be certain instinctive aspects of their behaviors that may be exhibited under certain circumstances. We also observe that these animals (and in particular, mammals) also have an intellect that helps them navigate their world in a far superior way than would be the case if they were exclusively driven by purely blind instincts, or even a feelings brain operating by itself sans an intellect. We observe that although most mammals exhibit some degree of reasoning capability, none even remotely approximate that of human beings (although dolphins and orcas may yet surprise us).

All mammals possess reasoning abilities which can restrain impulses of both an instinctive and emotional nature, and all mammals are, in greater or lesser part, impulsive. Controlling a powerful impulse is one of the hardest things a mammal can do. Impulse control can be uniquely exhausting. We all know this as we all do it regularly. When, for instance, we defer to our boss even though he's totally wrong, when we tell a loved one that *of course your purple Mohawk looks great*, or when we restrain ourselves from throttling the obnoxious, we are using our reasoning abilities to directly oppose impulses which, if unopposed, might easily get us in trouble.

Our mind is informed by our experiences, many of which are committed to memory. In this way, the reason becomes an ever more effective countervailing force against potentially problematic emotional impulses taking hasty or ill-considered actions that might be detrimental to the person involved. Humans do have a lot more reasoning capability than any other mammals to employ in this endeavor, but it is really only a matter of degree. Having such highly developed intellectual capabilities allows us to unconsciously and consciously modulate impulsive reactions of all types to best suit the plans and purposes of our conscious minds.

It's not easy to be a brain, but a constant feature of all brains from crude to human is that they are incessantly attempting to achieve order, maintain smooth operations, and spread the workload. As well, it must integrate separate components into a single coherent whole, and promote efficiency of operation despite the inherent chaos surrounding it. Consider that what has emerged as the human brain has integrated innumerable changes into its very structure *on the fly* through hundreds of millions of years as it evolved from its reptilian origins through the long period of emotional dominance to its current cerebral state. Neocortical contributions to the far-stronger feelings brain must have been sufficiently helpful to ensure not only its continued existence but its growth in complexity and influence as a favored adaptation.

In our modern human brains, the situations have reversed, and the bottom rail is now on top. The emotional system of our brains is, for the most part, now in a subservient position to our reason. What we experience inside our minds every day is a reflection of the process wherein the initially less powerful and the initially more powerful components have reversed their respective positions. We should thank evolution that they have!

At the inception of the neuronal circuitry in fish, amphibians, or reptiles that would eventually become the neocortex, it would've had almost no power, as it would have had very few neurons dedicated to its construction. To become more powerful to better serve the dictates of natural selection, it would have had to adapt the ability to grow untold millions more neurons, adapt existing neuronal structures, and evolve other new structures in order to best work with the feelings brain. It wasn't like the burgeoning neocortex was plotting a coup to take over. It was evolution's call to make, and it did. It naturally selected mammals to be this way. It is only in the last few million years that Homo erectus and others have added a distinctly new factor of highly capable intelligence to the equation.

The development of the neocortex is about many things, but one of those things primarily has to do with the sheer number of neurons that went into its makeup at any given time. More neurons, in the main, equates to a more capable and powerful neocortex. This addition of more neurons occurred over many millions of years and slowly but surely caused mammals to grow in reasoning ability, as well as most of the other components that we associate with the reasoning parts of our minds. It would've taken a myriad of adaptations and mutations, of trials and errors on a grand scale for this to come to fruition. Eventually, though, it did indeed bear fruit as it became the neuronal component that occupies the chief executive position in the modern human mind, and a seemingly significantly less powerful position in most other mammals.

The emotional system was also adapting and developing simultaneously. Its component structures were becoming better integrated so that they could excel at all of the functions required of a feelings-based brain. This would, of course, include interconnecting with the neocortex. In so doing, the pattern that would persist in humans to this day was established. When there is a conscious mind, you have to make a connection to it on a conscious level, or it cannot communicate or respond. It was incumbent on both components to make this happen as effectively as possible. Apparently, it was done successfully, as we are still connected hundreds of millions of years later.

Although the individual structures formed neuronal connections to each other, they did not truly amalgamate[120] or fuse into a single structure. Each kept its own identity and continued to provide the services for which it had originally evolved. As all brains innately do, it continually strove to better order itself so that it could more effectively coordinate its various activities to increase the efficiency of each component. Its ultimate purpose was to improve the overall maximum efficacy of the entire resulting feelings brain, while simultaneously maintaining those brain operations for which it had initially evolved.

The emotional portion of all mammalian brains (including those of humans) makes its feelings assessment of a given situation far more quickly than the intellectual portion[121], as a rule. The neocortex then adds its reasoning assessment to the blend, but by this time the feelings assessment has already informed the reasoning mind. As every conscious person knows, their intellects invariably engage only after their initial emotional reactions have already occurred. It provides a sort of built-in prejudice in favor of the feelings, doesn't it? I can only speak for my species (although I suspect most mammals also experience this phenomenon), but feelings occur quickly and powerfully before we have formed any opinions as to what we *think* about something. Our brains are designed this way, and our most current neuronal adaptations still conform to this pattern.

In the case of a higher creature such as humans, however, the intellect has nevertheless grown far stronger than the feelings aspect of our conscious mind. As such, it is *usually* able to assume command authority. When there is an emotional reaction, the intellect is fully aware of what the emotions require to be satisfied, and the same is true in reverse. The reason, in the main, remains fully capable of exercising a controlling influence over the emotions in such a way as to squelch their demands (that is an example of willpower). The reverse, however, is not true except in some extreme situations, as all humans know only too well.

As much as the emotions might make one feel bad, the reason is not compelled to harken to them. If it knows what's good for it, though, it will *attempt* to placate the emotions so that it will not be subjected overmuch to the incredible array of possible negative and truly hurtful feelings that your emotions can engender in you. It is more than merely interesting how there is a built-in counterbalance to the reason's dominance in this arrangement.

From the point of view of one who is in perpetual awe of the majesty of evolution, I honestly feel that this arrangement is one of the most perfect things I have ever seen in my life. When a mere human looks upon the flawless elegance of evolution, they are glimpsing the closest thing to perfection they will ever see. What is the proof of that? How about 220 million years of success and counting?

Although reason ultimately has overall authority in the area of decision-making, the emotional system has in its possession a trump card composed of the feelings that it can generate to influence the decision-making of the reason. It is a wise person who heeds the counsel of their feelings because the emotional system can keep playing its trump card all day...and all night. It won't get tired. It won't move on. It will just cause a crisis of conscience until you become too exhausted to resist it (or so it hopes).

Do you know why you'll probably eventually give in? Because, if a particular crisis is still tweaking your emotions at this late point in the deliberations, it's probably because you're reason is in the wrong. Let me provide an example. You are driving home, and see a lost little kitten by the side of the road. You know you should stop to see if the kitten is all right, but you're in a hurry, so you don't. Immediately, your emotional system resists you. Never using a single word, armed only with the feelings that are the pure essence of emotion, it demands that you stop, but you keep driving despite how you are being bombarded with vexation.

Once home, you eat dinner, but in the background, your emotions are sending you even more stark images of the hungry kitten forlornly watching you slurp gravy off your chin. For whatever reason, the food just doesn't taste that good anymore, so you go to bed; but a monster awaits you there. You snuggle down into the comforter in that certain way you enjoy so much, only to be confronted by dire images of a terrified kitten looking up at you beseechingly as coyotes howl menacingly in the background.

Go ahead; try to sleep. I dare you. More importantly, your emotional system is daring you. Try to just let all thoughts of tiny helpless kittens being gobbled up alive by rapacious wolves calmly dissipate as you prepare for a luxurious night of tranquil slumber. Five hours pass, though, and you just can't get comfortable. No matter what you do, you keep getting bombarded by incessant and increasingly strident demands from your feelings that are making you feel perfectly terrible, and your mood is at low ebb.

You are suffering an acute attack of conscience, courtesy of your emotional system. You are suffering because *conscience is an emotional projection*, and in this instance, it intends for you to suffer. It is making you suffer because it is displeased with your decision, and it has caused an emotional crisis. It uses its power in much the same way that it did 200-odd million years ago when it was in undisputed control of the organism (or, as it would term it if it used words, *the good old days*), and its emotional brain forced it to make its body rise up and exterminate that loud, snarling jackal that had enraged it to a homicidal fury. The entire world was a tough neighborhood back then, lest we forget.

Sigmund Freud believed that the above example of a crisis was a result of the superego[122] trying to force the ego to behave morally. It was doing this in the same way it had always done since it formed at the end of its owner's Oedipal[164] Stage around the time they achieved the age of reason. Another belief Freud espoused was that the superego doesn't take reality into account as it strives for an ideal[123]. Full stop! He just described the normal emotional system of a human being by describing the superego.

Freud thought the superego[163] developed as one grew from childhood, but I believe he was mistaken, in my humble opinion. It is not your superego. It is your emotional system, and *it* is what is developing as you grow. It knows how and what you think through its interconnection with the conscious mind.

It understands what you value, and not at all oddly; it reacts with feelings toward all things, because, well, it's an emotional system! It doesn't have alternative ways to express itself. It isn't like it can write a poison pen letter to the editor exposing your kitten-cide! It must improvise. Would you, the holder of a golden ticket entitling you to a free sleepless night, mind very much if your own emotional system were to bombard you with visions of your own inadequacy as a kitten wrangler? You would? Awesome! Then let's do this!

Fast-forward to 4 a. m., and you are now crawling on your belly through muddy ditches while meowing in such a reassuring tone so as to encourage even the most recalcitrant kitten in creation to come forth; because you, a member of the most deadly apex predator species on the planet have endured a vicious beating by an aspect of your own mind, and it won't let you sleep until and unless you can find and console one very specific pussy cat! That will be the cost of a good night's sleep for you.

Metaphorically, I've been in that ditch, and so has every other human being in the world, unless they have been so unfortunate as to have received something such as a traumatic brain injury, or are suffering from a condition that has resulted in a breakdown in normal brain function. If there was a moral to this story, it would be to just accept that there is more to this human mind of ours than either Sigmund Freud or your emotional system can ever tell you.

Remember, though, that your emotional system does know at all times what is going on in your head, because it also lives there, too. It cannot speak to you using words, because it does not have that capability. When its constituent parts were created, words were still half a billion years away from being invented. So no, you cannot have deep conversations with your emotional system as if it were a college roommate, because that's not how such things function. You might as well try striking up a conversation with a goat.

If you had just walked several miles through broken countryside in the dark of night seeking and ultimately finding a kitten (surprise happy ending!), and your right foot was sore where you fell into a woodchuck hole (because this is my story, and it's occurring in Vermont), wouldn't you rub that foot? Wouldn't you look it over, and see if it was all right? Words are neither necessary nor helpful, but making sure all parts of you are doing okay is part of your job, isn't it, reasoning aspect?

After your emotional system has been that agitated, it and the rest of your body feels as though it has been through something traumatic, doesn't it? It will take some time for the brain chemicals alone to dissipate from your system, and you're going to be pretty jumpy until you calm down, anyway. So sure, send your tattered emotional system some calming images of the happy kitten playing with a ball of yarn. Emotions love that (but don't get gushy and make promises you can't keep because they still know where you live).

It must've been a bit weird in the times of the early mammals, as two entirely different neural mechanisms were attempting to combine their respective abilities to the task of making daily life-and-death decisions. One mechanism was based in feelings, and one was based in abstract reasoning. The two are seemingly not things that fit together well.

Our reason tends to resist and abjure the illogic of purely impulsive emotional declarations (such as what happened with the lost kitty), and our emotional system (for the most part) is created in such a way that intellect and higher reasoning are entirely alien to it. It is as if they speak different languages with no common referent. Yet, they nevertheless developed what became extensive neuronal connections that provided them a mechanism by which to interface and communicate.

If a mammal is in relatively calm circumstances, then both the reason and emotions are also generally calm. Reason is more likely to prevail than it is in a time of stress. Say that you have a dog, for instance, and its emotional reaction to the presence of another dog is such as to create pressure on your dog's reasoning faculties to bark at him. The dog's owner, however, will scold him if he does; so he doesn't. The dog's reason is sufficient to curb the wayward impulse. Then, in the next 10 seconds, the other dog aggressively advances toward your dog, and your dog's emotional system completely and absolutely takes charge of the beast for the duration of the conflict. Just like that. Quick as a wink.

If you, the gentle and loving owner, were to be so rash as to attempt to intervene, your dog would also tear a chunk out of you without hesitation. You cannot blame the dog, as his reasoning faculties are no longer in his control[124]. His reason has been hijacked by his emotional system. That is how he is designed (and so are humans, to a lesser extent). If it is any consolation, though, the dog will feel just terrible about it afterward.

The dog's reason makes its decisions on totally different criteria than its emotional system. It is exactly the same with humans. The difference is in the amount of control that a mammal has compared to what a human has. Although there are individuals who do not have much control over their emotions, lord knows, most of us have far more than that which any other mammal could ever claim. It is in our nature, one could say, and they wouldn't be incorrect. Mostly, though, it is in that huge pile of 86 billion very capable neurons up there. In the words of Josef Stalin: "Quantity has a quality all its own."

A mind unified to have the ability to successfully integrate both capacities is a marvel of adaptation. What an incredible evolutionary achievement it is that there are two such distinctly dissimilar aspects created in fundamentally different ways over millions of years. Yet, these two have somehow managed to order themselves into a single mind, and for the most part, interact with equanimity, knowing that their concerns can be heard, each by the other. If you are engaged in lofty rhetoric with a peer, your reason is in control; but if a mountain lion should happen to leap down upon you from a nearby ledge, it's time to tag out with your emotions, and let them do what they do best: keep you alive.

Few organs have undergone such profound changes as has the human brain. It is a testament to the power of this miraculous conglomeration of structures that it has been able to establish and maintain order over its trillions of neuronal connections even as it integrated new parts into itself. It must always be remembered that the brain is constantly reorganizing itself for maximum efficiency, so that the areas of the brain that we associate with many activities do not necessarily occur exclusively within these areas. They can be *farmed out* as is determined to constitute the most efficient use of the facilities, as it were. The brain is quite adept at integrating its multitudinous activities and spreading its workload. We as humans are the ultimate beneficiaries of what is arguably one of the most incredible creations that ever evolved on Earth.

My education is in psychology, as I've pointed out, and psychology is principally concerned with the mind, and not the brain. The mind and the brain are quite distinct from each other. It would be accurate to say that the mind is primarily produced by the brain. The brain is part of the body, though, so the body is also involved in the production of the mind in a very real way. I'm certainly no expert in the physical structure of the brain, beyond the coursework I've taken in pursuit of the psychology degrees I've received and some reading and study I've done on my own. I leave the physical science to the many experts of all types with which the world is blessed. I am constantly amazed by the extraordinary insights that they reveal[173]. I rely on their pronouncements to provide me the knowledge I need by which to better understand how these physical structures have influenced the development of the human mind. Without their hard work, I wouldn't be able to employ their knowledge and understanding of our past and present worlds to inform my own thought process. My sincere thanks to them all for their incredible efforts.

The term "Dualism" is often used in different ways to describe specific beliefs about the relationship between the mind and the body. I'd like to qualify my use of the term to refer to the concept that the two entities under consideration here are the body (which includes the brain) and the mind. One is physical, and one is not. They are totally distinct, and will always remain so. At the same time, they are also forever linked. It's like the old song says: *you can't have one without the other.* That's the full meaning I intend, with no inference of any "greater" belief system which guides my steps, religious or otherwise. To paraphrase Groucho Marx, *I could never belong to an organization that would have a person like me as a member, anyway.*

The brain is a physical structure, but the mind is less substantial than a cloud, infinitely so. It has no physical substance whatsoever. As all of us humans know in our own conscious minds, though, it is the *most real thing* in the world to us. It *is* us, and we are it.

BECOMING HUMAN
A New Perspective on the Origins of the Human Mind
Chapter 6

The Genesis of the Human Mind

*"Man cannot remake himself without suffering, for he is
both the marble and the sculptor."*
-Alexis Carrel-

At a profoundly unfathomable depth of the human
mind lies the intersection between reason and emotion.
That is also where the inevitable conflicts between the two
occur. How and why did our minds develop this way? Why
do we have these two separate aspects combined in one
mind? How did this happen? It is a very interesting story
that unfolds over deep time as amphibians evolved reptiles,
who then evolved mammals.

Reptiles are primarily directed by their emotion-
based feelings brains, which determine the specific
emotional behaviors and reactions of the animal. Reptilian
emotions tend to be centered around basic needs, as reptiles
themselves are basic creatures in many ways. Reptiles had
been developing for around 100 million years before
speciating mammals. All reptiles are referred to as amniota
because they lay eggs (but not all amniota are reptiles). The
mammals who developed from these reptiles, on the other
hand, delivered their young alive.

Mammalian needs are far different than reptilian needs. Because mammalian needs are different, their emotions also needed to be different. Evolutionary pressures caused mammals to rapidly develop appropriate new emotions so that they could better care for their young. At the same time, the reptilian emotions they inherited remained in place, because they had proven themselves to be effective over a very long time. The new emotions were added on top of the old ones, and they have all merged over the succeeding eons. This is true for all mammals, including humans. The primary difference between humans and other mammals is the vastly greater amount of authority that our neocortex has over our emotional system. Reason is now in firm control.

By approximately 100,000 years ago[149], Homo sapiens had achieved their maximum level of intelligence. There is scant evidence to suggest that human beings have become any more intelligent since that time. Homo sapiens first appeared about 300 thousand years ago, and early Homo sapiens have been determined to be less intelligent than modern Home sapiens as (primarily) determined by cranial capacity. 100,000 years might seem like a long time, but compared to the sort of time periods that we're regarding in this entire matter, it isn't that long. When you consider how long mammals have been around, it makes a measly 100,000 years seem rather insignificant.

When you consider that the human brain has become larger and more capable over the mere 200,000 years between when we first speciated from Homo Heidelbergensis and 100,000 years ago, that is very significant. How much, then, can we suppose that our intelligence increased in the *220 million years* before that? That is over 1000 times longer than that in which present-day humans became identifiably more intelligent than early humans. Of course, this is not to say that intelligence increases at any kind of fixed rate, because it doesn't. Evolution doesn't work like that.

Generally speaking, there need to be evolutionary advantages to be gained that offset the risk of the organism needing to change itself to accommodate new adaptations to its brain, primarily through mutation. All changes can be potentially risky, as unforeseen circumstances can arise as a result of any adaptation. The problem with mutations is that you need an enormous number of them if you hope to get anything of substance accomplished. Small changes do accrue bit-by-bit over deep time, though, making nearly anything possible. Adaptational pressures exert themselves to promote change when change is necessary. If change isn't required to improve survival chances, it should not be expected.

The small differences in intelligence that slowly accrued over more than 200 million years caused our neocortical abilities to increase dramatically in what were fits and starts. Judging by some of the predecessor species that came before humans that we have encountered elsewhere in the text, we have certainly seen an incredible increase in intelligence throughout this time. Most of the greatest changes occurred in primates[150] over the last several million years.

While the neocortex has grown into its most advanced form in the human brain, the emotional system inherited from early mammals has also been passed on to us. It has, of course, been made to conform to human needs, but largely remains similar to its early mammalian configuration. The emotions that are harbored in the human emotional system are presumably as unalterable as those of our ancestors from that time. Encoded into emotions, I believe, is the power to prevent them from changing, even over incredibly long periods of time.

While it's impossible to know what the emotional state of a creature that lived over 200 million years ago was, we do know the sorts of emotions that would be required by a mammal to successfully raise young. Although it is also not possible to know the mental state of a paleomammal, we do know that their neocortex was very small and undeveloped compared to that of more modern mammals. As their feelings brain was still providing executive control, we know that their emotions were able to express much more direct control than can ours. This is because they didn't have a highly developed and powerful neocortex capable of squelching feelings in the same way as can humans.

The relative power differential between the neocortex of a mammal and a human being is staggering. Modern mammals retain an emotional system that is far stronger than humans, *in comparison* to their neocortex. Even though they have had exactly the same amount of time as humans in which to develop a massively inflated neocortex like us, they have not. Why? The most likely answer is that they simply were not under adaptational pressures to do so, and so; they didn't. We can't blithely assume that it would be in *all* mammals' best interests to do so simply because it was in ours. Arguably, it is quite to the contrary. It can be posited that their lack of extensive intellectual development *is* proof that it wasn't a necessary development for them. It would appear that they found their evolutionary *sweet spot*, and stayed in it. It was only we humans who needed more.

Most mammals are fairly intelligent creatures in terms of the numbers of neurons in their brains, but none are even vaguely in the same neuronal league as humans, excepting several species of large mammals such as elephants and whales. Aside from them, we are in a class by ourselves, and it is doubtful that they have anything even close to our level of intelligence. It is not simply a matter of the total number of neurons involved. There are many additional considerations. There is the efficiency of the neurons to be factored in, the number of connections each neuron can create, the neuroplasticity[151] of the entire brain, as well as many other characteristics.

This massive human brain, however, didn't evolve just to lord it over the feelings brain. Research indicates that increased intellectual capability was necessary to assist in the creation of ever-more-complex human societies. More complex societies would also contain an increasing number of individuals with whom one would have to become familiar. There has been a positive correlation between brain size and how complex societies can become, and this is borne out in studies[152]. The more people with whom one is in contact, the greater the brainpower needed. To accomplish this task, more neocortical area was evolved to be filled with yet more neurons. We did indeed develop an incredible cortical ability, and it appears that it was largely for social interactions with a greater number of other humans.

Human brains do possess six cortical layers that we share with all mammals. Six layers[153] seem to be adequate to the task for both of us, so there would be no reason to evolve more. Reptiles have only three cortical layers[154], and mammals' extra three evolved from their dorsal pallium around the time of the transition from the Jurassic to the Triassic periods.

Because our brains evolved from those of reptiles, we still share many brain structures with them. Some of these structures remain quite similar to those of reptiles, especially within the emotional system. The human hippocampus[155], for example, being one of those adapted structures, still exists in its original three-layer form, as do other limbic structures.

Additional cortical area is obtained within the six layers of the human brain by convolutions[156] that increase the surface area, as well as by the thickness of the cortical layers, and the neuronal density within those layers. In the early hominin lineage, the brain went through a quiescent period, thought to be indicative of a period of neural reorganization[157]. My use of the term "fits and starts" to describe the evolution of the human brain is based on such events as this. Human brain evolution was not at all a constant or steady process.

Humans, like all creatures, would be unlikely to continue to develop what would be extraneous mental abilities. As the human brain already takes about 25% of a person's total energy to operate, over-sizing it further could do quite a lot of harm. By siphoning off an even larger percentage of finite available energy, there would remain less available for all other purposes. How many people would have starved because they weren't able to spare the extra energy to power their unnecessarily overpowered brain?

Whatever the purpose, any significant increase in cortical neurons would've also necessarily affected the power dynamic between the neocortex and the feelings brain, presumably as a dysfunction (in the sociological sense of the term). If that was the case, then the feelings brain must have been in for a rude awakening when this hitherto minor neocortical structure steadily grew into a goliath. Overshadowing the emotional power of the feelings brain in every respect, we can only guess at the dramas that must've played out during this prolonged transfer of power. It's probably better that we don't know all the gory details.

What we do know, however, is that humans now have a reasoning aspect exercising executive control of our mind, and the emotional brain has been reduced in rank to that of an *emotional system*. That in no way infers that it is not a major player in the game, though. That is because our emotional system has certain capabilities and prerogatives which must be respected. The penalty for disrespect is emotional opprobrium of the sort no human enjoys. A variable balance of power is certainly evident in the day-to-day operation of the conscious mind. The only time the emotional system asserts itself to the point that it actually takes control of the mind, however, is in an emergency, or a situation that the emotional system deems to be an emergency. The fact that it may *not* be an emergency is completely irrelevant and is not taken into consideration in any way, shape, or form. This is because, as we know, the emotional system is not burdened by the need to be reasonable. It is incapable of logic of any type, as logic is a reasoning ability. Nevertheless, it has adapted to be capable of *limited interaction* with the reasoning aspect of the mind.

It is a difficult concept for some person to accept the idea that their mind has two aspects to it; aspects that would never be apparent if you were to examine a human brain on a microscopic level. This is not something that can be determined with a microscope, though, no matter how powerful it is. The brain, not the mind, is the area for physical scientists.

Let me make very clear what the distinction between the mind and brain is, because this is an area of some confusion, even among some trained people. The brain is an organ. It is the hardware without which the magic of the mind cannot function. The mind resides in a primary physical location called the brain. The mind, however, is not physical, but is that which creates and manipulates thoughts, memories, images, and other such insubstantial manifestations. As mentioned earlier, most people have adopted an outlook known as 'Dualism,' which is the belief that the mind and body (including the brain) are separate entities.

This book is about the human experience of living, and how we apprehend our own conscious minds every day. This is not something that can be studied objectively from afar. This is something that constitutes the very essence of *subjectivity*. This is something that can only be understood by experiencing it in one's life, and hopefully having a good understanding of what it is that you're experiencing within that life.

There is a single unified mind bouncing around within our pates, with reason being the primary executive within the conscious mind. There is, however, an emotional component that exists as the other aspect of our minds, although it exerts a far less important role than it once did in terms of being the *decider*. Nevertheless, it remains a very powerful and influential system in the human mind that is responsible for numerous critical operations.

In the development of most brains from Hylonomus onward, a simple brain has usually integrated new structures into it, becoming more complex and powerful as it does. Since early times, all mammalian brains have been working constantly to maintain the optimal function of their species for hundreds of millions of years. Who are we to say that they weren't perfectly capable, especially since we would not be here if they weren't? They have been proven over time.

It is this clever human brain that is the new development. We humans are still here because we also have these reptilian and early mammalian emotions-driven structures, along with a few later customizations. So thank you, feelings brain, but we can handle the executive duties from here with our reasoning mind, while still relying on your constant assistance. Our emotional system remains a critically essential aspect of our minds, however, and although its role has changed and somewhat diminished from its glory days, we would be lost without its guidance, even in those times when we really resent it.

The human mind is usually divided into the conscious, the unconscious, and the pre-conscious. The pre-conscious is something that some people are not as familiar with as the other two, so let me just say that the pre-conscious contains the things that aren't in consciousness at a given moment, but which can easily be recalled into consciousness when requested by the conscious mind or the emotions.

The emotional system, however, is not all entirely conscious, either. Every one of our lives is replete with examples of how our emotional system is most definitely functioning on an unconscious, as well as a conscious level. The conscious level is obvious, in that it is something that is directly interacting with our reason. Sometimes, the emotional system seems to be wheedling, cajoling, negotiating, and sometimes even deferring to the reasoning aspect, though it might not like what the reasoning aspect of the conscious mind is intent on doing.

If the emotional system did not have an unconscious component, then from whence would its emotionally laden feelings emanate without notice? It certainly isn't as a result of a dialogue with the rest of the conscious mind, as the emotional system isn't a big talker. It feels; but it doesn't think, as such. It does interact with the reasoning aspect, and the two components have obviously grown substantial neuronal connections between each other dedicated to *smartening up* some emotional attributes. This is apparently limited to its interactions with the conscious reasoning mind. Given the present progress in human understanding of our brains, I would guess that it will still be a decade or two before stronger physical proof is available to show the true extent of this connection.

Emotions are feelings incarnate. The emotional system communicates using its feelings, and can often do so quite effectively, probably because the neocortex has become so good over the last 200 plus million years at interpreting its feelings. Its concerns come welling up from what is perceived by the conscious mind to be an unconscious level of the emotional system. That's why these emotions frequently blindside the conscious mind. That's why we are often surprised by where a certain feeling might have originated from when it is presented to the conscious mind.

Why shouldn't there be an unconscious emotional system component? There already was an unconscious emotional component before the neocortex appeared. Insofar as our reasoning conscious mind is largely a product of the neocortex, and in that it was not powerful in the early days of reptilian and early mammalian existence, it is obvious that the neocortex and feelings brain could develop only a somewhat limited communication confined to common concerns. It appears to have remained like that to this very day, with some embellishments. Our brain has an unconscious component of which we are largely unaware, as well as a conscious component we identify as our conscious mind.

The emotional system[137], likewise, has a conscious component that it partially shares with the conscious mind, as well as an unconscious component, which is forever unknown to the conscious mind. When the unconscious component of the emotional system wishes to make a concern known, it does so of its own volition by presenting the conscious mind with powerful feelings which it effectively employs to depict its concerns. The conscious mind is fully aware of this, and often thinks to itself: *Where did that feeling come from?* If there was any doubt before, now you know that it comes from the unconscious of your own emotional system.

When the emotional system wants to make its feelings conscious, it will, and there is little that the conscious mind can do about it. It is the prerogative of our emotional system, and it does not necessarily desire that the conscious mind likes it. It doesn't answer to the conscious mind simply because it is more powerful than it. If the reasoning mind doesn't like what the emotional presentation consists of, it should consider why the emotional system is vexed. Let us recall, the conscious mind does not have the capacity to squelch emotions, only emotional *reactions*.

We must remember that there was never a complete uniting of the limbic structures in either reptiles or mammals. They have not melded with each other to this day. They are *extensively interconnected*, but they have never become a single structure[160], with all parts being subsumed into a greater whole. They have all continued to maintain certain tasks that they do alone while combining their information and power with other limbic structures to complete other tasks. Very often, what they are doing is communicating what they have perceived or accomplished to the other structures, as well as to the neocortex and other appropriate parts of the brain. It all depends on what needs to be accomplished.

If the limbic system has not truly joined into one system from its constituent structures, why would it be assumed that it would unite with the neocortex in that way? Especially when it might turn out that it was actually a good thing to have two aspects in one conscious mind? Because of the way that the feelings brain had become so developed before the neocortex arose, there was an inherent separateness to these two aspects that were obviously evolutionarily intended to be permanent. I believe that their presence is actually a good thing.

It is a personal choice what any individual believes, and it is up to everyone to decide for themselves what they think. It is always best to do this from an informed perspective in which one has considered many viewpoints and theories. If one is not aware that something is affecting them, though, it's going to be very difficult or impossible for them to do much about it. That is why we all go for annual checkups. If something is wrong, then it's good to know.

The same thing is true of our minds. One may consider the human condition in innumerable ways. The more ways one has in which to consider the nature of their existence, the better off they are, in that more information of self is generally helpful. By considering how our conscious minds *seem* to have a natural duality, we can (at the very least) entertain this as a possibility. I think it is very helpful to consider the many implications of this arrangement, whether one agrees with it or not. Aside from everything else, it is an interesting and compelling thought experiment.

Not to acknowledge it does not in any way make it go away or decrease in its effect. In fact, we tacitly defer to this duality every time we evoke our emotions and encourage them to express themselves, either directly or indirectly. Likewise, they can also get our reason to express itself, whether it wants to or not. It is just that our emotional system doesn't comprehend the abstract reasoning by which the neocortex functions. Neither does our conscious mind comprehend the unconscious parts of our emotional system.

These points notwithstanding, our human mind has nevertheless learned to adapt to communicate using the unspoken emotional language of feelings and numerous symbolic interactions[161]. The reasoning mind, however, does have the capability to understand what the emotional system presents, and it can communicate back to the emotional system utilizing its neuronal connections. The emotional system is far too crude for any non-emotional comprehension, and this level of understanding doesn't need to occur. If it was necessary, evolutionary adaptations have had hundreds of millions of years in which to make it happen, but it hasn't. That is all we need to know.

We have to consider that emotions themselves arose not as feelings per se, but as initially crude neurological circuits to evoke reactions and responses from a feelings brain to promote the interests of its owner. Emotions provided a reason for the creature to react, as well as the motivation to perform whatever the emotions determined, should be the response by the creature. That was their entire purpose, in the beginning. That was why emotions evolved in the first place. Like most things, though, their story grew in the telling. We will be discussing this in much greater depth in succeeding chapters, but especially in Chapter 10.

Emotion's raison d'etre in humans remain every bit as essential as it has always been in all other creatures both gifted and cursed with them. Human beings need their emotions as much as they need their intellect. Everyone agreeing with that last sentence (I cannot help but note) is already demonstrating at least a tacit acknowledgment of this inherent duality by noting that there is indeed a definite distinction between the two. This duality is deeply embedded as a part of our conscious mind, and yet; it is very easy to remain unaware of it. Even so, we unthinkingly acknowledge its existence numerous times every day. It is us, and we are it.

Emotions inform and help guide us in our complex modern societies. Their *innate immutability* (which we will also be discussing in much greater depth in Chapter 11) ensures that all members of a species remain uniform in their emotional responses through hidden processes deep within the emotional system. I believe in the existence of such an "immutability" structure in whatever form it might take. I very much doubt that anyone is going to point to such a neuronal structure in the near future, and exclaim: "Eureka!" I am postulating it as a *construct* to explain the action that results in emotional immutability, and I qualify the term to be considered on that level. I believe that it is something that is critical to ensure emotional and behavioral uniformity both within and between species over time.

In their final configuration, the two aspects have *partially* joined their collective capabilities. There is a limited area in which both commune, each with the other. The reason has little trouble conceiving of an unconscious aspect to the mind. Most people accept this in stride. It is hard to know how some people would react to the idea that their emotional system also has an unconscious component. One could say that this is simply part of the entire brain's unconscious, and I agree with that. I see no reason to make a distinction between the two unconscious components of both aspects of the mind. Together, they are both simply part of the human mind's unconscious.

There are both conscious and unconscious components of the human mind. It is neither necessary nor desirable that these two aspects of mind share everything. They have evolved to share what they need to share. A far more important question is how they accomplished this ability to communicate and share information in the way that they do, given that both components of the mind are so radically different in design and construction.

The feelings brain and the neocortex interconnected by growing vast neuronal circuitry between them. They both have components that will always remain unconscious to the other, as well as conscious components that they share. Nevertheless, they have impressively adapted over deep time to combine their efforts and abilities, and both can do far more than that for which they were originally intended. It is a glorious thing for humans that we do have these two aspects to our minds. A human without both aspects would truly be a lost soul.

If we intentionally try to cooperate with our emotional system, we will usually find our life goes much more placidly than if we place ourselves in opposition to its dictates. The more we try to resist emotional pressure, the more it appears to us to be opposed to our purposes. We feel this way because we perceive that it's being hard on us. What we generally ask, of course, is: *why are my feelings berating me?*

Instead, the question probably should be: what have I done to irk my emotional system in this manner, and how can I accommodate it more sensibly? It seems to me that that is the better question. Sometimes, though, there is no responsible way in which one can accommodate an inherently irrational emotional system. In those times, the reasoning mind has no choice but to resist the desires of the emotional system, for the very reason that this system *is* irrational.

Simply feeling angst because our emotions appear to have risen up against us suggests that they are our adversary, instead of our ally. While I realize that they can sometimes show that side of themselves, it is for the reason that they are trying to keep us on *their* straight and narrow, emotionally. They are responding on the conscious level, within that conscious interface that they share with our reason, and they are sharing the same conscious experience as is our reasoning aspect every moment of every day. That is how they know *when* to feel something; they already know how.

That is what they do. What remains unsaid by the emotional system (because the emotional system does not speak) is that it is relying on the reasoning mind to be the executive. When the emotional system is concerned that the reasoning mind is not duly performing its executive functions, it is invariably going to let the conscious mind know that it is perturbed. At such times, it will make you suffer, sometimes deeply.

It only took us 220 million years, but we have, mostly, worked out our difficulties with our emotional system. Most problems we may personally encounter with our emotions, therefore, are usually of our own making. May providence show mercy, because our emotions will show none.

BECOMING HUMAN
A New Perspective on the Origins of the Human Mind
Chapter 7

Thinking and Feeling

About 220 million years ago, you will recall, paleomammalians that evolved from Cynodonts had survived the Permian period primarily due to their warm-bloodedness. They did not have much reasoning capability yet, but they did possess a highly developed feelings brain. Although these early mammals inherited the feelings components of their brains from reptiles, they also inherited a limited neocortex.

The same neocortex that mammals originally shared with reptiles adapted to become ever larger and more complex in mammals, however, increasingly making them very different from reptiles. Reptiles' brains just never grew to large sizes or possessed the reasoning capabilities of mammals. The skulls of most reptiles literally have extra space in them[125], whereas the skulls of most mammals are packed full enough to leave an impression on the inside of the skull[126]. A type of reptile named Anolis evermanni has about 5 million neurons in its brain, while a smoky shrew (not known as a towering intellectual even among other shrews) has about 36 million[127].

While neocortical structures have equivalent structures in the pallium (which serves the same general purpose as the neocortex in reptiles and birds, as well as some other species), that doesn't mean that these similar structures have equivalent power. It does indicate the convergent evolution of similar neuronal structures in the brains of very dissimilar creatures. This indicates yet again the necessity for intelligence as an essential survival component for many species. Many birds are highly intelligent, especially compared to reptiles. A pigeon, for example, has about 131 million neurons in its brain, or more than 25 times more than some reptiles. A pigeon's brain is large compared to that of a reptile, but tiny compared to that of a human.

We can make several conclusions from these points. Reptiles have apparently not found it necessary to evolve large brains in order to survive in their environments. Although reptiles are probably not very much more intelligent than they were when early mammals branched off from the reptilian line, they are certainly *no less* intelligent than they were then. As such, they can provide a standard of comparison when considering matters such as how brain structures have developed in reptiles, as opposed to mammals.

That is exactly what they are doing at the Max Planck Institute, where they have used their advanced sequencing techniques to discover that two large reptilian pallial areas are very similar to the mammalian amygdala and hippocampus[129]. This really shouldn't be that surprising, as we have earlier recounted that these mammalian structures developed long, long before reptiles themselves had evolved. Once again, new and improved investigative devices have allowed the boundaries of what we know to be true to expand, even as this new knowledge informs many other related areas of inquiry.

Like many other creatures, reptiles tended to seek out stable ecological niches in which they could thrive without great adaptational changes being required for survival. It wasn't so simple for mammals, though, because their offspring-raising requirements demanded that they develop numerous other attributes in order to successfully raise their young.

As well, many mammals adapted to more communally-based social groupings than did reptiles, and these require yet more changes. Both of these adaptations provoked a dire need for entirely new emotions to evolve by which to support their new lifestyle as they raised their young. Often, this happened in more advanced social groups than that with which their reptilian cousins were familiar. The new child-rearing and social organizations required far more neurons in their neocortex than they had at the beginning of their adventures in lactation. As time went by, the mammals did indeed evolve both new emotions and lots of extra brainpower.

When the early mammals first appeared, they certainly had their work cut out for them. They immediately began to feverishly adapt to better serve these newly established priorities. At the very time that their neocortexes were becoming stronger and more capable; their feelings brains were being tasked with the actual creation of new emotions to accommodate their new parenting and social roles. How did mammals respond to this double challenge? They simultaneously developed both their emotional and neocortical structures. In so doing, they developed new emotions while revising old emotions as necessary. At the same time, the neocortex kept adding more neurons and enhanced capabilities. Multi-tasking did not arise with the invention of the personal computer.

It is fair and accurate to say that the feelings of the emotional system increasingly evolved alongside the reasoning abilities of the neocortex from this point forward in mammalian evolution. In the beginning, the feelings brain functioned as the predominant executive authority of the animal. It made the decisions in the same way that it had for over 100 million years. As time went on, though, this changed.

In many respects, emotions remain a very primitive system, when compared to the lofty intellect. It is indisputable, though, that the emotional brain did quite adequately serve a similar function to that of a primitive intellect, up to a certain point of development. Beyond that point, though, the machine can break down. A creature behaving only under the executive authority of emotions is going to be able to modulate their feelings to a very broad degree with enormous power, in the same way as can humans. The problem with purely emotional reactions, however, is that they tend to not necessarily be well thought out, to put it mildly.

That is also precisely how emotions tend to work in humans. Most of us recall only too well how good our own decision-making has been when we have given in to our most deeply emotional selves. Yes indeed, most of us can recall how well that worked and then be very glad that we also developed a powerful cerebral cortex so that we would not have to rely on our feelings brains alone.

Evolution determined that the creatures that became human beings would try an approach other than a purely emotional one through the development of more powerful intellectual attributes. These reasoning abilities, however, did not develop in a vacuum. Rather, they developed in a milieu in which the emotional brain was still in executive control. The really interesting thing about that is, as the intellect gained in power, it would have to be in more or less constant negotiation and renegotiation with the emotional system. Again, that seems to describe the human condition to this very day. Some things don't change, especially if they work well.

Consider this. At one point in our evolution, our distant ancestors had no meaningful neocortex but did have an emotional brain. Humans today, though, have an intellect that is (tenuously) in control of their emotional *system*. So, between then and now it is indisputable that there must have occurred some very tenuous times in which both aspects of mind vied for supremacy. Don't look now, but they still occasionally do!

Imagine an ancient mammal of around 150 million years ago with a now highly developed neocortex and a very powerful feelings brain that work together to assist their owner's survival. These two separate entities, evolving in pieces scattered across 400 million years, borrowed a hypothalamus from a sea worm and a neocortex from a fish, and through the miracle of adaptation, these structures somehow coalesced into a new kind of brain. Not an everyday sort of brain, but a brain with two powerful aspects.

If they worked together well, what a wonderful combination that would make. Who would be in control, though? Given that the feelings brain of that era had 100 million years of seniority, we can imagine it might have gotten bumpy at times, but that is all lost to deep time, and we will never know for sure. Perhaps there were times when *neither* was in complete control? That would be a recipe for disastrous internecine internal conflict. That circumstance could not have lasted long, or I don't think we mammals would be here today.

Somehow, an accommodation between the two aspects of mind was achieved in humans. That accommodation has resulted in humanity's current state in which reason exerts executive authority, while a strong emotional system helps guide and inform decisions made by the reason. Although we will never know exactly how any such hypothetical conflicts might have developed, we do know the outcome.

Reason, informed by emotions, enables humans to make the great majority of our wisest decisions. The intellect makes abstract thought possible. All alone, though, it has little heart and does not feel deeply without guidance from its emotions. A purely intellectual response to a question or situation which does not take into account the attendant feelings and emotions that it will give rise to is unlikely to produce wise decisions.

It was through the extensive interconnection of the reason and the emotional system that humans have reached the top of the food chain. It has allowed our species to evolve into the highly social creatures we have become. We are still able to experience a full range of emotions while retaining the ability to use our highly capable and informed reason as a check on what otherwise would tend to be emotional excesses. Together, these two aspects of our conscious mind have formed a highly capable team in the game of survival for the human species.

Most people would agree that reason reigns supreme, and they might be correct. Few, however, would suggest that the emotional system isn't as important to our sense of who we are as a species as is our reasoning faculty. We are thinking creatures, yes; but we also feel deeply. We have unique capabilities to create lofty philosophies and theorems by which we suppose the universe operates, and yet we retain the capability to show sympathy for the most basic of our fellow creatures. In the end, perhaps, those may turn out to be our best qualities.

Emotions can confuse us, let's recall, because they simultaneously exist in two realms of existence; that of the conscious and unconscious minds. We can, remember, only experience the out-flowing emotions. Our brains don't allow us to directly experience the internal emotional process, or any other emotional activities *until* they emerge into consciousness, which is something they only do when *they* choose. The reason, conversely, remains consciously able to evoke strong feelings employing purely intellectual activity to spur an emotional reaction. Want to put that to the test? Create a mental image of your most reviled politician's sweaty hand shaking yours. The test is over.

Another great example of this (not involving your hand, which you cannot seem to scrub clean for some reason) can be provided by simply watching a tear-jerking movie. Generally, people *like* emotions when they are both controlled and confined to an area of individual comfort, as emotions provide an inestimable trove of joy and pain in one's life. In the final analysis, however, the reasoning aspect of the conscious mind can summon emotions into consciousness, whereas emotions can emerge into consciousness whenever they are called up by external circumstances, reason, or whenever they feel like making an appearance (which is invariably at the most inopportune times and places). When an emotion is evoked for whatever cause, it can take a powerful and often decisive role in the initial response of a person, giving the reasoning aspect of your mind *time to think*, as the saying goes, so that it can formulate its optimal response.

We do constantly refer to our intimate interactions with our emotional systems in numerous ways. We might say: *I feel angry, hurt, bitter, sad, happy, joyful, relieved, etc., and I don't know why.* That's your reason speaking. In fact, you don't *need* to know why your emotions feel as they do, and that is by design.

You, the conscious reasoning mind reading these words, don't really need to know why your emotional system feels the way it does, and you often won't. Instead, it is more helpful to understand how the synthesis of these two aspects of mind cooperate to produce the treasures that result from this interaction. Most attempts to understand the inscrutable nature of emotions usually end up as futile and pointless exercises in intellectualization, anyway.

The early neocortex was, naturally, fully integrated into the feeling brain's apparatus. Although it is natural and inevitable that internal conflicts *will* occur between a dominant feelings brain and a subservient neocortex that realizes (on a reasoning basis that the feelings brain could not comprehend) that it was about to do something that would result in a world of hurt to the creature. In such instances, the neocortex must have had enough input to communicate, presumably in feelings, the angst that the feelings brain and the creature it was attached to would soon experience as a result of its unfortunate feelings-based action.

When presented with feelings of neocortically-inspired dread at what it conjectured was about to transpire, it would have certainly considered such a potent concern before acting as precipitously as it otherwise certainly would have. Presumably, given the obvious power of intellectual competency present in even a crude neocortex, the feelings brain would have at least heeded the neocortical warning, even if it didn't follow its advice.

After repeatedly suffering as a result of *not* heeding good neocortical advice, one would assume that the feelings brain would be more likely to listen more closely and attentively as time went on. Over millions of years, billions of experiences would also inform it to closely heed the advice of the reasoning brain. Mutation being what it is, and under constant evolutionary pressures to be especially efficient in the great cause of survival, the rise of the neocortex could have been relatively rapid.

A well-developed neocortex with a subordinate emotional system would create a magnificently powerful team. A world dominated by higher creatures guided by reason that is assisted and advised by emotion is truly a game-changing proposition. That is precisely what transpired to create the world as we know it today. It is obvious that there are advantages and inherent tensions which arise between these two aspects of mind that were evolutionarily made inevitable many millions of years ago. What was decided by Mother Nature was that it is good to have this sort of tension for numerous reasons, including that it creates an *ambiguity of response*. What I mean by this is that a creature subject to these inherently different outlooks is not always going to behave the same way and that in-and-of-itself provides a substantial survival benefit to a creature.

Ambiguity of response leads to unpredictability of an individual creature's behavior, making their actions harder to ascertain in advance. As such, it is a positive survival advantage. There are times when *predictability* is advantageous, but that generally applies to an entire species. We will be considering this at greater length in later chapters. Please just keep in mind that unpredictability of response tends to be a good thing for an individual animal, but a very hazardous thing for a species.

It is not a weakness but a strength that we have these two different aspects of mind that we regularly employ in decision-making. They form one system with two components. They have both evolved as they have for the simple reason that they make a pretty good team. Like any good team, the individual members don't always agree or see things the same way. Like any good team, though, the individuals within it know that their concerns can at least be aired, even if they are not heeded to their satisfaction. There is an established protocol for the airing of grievances.

Sadly for the emotional system, perhaps, reason ultimately rules. The reasoning mind can and does regularly overrule emotional dictates, but at a potentially severe cost to its well-being. If emotions are disregarded, the intellect will suffer guilt and possibly, even a troubled conscience as the price it must pay for its callous disregard of emotional concerns, particularly when they're well-founded. In my estimation, conscience proceeds from the emotions and is created as it interacts with reasoning capabilities. This is not, however, a topic that I can take up more deeply in this book, as it is a very involved theory, and needs its own book in which to fully explain. Please stay tuned.

As we've mentioned elsewhere, the emotional system far predates any neocortical structures such as gave rise to what our current mind views as consciousness. The emotional system existed long before there was any sort of concentration of neurons capable of doing much besides creating simple emotional reactions that provided sufficient motivation for basic survival-related activities. Feelings brains, like most other things, slowly improved through adaptation over time.

It was only much later, when the emotional system was out-distanced by the now overwhelmingly powerful neocortex, that the emotions learned how to guilt trip its reasoning aspect into submission. If the emotions couldn't get the intellect to do what they desired it to do, they could at least make it feel really bad about it. Sometimes, that was (and remains) precisely what is needed to nudge the reason from its abstruse plans. The emotions prevent us from becoming a machine-like abstract planner, a human abacus. Emotions humanize us.

I think everyone, upon reflection in their own lives, would have to agree that our emotions make us better in nearly every way than we would be if we were simply more intellectual and less emotional. At the same time, some people are very emotional but do not have nearly as much reason as they could use. Too much of either quality in absence of the other is probably not the best formula for a well-balanced individual. Together, however, these two aspects of mind both add great benefits to the mix. Together, they have combined to result in a unique creature with both qualities that make humans the creatures we are.

The two components of mind have long since successfully interconnected, but an internal tension between the two will always exist and is intentional on the part of evolution. Apparently, we are designed in such a way as to turn this internal tension into a benefit. We humans just naturally and unthinkingly accept that our reason is in the ascendant, for the most part. We can all quite vividly recall times in which our emotional system (for whatever reason, but a reason often involving alcohol or even more interesting substances) seized control, or so it would've felt at the time.

Inevitably, such times are fraught with peril, fear, angst, or other powerful emotions. This sort of occurrence strongly suggests to me that evolutionary pressures have caused humans to conserve this particular trait. One has to wonder how our emotions can suddenly rise up and, essentially, become the dominant force in our minds for a period of time. More importantly, though, is the fact that this evidently does serve a useful purpose, or else it would've vanished long ago from the human gene pool. This extreme emotional reaction is not uniform in everyone, any more than intellectual capabilities are evenly distributed among people.

There is no mathematical equation by which the relative strengths of our reason and feelings can be calculated, much less solved. There is no solution. They both exist on completely separate scales and must be examined that way. A good way to conceive of their relative power would be by visualizing a scale for each in your mind. Both intellectual and emotional scales would register the overall strength of each relative to the other, but this would only provide a personal reflection for an individual by which they might gain insight into themselves. What usually results from such an exercise is that there is little correlation between reason and feelings strength.

Some people have a well-developed and inherently strong intellect and have only a slight emotional affect. Other similarly intelligent individuals are incredibly emotional and are frequently overwhelmed by this attribute. The exact diametric opposite of this example is also true. If anyone stops to consider the people they know, they will be forced to agree that these two aspects of mind are uniquely individual to every person. If nothing else, it makes everyone completely unique from everyone else. I think that is a good thing.

Our neocortex essentially usurped the executive authority of the feelings brain which had been in more or less unquestioned authority for a hundred million years. As the neocortex increased in strength and decision-making ability compared to the relatively stagnant feelings brain, the mammalian mind was able to benefit for millions of years as adaptational forces tried to determine how to get the most out of both aspects of mind.

When all is said and done, the human mind is unified in the ways that really matter, whether we like it or not. Our enthusiastic acceptance of this reality is neither relevant nor necessary. Although emotional considerations routinely affect how the reason reacts, the emotions are frequently disregarded by them in the heat of the moment. Yet, our mind still retains these two separate aspects for critical reasons, some of which are known, and some of which are lost to deep history, and are therefore unknowable.

A large part of the reason must be because our mind simply developed with these two existential aspects in a situation in which the power dynamic between the two slowly shifted over time. I do not feel, though, that this is an adequate reason to explain why the mind has remained this way. It seems to me that the only reason that it would remain this way is that there is an advantage to be realized in remaining this way. What might that advantage be? I think it may be because it provides two seemingly separate ways to apprehend that which is presented to our senses by our full environment. It is almost like an eccentric, built-in second opinion perennially prepared to give us a *twofer*.

In the normal course of events, our reasoning mind is securely in control and making executive decisions as to what the individual *does*. The emotional system, diligently working in the background, considers matters from an entirely distinct feelings perspective and chirps up when it is concerned or vexed. What results is normally a product combining the strengths of both aspects, and both are very powerful influencers and motivators, taken individually.

What is it that occurs in a psychologically stable and relatively normal human being that might propel their emotional system into the ascendant over their reason? It has happened to all of us numerous times in our lives, often within every calendar year; and for some especially high-strung individuals, numerous times in a day! People in this latter category should first consider cutting back on their caffeine intake before seeking further treatment, I would suggest. In such a situation, emotion reigns supreme as if by prearrangement with the intellect that there are times and circumstances in which the reasoning mind needs to jump back in avoidance! Fear not, your emotions know what to do...sometimes.

Unsurprisingly, then, it is such emotionally-laden moments that not only excite the emotional components into prominence but unquestionably increase their power over the decision-making capabilities of the conscious mind[130]. Right in front of our eyes, the emotions seem to radically grow in strength and determination to such an extent that reason is swept aside like a leaf in a gale. This is a phenomenon that we've all observed and lived. This is a thing so close to our core being that we usually don't even feel the need to acknowledge that it's there. At the same time, it is there, and we know that perfectly well.

I suppose the only reasonable conclusion is that it is there for the same reason that all adaptations, however unknowable, are there. It is there because its presence is in the best interests of the person possessing them. It is there because the final result of this *symbiosis from hell* is that it is a very effective mind that arises from this bizarre merger. We think of ourselves primarily as creatures of reason, and we tend to relegate emotions to a subordinate position at the foot of life's table.

This is, of course, completely false at every level. These components, both the reasoning and the emotional, are, in the final analysis, always and forever truly two aspects of one mind. That is because the emotional and the reasoning viewpoints are each totally distinct in our minds. It is easy to see the advantages in having these two aspects of mind, especially at such times as they are working in congruence and harmony. The knowledge that highly dramatic occurrences can trigger such incredibly formidable emotional reactions when evoked by situations that *will* inevitably occur, better prepares us when such invariably memorable events *do* occur.

Most people emphatically do not want to be overcome by the sort of drama and strong emotions that dwell within all of us. Most people go to great lengths to avoid those very situations, with the exception, perhaps, of histrionic individuals. Most people intensely dislike not just the pure emotionality, but the adrenaline and cortisol and the entire chemistry set of brain chemicals[131] being dumped into our systems. They find this extremely unpleasant, and so they avoid them wherever possible. Most people also avoid other people who are prone to frequently being unable to control the ascendancy of their emotions over their reason.

The truth of the matter is that most of us are gifted and cursed with living a *civilized* existence. We have built our very lives and cultures around both spoken and tacit understandings which seek to decrease excess emotionality. We do this by saying please and thank you and indulging in both niceties and social graces to a ludicrous extent. This is strongly ingrained in every culture and social order that exists in the world today, in antiquity; and I dare say, probably back before the Paleolithic era began.

We are designed to be social, it is true. Perhaps more importantly, humans are designed to employ many distinct social mores and customs in an effort to *lubricate* our cultures uniformly across all peoples and societies of the earth. In that way, interactions between individuals flow with minimal emotionality being brought to bear, except in such times as it is truly needed. At such times as are culturally or socially appropriate, it is not only desirable but expected that one will allow their emotions to hijack their conscious mind.

No self-respecting mob would ever take the effort to think through what it was they were doing. No self-respecting mob has ever *had* a clear idea of what it was trying to do, anyway. Merely trying to think it through would immediately convert the most diehard lynch mob into a group of confused and slightly befuddled goofballs trying to understand why they were so upset. When the emotions flood in, reason shuts down. It happens to me and you and everybody else at regular intervals, and it does this because our mind is designed to do this. This ultimately happens because unknown multitudes of adaptations have meticulously designed this to occur in this very way.

We have evolved *to retain* the ability to perform this completely emotional sleight-of-hand. Suddenly, as emotions hijack our conscious minds; our brain devolves as it divests itself of the neocortical reasoning abilities it worked so hard to develop over hundreds of millions of years. This seemingly happens because evolution has made the determination that we operate best when this process occurs as needed. It provides a capability for our minds to, metaphorically, *break glass in case of emergencies.*

We all know it's going to happen on occasion, but most of us go to extreme lengths to minimize these sorts of occurrences. When they do occur, it is often referred to (when it occurs in public) as a "scene." No one of good breeding wants to be responsible for creating something as onerous as a *scene*. Humans have become so good at defining the situations in which it is permissible for over-the-top emotionality to bloom that we do it without conscious thought. *Don't be so emotional,* we are told. *Don't get excited, because you might hurt someone,* they say.

Then, when a war breaks out between your social order and another social order, someone hands you a gun, commands you to kill someone with it, and you are then rewarded and praised for doing so. No wonder people are so confused! The thing of it is that this tried and true duality of mind is adapted into us in an incredibly hardwired way that will not tolerate one to diverge from it if they wish to maintain their mental equilibrium. Both aspects are you, and you are therefore a creature who must learn to balance both aspects.

Look to the natural world if you want to see how the other 99% of life exists. Look to creatures that live in the wild. Not those fat and languid gray squirrels lounging in the park, but the smaller, quicker, cannier, and far more aggressive red squirrels that live in the wild, and which plunder your birdfeeders while terrorizing your chickadees. One of these ruffians experiences more drama and emotionality in a day defending *its* feeder from the depredations of nuthatches and other squirrels than you will experience in a decade. If a human could experience the overwhelming emotionality that a squirrel experiences in an afternoon, they'd suffer PTSD for the rest of their life.

We social humans have developed archetypal patterns across all cultures, such as Carl Jung[132] correctly hypothesized. Of course we have universal archetypes. All humans have the same brain, with the same mix of reason and emotion. Of course we have the same desires, and of course we express them in similar ways across cultures. We all do the same thing because we are *all the same creature*! It is surprising how some people don't simply accept the complete obviousness of this statement.

Evolution has determined, for whatever reasons (and I'm sure they are very compelling ones), that we be sentenced to labor under a duality which allows us to use both our reason and our emotions to best benefit. With this evolutionary bequest comes a result in which we are thereby promoting the best interests of individuals who will then pass on their genetic material to the next generation. It is a proven winning combination in the battle for survival that even creatures at the apex of power over an entire planet must subscribe to or perish.

161

Humans epitomize reason's ascendancy over the emotional system, most of the time, as we have described in prior chapters. In the evolution of humans, we have become forever distinct and separate from all other creatures through the development of our reason. It does not merely add to our capabilities. It allows us to understand the minutest intricacies of our entire universe, but it doesn't necessarily allow us to understand ourselves (I can't decide if that should be classed as comic or tragic irony or both).

Reason provides us humans with the ability to reach out among the stars, as well as inside our own minds to discover the attributes that make us who we are. I would also venture to say that it *theoretically* allows us the ability to understand ourselves. The fact that our reasoning minds also gives us so much such as abilities of object permanence, memory retention, and abstraction is an homage to the incredible ability of evolution to improve upon an existing creature to allow it to grow into something far greater than the sum of its parts.

Our reasoning minds are a miraculous evolutionary gift bestowed on all people at birth. Its presence guides virtually all aspects of our existence. Of course, I don't intend to suggest that because the neocortex partially arose to counterbalance the emotional system, that is all it can do. As the saying goes, "Giant oaks from little acorns grow." The *little acorn* that was the neocortex grew into something much greater than what it was originally designed to be. As a result, humans are poised to enter a new and exciting phase of their destiny, assuming that they can muster the reason to make smart decisions, and the feelings to make just decisions.

BECOMING HUMAN
A New Perspective on the Origins of the Human Mind
Chapter 8

The Human Mind's Dual Aspects

Emotions operate bi-directionally. They go from the unconscious to the conscious mind, but they also recede from the conscious mind back to their base in the unconscious. We remain unaware of this because, to us, emotions simply vanish when we're not feeling *emotional*. That is not accurate, of course, and is actually a false perception caused by our inability to perceive the unconscious aspects of our emotional system. We don't perceive the emotions residing in the unconscious because we *can't* perceive them, any more than we can perceive the electrical signals that cause our hearts to beat or the pulses our ears send to our brains after creating them from sound waves. The body is complex, but our understanding is simple.

As emotional creatures, we humans frequently describe emotions as constituting an "outpouring," as in; an outpouring of emotions. They appear to spontaneously emerge from our unconscious, much like an instinct. Also, like instincts, they are often triggered by external events occurring in the environment. Unlike instinctive reactions, however, emotions often trigger themselves for reasons which typically puzzle and confound us. Emotions make us feel, but they also do so much more by compelling us toward taking action.

Emotions precede intellect, and emotional responses *appear* to be virtually instantaneous. Humans feel before they think. That is because emotions are fast, and thinking is, by comparison, slow. If someone offends you, your emotional reaction is virtually instantaneous, while your reason must scramble to comprehend what has occurred. Then, it must determine a course of action in reaction to the offense, and decide exactly how to put that action into effect (if at all). Relative to intellect, emotions are arguably pretty dumb, but we all know how quickly they can arise.

When one contrasts the alacrity of an emotional response to the relatively lethargic pace of the reason, though, it becomes readily apparent that having both aspects of mind is a tremendously powerful combination for a creature to possess. Sometimes, one has to react quickly, and emotions promptly respond. Often, a slow initial reaction can be fatal in the natural world in which all creatures evolved.

After the initial emotional response has burst forth and bought precious time, however, the reasoning mind has had the opportunity to formulate a more thoughtful response which has an increased likelihood of creating a conclusion more favorable to the interests of the individual. At the same time, the emotions inform the reasoning response as to how it *should* feel. The emotions thereby assist the reasoning mind in the initial formulation of the response and continue to insinuate themselves into all decisions made by the intellect, from a thought's conception to its conclusion. In these ways and many others, emotions form a critical part of the *platform* on which the conscious mind rests, and are essential to its operation on multiple levels.

It is undeniable that there was a time when our distant antecedent species was governed solely by unconscious processes, instincts, and the unconscious and conscious aspects of the emotional brain. The emotional system was the first part of the mind that became *truly* conscious, some believe. It is a decidedly different kind of consciousness than what we humans experience in our daily lives if that is the case. It worked quite successfully for our precursor species, though, and if they hadn't been who they were, we would not have become who we are.

I sometimes wonder what Sigmund Freud[133] would theorize to explain the workings of the human mind if he was aware that there was a period of time lasting for many millions of years when the only working brain available was primarily based in feelings, and that our human mind evolved from that? It would've certainly been a primitive world that was driven by emotional impulses and the vagaries that seem to accompany all feelings. But Freud wasn't aware of those things for the simple reason that they hadn't been discovered yet.

If Freud had been aware that our reasoning faculties were a much more recent development than our feeling faculties, I'd like to think that he would've considered these facts as he formulated his theories, and adapted his theoretical constructs accordingly. Freud was very much a product of his era, even as I and my contemporaries are products of ours. This means that we can expect certain things from both Freud and me that are reflective and representative of the zeitgeist in which we live.

A more contemporary theorist, Paul MacLean, introduced the Triune Brain Theory[134] in 1949. This theory hypothesized that humans, in essence, have three distinct brains: the reptilian, the paleomammalian, and the neomammalian, with the paleomammalian also referred to as the "feelings brain." A brilliant theorist and pioneer of neuroscience, MacLean nevertheless made several errors that undermined his work in substantial ways:

"MacLean proposed that the most ancient 'reptilian brain' is composed of the basal ganglia, is involved in basic species-typical behaviors such as aggression, dominance, and ritualistic displays, and is present in all vertebrates. According to MacLean, the 'paleomammalian/visceral brain' arose early in mammalian evolution, and is involved in emotion and motivational drive required for offspring care, reproduction, and feeding. Lastly, MacLean proposed that the 'neomammalian brain,' or the neocortex, which arose later in mammalian evolution, is more developed and complex in 'higher' mammals, specifically primates and humans, and underlies higher order cognition and intelligence (MacLean, 1985). Despite the advances MacLean's theory brought to neuroscience, central to his theory was *the assumption that the emotional brain is a separate entity to the brain that supports*

167

reason and intelligence." (italics mine). *(Lew, C. H., Semendeferi, K., 2017. Citation #116)*

Although he was correct about there being a feelings brain that arose in the reptilian complex from which mammals descended, his belief that an "emotional brain" was a separate and distinct entity from the neocortex was not correct. They are both parts of the same whole.

He was also mistaken about some of his other premises, such as when the neocortex first appeared, and his belief that reptilian brains were constructed far differently than mammalian brains, among many things. His belief that the reptilian brain was so essentially different from the mammalian never appealed to me, as we descended from them, brain and all. This has been verified beyond all doubt since 2018[135], when researchers working under Gilles Laurent at the Max Planck Institute dispelled these myths:

> "Taken together, these comparisons showed that rather than considering the reptilian brain a distinct unit, separate from the mammalian limbic system and the primate neocortex, the three can't be clearly distinguished from one another. Instead, reptiles have primitive versions of both of MacLean's "higher" brain areas, all but proving his theories false. These areas didn't evolve from scratch after reptiles, but instead simply expanded out from their smaller, less well-defined reptilian precursors." (Howe, James R., *Human and Reptile Brains aren't so Different After All, (2018)*

Neuroscience and Genetics, UC San Diego. Citation #128).

I am fascinated by the formation of a brain based on the abilities of the emotions produced by limbic structures as they adapted and increased in power during the age of the reptiles. Without the reptile's initial development of a complete and serviceable feelings brain, the early mammals would not have had anything with which to work. Instead, they were gifted a completely formed and serviceable brain with an attached and integrated (if underpowered) neocortex capable of interacting with it.

Before the neocortex gained so greatly in power, there had to have been a long period in which this new reasoning ability had figured out how to coexist with a dominant but intellectually incapable partner. I find it most likely that the input from the neocortex to the feelings brain would be in the form of suggestions, rather than demands.

The intellect would naturally be canny enough, even in its early form, to realize the inherent limitations of the feelings brain, and to learn to work around them. I believe it would only be when the intellect perceived a big problem in following the dictates of emotional impulses that it would set up a howl.

Consider how the situation has reversed in human beings. The reasoning mind is now in firm control, in the *normal* course of events. The rule of the intellect is the law of the land. That's because the intellect is not obligated to follow the feelings of our highly evolved emotional system, even though both aspects of mind reside together within the confines of our human brain.

The human mind is evolutionarily designed to contain two separate aspects that are ultimately working in concert. Isn't that an extraordinary thing? Every human being experiences this natural duality of our minds every day of our lives. It is so close to us, so very intimate to our internal selves, that we are not aware of it until someone points it out. When someone does point it out, though, a great number of things can start to slip into place in terms not only of our own internal life but how we react to other humans and the greater environment beyond them.

We are all creatures of both feelings and reason. These two aspects of self communicate with each other only partially. The reason for this is historical on the part of the feelings brain, as it existed long before the neocortex was even a twinkle in the eye of an amorously aroused lizard. The reason that our reasoning aspect is unable to communicate well with the emotional system, on the other hand, is that it is a vastly different neurological structure than are the multiple structures of the limbic system. It would not be that dissimilar from one trying to explain physics to a chimpanzee, believing that it would be possible if only the material was presented *slowly* enough. There is an inherent disconnect between the reasoning and feeling aspects of our minds, reflective of their adapting so many millions of years apart.

The most interesting thing is that, in our entire human development, evolution has gone out of its way *not* to streamline that process, or correct that communication defect. It is as if it has been decided from on high that human beings operate best with this inherent duality of mind as part of their basic makeup. One might point out that two minds can indeed be better than one, although it could also be argued that two minds could be twice as confused as one. I have a strong belief that both points are probably correct. Nevertheless, it seems to me that the only logical conclusion is that there is an intentional balance between our reason and emotions because *evolutionary pressures desired to preserve this status quo*. That means it must be useful as it exists.

If I may create a construct to explain their interactions, these two aspects of mind interface in their own private forum of the mind, their own intimate mental agora. While there, they present, each to the other, what they would like to see happen in a given instance. They attempt to cooperate and are capable of compromise, When needs require it; the emotional system can usurp mental control (for a while, at least).

That is not to say that the mind is of such weak moral fiber that it simply succumbs to the force of the emotional system so as to be swept to the side. This is not the case, and all humans who still draw breath can attest to the fact that the reason can and does step in and tamp down what it sees as emotional excesses that can do damage to the best interests of the person involved.

An anecdote from history makes this point quite well. The psychopathic Russian dictator Josef Stalin would hold massive Communist Party convocations following the Russian Revolution. His murderous purges had already resulted in the deaths of tens of millions of Russians, many of whose relatives in the audience were broadly smiling as they enthusiastically applauded every comment Stalin made. Of course, their applause was enthusiastic because they were deathly afraid (with good reason) that their names were next on the purge list. So great was their terror that everyone in the room was afraid to be the first to stop clapping, lest Stalin see that as proof of their disloyalty, and have them killed. The problem was that they just kept applauding until Stalin had to vociferously quiet them down. Then, as he made another remark, however banal, the same process would instantly resume. In the end, the solution proved to be the installation of a buzzer that Stalin himself controlled, and that he would press to inform everyone that they could safely stop applauding, which they would immediately do with nearly military precision.

The point behind this anecdote is that every one of those people pretending to love Stalin hated and feared him to the deepest core of their being. Their purely emotional reaction, if it were heeded, would've been to tear that devilishly evil man to pieces with their bare hands. Instead, they *ostensibly* happily took part in a farcical, kowtowing display of obeisance that reflected little credit on anyone.

What does this demonstrate? It demonstrates the ability of reason to rule over the emotions while simultaneously stifling the emotion's desires when it is essential to do so. Of this, there is no doubt. This is for the best. The reason for the numerous adaptations to propel the power of the reason far beyond that of the feelings brain is that a reasoning mind is incredibly more powerful.

The fact is that the neural connections that comprise the emotional structures far predate the more advanced neuronal connections of the human cerebral cortex[135]. In the human cortex, each neuron can sometimes have over 10,000 synaptic connections *each*[136]! I rely on the expertise of knowledgeable scientists in this area to verify these statements, as I'm no expert on such matters.

A feelings brain can effectively operate and be wildly successful based entirely on feelings bereft of all intellectual influences. We know this is true because creatures *did* have such brains based in feelings for many millions of years before they developed any reasoning abilities capable of exerting any significant influence.

A feelings brain can be seen in much the same way as a fission bomb. A fission bomb can only get bigger and more powerful to a certain degree, but then it hits a physical limit as to how powerful it can become. A fission bomb can become no more powerful than that limit imposed by physics.

A neocortex, on the other hand, is more like a fusion bomb, which can grow ever larger to a theoretically infinite level, and which can thereby become commensurately more powerful, such as you might see in a sun a million or more times larger than Sol. The feelings brain hit its point of maximum expansion many millions of years ago, and presumably, has not evolved much beyond that point. A reasoning ability can get ever more capable, but an emotional ability can only get more emotional, and becoming overly emotional can be deadly. The emotional system did substantially evolve further in early mammals to better serve in such newly invented necessities as child-rearing and related activities.

It is, ultimately, a matter of intensity of feeling. If a creature with a purely feelings-based brain is not feeling especially agitated about something, they might choose to not take action about that thing. If, on the other hand, the same creature is feeling highly emotionally aroused by a matter, they are far more likely to take action. That is one of the many great strengths of reason over emotions. Reason can show good judgment and sense in a situation when the powerful feelings of the emotional system have been exceeded, and are no longer capable of exercising judgment on their own. In such a situation, the intellect steps in and relieves the melting-down emotional system from duty. Dilemma resolved.

This is extremely hard-wired stuff and is not subject to the vagaries of logical discourse. In such matters, one is dealing with a structure in your brain that is not in any way capable of understanding such things. You may as well try explaining theoretical physics to a guppy, as that will be every bit as successful.

At the same time, though, the emotional system always has its concerns heard (even if they are not heeded) by the reason, insofar as it is condemned to *always be available* to receive emotional input, whether or not it wants to be available to receive such abuse. If you ever find yourself doubting this, go ahead and try to simply *switch off* your emotional reaction to something in such a time as your emotional concerns are demanding to be acknowledged and heeded. It can't be done.

It would appear that this situation that has occurred in human beings is an unquestionably intentional evolutionary adaptation. As odd as it may seem, this Faustian bargain between the reason and the emotions is firmly established by innate protocols that allow each component of mind to have certain perquisites and commensurate responsibilities. Visualize it as a sort of

"Treaty of Versailles" of the human mind in which hostilities have been replaced by established protocols designed to preserve the interests of those involved while being equally unfair to both sides.

The reasoning aspect is in nominal control of the emotions most of the time, with the express understanding that the emotional aspect has the authority to bombard the hapless conscious mind with constant carping, chiding, subtle redirecting, and occasional outright demands that the reason does its bidding, irrespective of whether the bidding of the emotional system is at all sensible or not. Ultimately, the emotional system has a right of usurpation of the intellect when it feels that it has been sufficiently abused. An outraged emotional system is not a thing to take lightly, as it might force ill-considered actions that conclude with you in a hospital or jail.

More commonly, though, the emotional system simply makes the conscious mind feel bad when it doesn't get its way because it has concluded that reason has allowed a situation to exist which concerns or perturbs it. In such moments, the emotional system is capable of causing truly unpleasant and even horrific feelings to assail the conscious mind in such a way as to strongly motivate it to comply with its dictates. If it refuses, it will continue to suffer, as it cannot intellectually convey to the basic, non-reasoning emotional system the reasons for its actions. Nevertheless, it is charmingly human of us to unsuccessfully try, anyway.

Perhaps the reason cannot comply with emotional dictates because to do so would be impossible, or present an avoidable hazard to the person who owns the brain in which these dual aspects of mind are in conflict. The emotional system does not understand or care why its feelings are not being assuaged. Ultimately, there is a confrontation with the intellect in which the emotional mandate continues to demand compliance. When this occurs, it is often referred to as a *troubled conscience.*

In my theory, conscience is, at its core, an emotional and reason-based creation of accommodation in which the dictates of both components of mind interface. Sometimes, the reason will extend itself to resolve such conflicts, but sometimes it cannot or will not allow such a resolution. In such times, most people can easily become embroiled in an internal conflict as both aspects of mind exert their influence, each against the other. What a curious fate! To forever be locked together, while being innately unable to fully comprehend the other. Yet, these two partners in this (occasionally) unhappy marriage are unable to divorce without the assistance of a brain surgeon.

Destined to be unable to understand the other on a fundamental level, these two aspects of the human mind are nevertheless in constant dialogue in the imaginary forum of our minds on a conscious level. The emotional system was simply not designed to naturally interact with a reasoning mind, as it reacts to stimuli in non-reasoning ways, and feels instead of thinks.

Feelings seem to primarily interact with the conscious reasoning mind; although in an extreme situation, feelings can dredge up pre-conscious thoughts into consciousness, where they can be dealt with appropriately before being emotionally tortured. These two occasional contenders, though, are more often cooperating

176

compatriots that together have created a synthesis unique among all creatures of the earth.

The fact that we are this way, let us remember, is because myriad adaptations have decided that this is how the minds of us humans function most effectively. This duality of mind is experienced every day of our lives. We have evolved to accept this duality so naturally and seemingly effortlessly that we are unaware, in the normal course of events, that there is anything there to perturb our mental equilibrium in the first place.

It is a strange thing, to realize that in all of us there exist two vastly different aspects of mind that use such radically distinct means and methods by which to arrive at conclusions and decisions. We humans are forced into a sort of shotgun marriage dictated by evolution. Yet, here we are, and here we will stay until mutations and new adaptations provide us a new direction that bestows benefits that evolution decrees we must accept. Such is life on planet Earth for us humans now and (presumably) until the end of time.

As the mammals continued to evolve over the succeeding millions of years since their speciation from reptiles, they evolved more and more neurons in their neocortex. As a result, there were exponentially more neuronal connections that could be made, resulting in exponentially more computing power. The feelings-based brain had evolved to go as far as it could go, but it was shackled to an ever-growing reasoning brain that *could theoretically* continue growing in complexity and power indefinitely. The final act of this dramatic struggle for power occurs as the intellect overwhelms and preempts the control of the feelings brain. In the end, reason rules while the emotions feel. Those feelings have evolved into the tools and weapons of the emotional system, which in turn has adapted to function under the dominion of reason.

Sometimes, we allow ourselves to be primarily directed by our emotional system. Such times as these are often accompanied by bad decisions and over-reactions. That is not to say that there are not moments to let a purely emotional response govern. There is a time and a place for purely emotional reactions, both as a survival mechanism employed by a species and as a personal choice. The reason will sometimes gladly allow the emotional system to be ascendant in the relationship.

These are usually times involving great joy, fear, or other extreme emotional states. That is because emotions are extremely powerful in all of us. As individuals, we usually do best when we heed our emotions, and we generally suffer when we do not. There are times in life when anything but a purely reasoning response would be odd and contrary (such as might be the case when regarding the transfer of information of a technical nature, or such like). An individual in society without a requisite amount of emotionality, though, would accurately be viewed as shallow and cold.

It is good that we have two interacting systems of such great capability. With both, we can create lofty intellectual insights, and simultaneously imbue them with all of our emotional fire and zeal. The interactions between the emotional system and the intellect can be both profound and breathtaking. It is what makes each of us unique and special. The sheer possibilities are virtually unlimited, if not truly infinite.

In some situations, the emotions might pitch in 75% of the effort, and the intellect, 25%. In other situations, the reverse can be true. Some people tend more toward the emotional, while others are naturally more intellectual by nature. That is as it should be as each individual expresses their unique personality. With the rarest of exceptions, however, all humans are creatures of both emotion and reason.

Emotional reactions lack thoughtfulness, it is true, but purely intellectual responses can be equally costly and contrary to the true desires of the individual when they are badly conceived, or simply based on incorrect facts or assumptions. For good or ill, reason retains ultimate control over the emotions and can exercise command authority to protect us in the most precarious of times.

No wonder we're the apex predators of planet earth, with a team like this in our heads. We've earned this dubious distinction the hard way by vanquishing all who have dared to come against us. The fierce beasts that once filled our nightmares now shrink from us in fear, if they value their hides (literally). Now that we have won the king-of-the-hill contest which is life on earth, though, we need to figure out how we will use our power. How do we *feel* about that, and what do we *think*?

BECOMING HUMAN
A New Perspective on the Origins of the Human Mind
Chapter 9

Human Motivation

Life is really simple, but we insist on making it complicated
-Confucius-

There are so many theories of motivation; it is a testament to human ingenuity. Some of them are quite abstruse to most of us (myself included). I have read some fascinating things from numerous researchers in this area, and I have been duly impressed with those parts (that I've managed to comprehend). There are many components to the question of motivation, lord knows, and especially human motivation.

There are many and varied theories of both animal and human motivation. Some theories focus on the molecular level at which motivation operates. Some theories focus on the importance of societal influences, and even facial expressions[138]. These numerous approaches to understanding the neurobiology and social influences of motivation are absolutely essential for a complete understanding of this topic, but none of them factor into my theory of human motivation in any way.

I accept that many things must be understood on multiple levels, and motivation *can* certainly be one of those things. Even such great luminary geniuses as Charles Darwin[147] proposed a theory of motivation[139], and he is in very good company.

I believe that human motivation inherently proceeds from two primary sources: our reason and our emotions. The motivation from our reasoning aspect differs from emotional motivation in the same way that these two aspects of mind differ generally.

Reason-based motivation comes from an intellectual understanding that certain things have to be done. When we do not complete those things which we know have to be done, our reason chides us initially and then excoriates our very conscious mind with images portraying our motivational dereliction of duty, and the dire consequences that could accrue as a result of this failure.

As all of us know, our reason can be completely merciless in its excruciations of what it perceives to be a failure on our part to complete the things we know need to be accomplished. How does our reason decide what the object of its derision should most properly be? It learns through a lifetime of experiences, both positive and negative.

The reason, for example, comprehends what the ramifications of not splitting wood for the evening fire will be. It does not require emotional entreaties to make it cognizant that the conscious mind's owner or others that are loved or dependent upon the mind's owner will directly suffer as a result of a failure in motivation that might have dire consequences. The reason, aware that it is going to suffer severely for its deficit in this area, experiences self-imposed pressure to complete the necessary task. In all respects, this is the definition of motivation.

What person is so blasé that they are willing to incur the wrath of everyone around them just to avoid a task on which they would prefer to procrastinate (except, of course, a teenager)? Initially, a person might be able to use the power of rationalization to allow them to defer that which they desire to avoid, but it isn't as if the conscious mind is going to allow them to simply forget about it. Reason doesn't work that way. It will, in most cases, hound its own conscious mind mercilessly until the task at hand is completed, at which time the motivation will disappear because the job is complete. Until the task is completed, though, the reason will continually *tighten the screws* until the job is accomplished, and the pressure relents.

At that point, the conscious mind (metaphorically) heaves a great sigh of relief, as it comprehends that the task's completion results in reason ceasing to perturb its equilibrium. At the same time, the reason is also aware that all of the other people affected by this decision will be likely to praise their efforts to complete it, rather than curse them that failed to complete it. Thus, we see that the abstract abilities of reason to visualize the positive benefits to be derived provide yet more motivation.

This is a more or less constant process within the conscious mind that we all deal with every day of our lives. It is also a profound study in obviousness. Quite frankly, I find it amazing that there is such a wide diversity of opinions as to what human motivation consists of, and from whence it emerges. I do not understand how the concept of what motivates an individual can be seen as so obscure. The same people (including me) who are actively researching, studying and creating theories experience these same motivational kicks in the pants as does everyone else. Those very people who are proposing the theories, in other words, are experiencing the same pressures within themselves that constitute motivation! An individual who is creating a theory of motivation has to motivate themselves to write down their thoughts, and arrange them into a theoretical framework, or else be subject to pressure to complete the task by their own reason. It seems to me that a person hypothesizing a theory of human motivation is actually creating a human motivation experiment, however unwittingly.

We can be quite sure that the person's reason is informing his or her conscious mind that they don't seem to be motivated enough in the construction of their theory of motivation! Therefore, the reason starts to assail the theorist's conscious mind with dark and forbidding images of all of the negative elements which may transpire if they don't complete the work to which they have committed. It excoriates them: *You're going to lose tenure and your wife will leave you!* This is deeply ironic on several levels.

The other, even stronger basis for human motivation is *emotional*. Our feelings can be far more relentless than our reasoning aspect as it seeks to implore us to do the things it ascertains we must. Most of us would rather have the Sword of Damocles over our heads than an upset emotional system that will constantly confront the conscious mind until its demand that we complete a task is fulfilled.

Our emotional system is utterly remorseless and completely without mercy in its demands that we do those things that it finds absolutely essential. Usually, this is for very good reasons. Perhaps the emotional system feels that we, the provider, have been remiss in bringing food to feed the hungry children that we *claim* to love. Perhaps the emotional system is assailing us because we are resisting standing up to something for the reason that we deem it to be hazardous, and that is why we are reluctant to become motivated to confront whatever issue is making us feel that way. As a rule, that does not matter one iota to our non-logical feelings. The emotional system, let us recall, is not known for its deep insights and thoughtful conjectures[140]. It feels an impulse and demands that the conscious mind act on that impulse forthwith.

There is very little reasoning to be done with the emotional system on any level, as the emotional system is not something that responds to reason. The emotional system does not have the capability to intellectualize or rationalize things away. The emotional system, while being a highly sophisticated and integrated part of our mind, nevertheless can bombard the conscious mind with its demands on a more or less incessant basis until it gets its way. At some point, humans under this sort of emotional pressure will become highly motivated to complete the task demanded of it for the simple reason that that's the only way to get it to shut up!

The thing of it is, we all know only too well what the emotional system is willing to do to accomplish its ends, don't we? While it would not be mentally healthy to fear or live in trepidation of our own feelings, we are nevertheless forced to take them extremely seriously. The alternative is to suffer while our own feelings belabor and bully our conscious minds with a host of increasingly unpleasant feelings and images. If a person is so foolish as to attempt to avoid or evade the motivational pressures emanating from the emotions, at some point the reason also becomes involved and imposes its own additional pressures in the shared forum of the conscious mind. A person can indeed *attempt* to withstand pressures coming from both the reason and the emotions, but I guarantee that that person will not be happy.

The two aspects of mind are rarely more powerful than when they team up on the poor conscious mind in this way. In the great majority of cases, it screams uncle, and simply complies with whatever the demands of these two influences command. To avoid or attempt to evade doing so would occasion ever-greater sanctions that would quickly result in intense personal suffering. The poor conscious mind is in a situation similar to a parent in a candy store with a young child on each side of them loudly demanding their favorite confection.

What on earth could be more motivating than a combination of our reasoning and emotional systems combining in the forum where both forces can hold forth in a combined effort to punish our very psyche? I believe that there are no greater motivations possible for any creature that has ever lived on this planet than that which these two aspects of the human mind provide. While it is important and edifying to understand the neurological bases of motivation, it is even more important to simply realize the incredible strength of these two aspects of mind in our own lives. Either of which is perfectly capable on its own of figuratively (and sometimes literally) bringing us to our knees.

Reasoning learns to be a more effective motivator over time. Feelings, as well, develop in depth and complexity over time. People naturally develop both positive and negative feelings about other things and other people through their experiences. Some people are loved by a person for certain reasons, and others are hated for yet other reasons. These intense feelings do not arise without cause. The intellect provides the reason based upon its experience and communicates this to the feelings in the ongoing dialogue between these two entities. It cannot speak, it may be true, but it still does communicate bi-directionally in an ongoing way, whether or not we are aware of it. When you really take time to meditate on it, though, you can learn to become quite aware of their interactions. It is a fascinating exercise in self-awareness, and I'd recommend it for those so inclined.

Let us not forget that this is a dynamic dialogue, in which a reasoning assessment (as well as the feelings resulting from this assessment) is constantly changing. A good example of this is provided in the case of a politician that we might intensely dislike but then come to revere based on a vote that they take with which we strongly agree. In such an instance, this politician might transform from a devil to an angel by both our reasoning and emotional systems in the blink of an eye. I cannot imagine how anything could be more dynamic than that.

What a strange creature is a human being. Gifted and cursed with two sometimes convergent and sometimes divergent aspects of mind. It is hard to believe that evolution made specific adaptations that allowed us to retain these ostensibly separate components which, in the final analysis, are both aspects of a single, highly unified mind. The reason that we have evolved this way is that there is an advantage to evolving this way. There is no reason to go to extreme lengths to explain that which inherently provides its own explanation to all humans daily. It makes a lot more sense and takes far less energy just to accept the obvious than to continue to question why it is the way it is. It is because we have evolved that way over hundreds of millions of years. That is why. It is as simple and complex as that.

Because human being's emotions and reason are capable of *double-teaming* a reluctant mind to do things that satisfy the demands of both aspects of mind, humans are without a doubt the most highly motivated creatures on earth. Intellectual motivation is powerful, and so is emotional motivation.

Together, though, they provide an extreme range of motivations of both a reasoning and feelings basis that most people are unable to resist. In most cases, people shouldn't usually try to resist, as the force that is providing the motivation is usually spot-on as to what they demand to be done in a given situation. I am reminded of an old saying that goes: *Don't push the river, it just flows around*. In the same respect, one is metaphorically pushing the river when they attempt to deny the authority and power of our own dual internal motivational structures.

One might say that motivation also comes from outside, but that is not correct. If an employer demands that you perform an activity to which you are averse, you might perform it, but not because you have been instructed to do it by an outside authority. You would perform it is because your internal motivational system is wise enough to reason that you will lose your job if you do not do it, and this would have other deleterious effects on your person and those you care about.

Your emotional system would also chime in at this point, making you feel inadequate and disconsolate in that you would be letting others down by your decision, and would further retaliate by bombarding your conscious mind with dire feelings of the possible negative consequences of your poor choice.

Ultimately, if one is still intent on noncompliance, both your reasoning powers and your feelings will beat on your conscious mind like a rented mule until your compliance is obtained. Now, *that* is power like no other creature on earth can bring to bear. That is an example of why human beings are the most highly motivated creatures on earth. No other creature has a powerful enough reasoning mind to add such significant reasoning prowess to the equation.

Adele penguins in the Antarctic[141] always return to a certain area to hatch and raise their young and have done so since time immemorial. The area in question was originally very close to the water untold thousands of years ago when this instinct developed. Now, however, they sometimes have to trudge over 100 miles to reach their hatching grounds, overcoming numerous and daunting obstacles as they attempt to accomplish this feat. It is indeed a very powerful instinct that is driving these poor sore-footed birds, but a very powerful instinct is still not equivalent to the double-teaming motivational abilities that human beings demonstrate regularly.

The Adele penguins follow the dictates of their instincts because they have no choice. Let us consider the sorts of things humans will do as a result of being internally motivated, without there being any instinctive imperatives of any kind being exercised. 300 Spartans held the Pass of Thermopylae in 480 B.C. against hundreds of thousands of Persians until they were all killed.

American bomber crews in the Second World War regularly went on missions during which large percentages of them were killed, fully realizing that their deaths were the inevitable price of victory. 343 heroic firefighters in New York City on 9/11 intentionally ran into the burning and collapsing twin towers, taking one last look at life over their shoulders before reconciling themselves to the imminent death that they knew awaited them inside those buildings. I could go on regaling you with such stories as these all day, and I daresay that you could do the same to me.

In the end, though, the mere submission to the instinctive imperatives of the penguin appears amateurish and bumbling compared to the conscious acceptance of imminent death which human beings normally accept in circumstances requiring extreme sacrifices. Our own motivational apparatuses often force us to accept horrendous outcomes of which we are fully cognizant *before* we embrace them. *There is no other creature that has ever walked this earth that is capable of exerting this level of control over their motivational*

189

behaviors as are human beings. Perhaps, I conjecture, this attribute is a good thing for the species, but it can be a very bad thing for an individual.

Our mammalian cousins, partly driven by instinct, but also motivated by their relatively more powerful emotional systems over their reasoning abilities are also capable of very high degrees of motivation. The main thing that is different is their far less capable abilities to be able to realize the full implications of what responding to a motivational imperative can sometimes result in (such as a horrible demise).

Although I generally avoid sharing personal stories, I would relate to you a tale that changed my entire understanding of how deeply mammals feel and can be motivated, although the sentiments of the story have already been revealed to many other people, I realize. Many years ago, I was driving from my back road onto a main paved highway, and as I stopped at the intersection to look both ways down this busy thoroughfare, I saw a squirrel that had been run over by a car very recently. I could tell because it was still twitching. What was incredible to me, though, was that there was another squirrel who was frantically trying to pull the flattened body of the deceased off the highway. Over the space of five minutes, this desperate creature repeatedly risked its life in a vain effort to rescue its child (or mate or friend or parent).

I watched, transfixed, my heart in my throat as the squirrel would leap out, grab the corpse in its teeth, and pull for all it was worth to get it off the road as trucks and cars sped by, their tires coming within inches of it on every attempt. Repeatedly, it made last-second leaps out of the jaws of certain death, and then it would leap right back in again, never stopping in its efforts while there was any hope left remaining, and never quitting in a desperate situation in which most humans would have just given up.

Finally, after the squirrel realized that any further action was futile; it went into the edge of the tall grass growing by the roadside and sat back on its haunches, its quivering little arms held helplessly before it, staring unmoving at its deceased love for long minutes from the grass's edge. The intensity off its stare gave no doubt as to the immensity of grief it was experiencing. It was in shocked mourning for one who was much-loved and deeply missed. Very slowly, I got out of the car to stand near the deceased so the cars would swing wide of it.

Waiting until there was a break in the traffic, I ever-so-slowly and carefully knelt, and eased the tiny body up off the pavement. Holding it in my open palm, I gingerly set the body down at the edge of the tall grass only several feet from the observer, and then backed away as it turned its gaze to me. The squirrel certainly showed no fear of me, but then; it had also showed no fear of trucks and tractor-trailers, even when it was under them.

After regarding me for several long moments, it abruptly disappeared back into the tall grass, only to re-reappear several seconds later by the recently departed. It came up very close to the body, and sniffed and touched it to verify that it was indeed gone. Then, it again settled back on its haunches, and went back to staring. I had unintentionally become part of a memorial service, and I felt extreme sadness in this tragic moment for my new friend's loss.

I slowly backed away, returned to my car and somberly pulled out, as I felt that I had not earned the right to be present at such a moment to view the hero in their agony, like Hector before the walls of Troy. In this world, the most courageous don't always get a statue, and sometimes the bravest and noblest among us have fur, and never speak a word. They live, die, and are forgotten as though they'd never been. We humans might not understand how they feel...but they do.

Many folks with whom I've had the pleasure to work in my quarter century in human services have helped me to understand that people can quietly be as brave as even the most heroic squirrel, and that is probably the highest compliment I can give. Like this noble beast, they bear their grief and move on through life. In the same way, every species of animal that has lived in this world, including humans, could tell similar stories of pain and grief and loss and unbearable trauma. We mammals aren't as different from each other as some of us humans might think. A friend of mine who was a squirrel taught me that.

Mammals have a motivational system capable of driving them to extremes, but they do not generally have a powerful enough reasoning aspect to provide motivation from two simultaneous directions to the extent that humans can. In addition, they lack the full intellectual cognition of the results of following their motivational imperatives to the same extreme level as do humans.

Humans will regularly combine thoughtful input from the reason along with emotional input to create what is *usually* a reasonable balance of motivation between the two that *generally* accrues to the benefit of the individual. Following this train of thought, human motivation can be seen to spring from a combination of reason regarding what a person should be doing mixed with feelings that impel them to satisfy those motivating emotions through completing such tasks as are necessary to cause those feelings to be assuaged.

Our two aspects of mind excel at teaming up to create all the motivation most people need or want (and a little bit more). At that point, the hapless human is being assailed from two aspects of mind. Together, both compel one to act to get things done that will benefit the person or others within their purview that they care about. That includes ourselves, our loved ones, our culture, our social order, and all of the many things that we venerate.

That which we most value supplies both our reason and emotions with the raw material that they transmute into motivational gold. Our dual aspects of mind take these factors and bombard our very selves with them to make us act in a multitude of ways to satisfy the demands they impose. A lemming (it is falsely believed) might run into the sea, but humans will actually walk through fire, if the situation demands. There have never been such creatures as humans, whose motivations arise from within the two aspects of their mind and strikes with the irresistible force of a hurricane.

Humans, unlike all other mammals, have two powerful and sometimes pitiless masters to provoke and prod them into doing their bidding (poor things). These separate and vastly different aspects of mind, forever joined in the purpose of making motivational demands of the self, *force* the individual to take action. Those powers emanate from both the reasoning mind as well as the emotional system from which feelings proceed. That is a lot of motivation! It should be both a matter of pride and sorrow that we humans will bear such burdens to accede to the dictates of that which internally motivates us to such extremes.

Ultimately, it makes us far more capable as creatures able to manipulate and control our environments to serve our needs and desires, but it usually comes at a terrible price in human suffering, loss, and death. We are a unique species because of this. We are capable of being internally motivated to fulfill the direst, most horrific, and even fatal endeavors to satisfy motivators that arise entirely from within ourselves. It is both glorious and incredibly sad, and this is reflected all too well in our equally glorious and incredibly sad human history.

BECOMING HUMAN
A New Perspective on the Origins of the Human Mind
Chapter 10

The Origins of Emotion

Do not go where the trail may lead,
go instead where there is no path and leave a trail.
-Ralph Waldo Emerson-

A lot has changed in the hundreds of millions of years since limbic components performed all of their activities as exclusively separate structures. In human brains, many of the emotionally related activities are now processed in neocortical areas, simply because they are more efficient at completing such tasks. We are not the creatures we were when mammals first speciated from their reptilian ancestors, but our human brains include the various components and structures that earlier brains did, for the most part.

When one is forced to choose between reason and feelings, reason usually provides better outcomes than feelings. Imagine what it would be like, using your knowledge of your own emotions, to have them operating without the restraining and constraining influences of reason. When you got angry, you could act out the anger to your heart's content without reason stepping in and quashing your demonstration of emotional pique.

How well do you think your decision-making would be, based upon your own emotions? Would you tend to make sound decisions bereft of your reasoning faculties? Would the feelings washing over you prepare you to make long-range decisions of any merit or value? Or wouldn't you more likely be making rash decisions that could easily result in unforeseen negative consequences? I have personally made far too many impulsive emotional decisions in my life that haven't turned out well, and I suspect that most people would have to concur with my experience. We humans do have reasoning minds, and we still make foolish, impetuous decisions with great regularity.

The feelings-based brain that evolution gifted to our reptilian and early mammalian ancestors had evolved a neocortex for the simple reason that it desperately needed one. Until it developed, though, mammals would remain under the primary control of their emotions. What else were creatures supposed to do in the meantime? Perhaps they could hibernate until something better came along? Luckily for them, perhaps, their intellectual limitations made them unaware that they were in such a tough spot.

Obviously, nearly any brain is better than no brain, and a feelings brain is infinitely superior to even the most advanced neural net. Our even more distant ancestors were successful using only crude stand-alone limbic structures to help them make decisions, follow impulses, and manage instinctive displays and responses. In the absence of any brain at all, neural nets have proven themselves very capable structures over hundreds of millions of years. There are still creatures on earth with nothing more than a neural net to act in an executive capacity, such as those of phylum Coelenterata class Hydrozoa (hydras). Although some creatures can survive and thrive with such a limited structure, they will nevertheless have to reconcile themselves to very primitive existences. It is hard to imagine the kinds of decisions that such a creature would make, considering the extreme limitations of such crude neural structures. Suffice to say that they would be able to complete only the most basic of interactions with their environments, as well as with others of their kind. There would be little sophistication, and such a creature would be capable of only a very simple life. A feelings-based brain, by comparison, would create a much greater ability for an animal to cope with the many vicissitudes of their very unforgiving world.

Certainly, the emotions of any creature would be formed by its interactions with its environment and the other creatures within it. Many things must be considered regarding how a species would evolve a specific universal *emotional* reaction roughly identical in all creatures of that species. The emotions that the creature was employing to make decisions would necessarily have to be supportive of outcomes that would tend to favor the creature's survival, or they wouldn't be there in the first place.

Let me be perfectly and unambiguously clear. My theory of the origins of emotions state that *emotions were not originally here to make us feel, but to act!* That is the great secret of emotions! Why on earth would a capacity to

197

feel anything for its own sake spontaneously arise in a primitive creature that was just trying to survive? That makes no sense.

It is our natural human inclination combined with hubris to view things through the lens of our own experiences that cause us to always seek out answers in terms of ourselves. *We have emotions,* we might reason, *so wouldn't other emotional creatures be much like us, but in a lesser way, given our inherent superiority?* Well, no! In this case, we are used to looking at other creatures in our usual anthropomorphic way, and that is where we go wrong. It is only by developing a fresh perspective and tracing emotions back to the root of why they exist in the first place that their true initial intent becomes apparent.

Perhaps the best way to look at emotions is more from the standpoint of what benefit or specific positive outcomes might develop from a specific emotion. Let's consider what would undoubtedly be one of the most common emotions of a primitive reptile from, say, 250 million years ago: anger. This period was about 30 million years before the early mammals made their appearance, and occurred long before the emotions of the mammals developed, for the simple reason that the mammals themselves had not speciated from reptiles.

An emotion of anger can be extremely powerful and is an excellent way to create havoc in the existences of those that might seek to vex, compete with, or enrage you. The emotion of anger, then, becomes important and even essential to the health and well-being of a creature, as it inspires and motivates them to "mess up" anything that tries to mess with them.

As is often the case when we ascribe human characteristics to other creatures from which we originated, we humans are looking at emotions in the *exact wrong way*. We are considering the *feelings* generated by an emotion as the primary area of focus, when we should be regarding the *action taken* as a result of the ensuing emotional reaction. That's what matters in this equation. In other words, when considering the benefits of a given emotion, that benefit only accrues a survival advantage for the creature through the expression of the emotion outward into the environment. It is almost the same way that an instinct is directed outward into the environment.

Of course, it is mostly in primitive creatures that interactions tend to be primarily aggressive, and otherwise basic. Sex, food, territory, and other such survival-based considerations would be the formative elements that would determine the composition of an emotion to elicit the most effective and powerful motivation from the feelings brain to encourage it to respond in a way that is congruent with the emotional impulse to act. In this respect, *we should regard a specific emotion as an impulse-spurring motivator, but* ***the outward expression into the environment is the true reason for the evolution of that specific emotion.***

Although we humans inherently value our emotions for the good and bad feelings that they bring into our lives; to a creature with a primarily feelings-based brain, the emotions themselves were *secondary* to the feelings-based motivation and direction they provided. They were simply there to produce the desired result in the *expression of the powerful feelings* that the emotions give rise to, and for which they were initially created.

Would we rather suppose that emotions just spontaneously sprang into being to satisfy some spiritual or "feel good" purpose? Do we think they would evolve just to allow us (and our reptilian ancestors) to experience a more complete existence so that we might feel better about ourselves? In the actual hardscrabble existence of an animal struggling for survival in a world that guarantees it a 90% chance of extinction, the name of the game would be simply surviving to pass on your adapted genes to the next generation, so they can do the same, and that is the alpha and omega of it.

We humans fall into this trap constructed of our own false beliefs and assumptions. We truly do have emotions that originated in reptiles, but our emotions do not serve the same purposes as theirs did at that time. We mammals have had 220 million years in which to derive new purposes and re-purposes for old emotions, and where necessary, evolve entirely new emotions.

In this hypothesis, then, I am strongly suggesting that we are spending too much time considering what the emotional states of ancient creatures might have been. Instead, we should be spending our energy considering that their emotions are only the motivators and instigators of feelings that result in very specific actions being taken. This can't be overemphasized. A primitive, angry creature is a creature that is probably a lot more likely to get its way than one that isn't because an angry creature will invariably act out its rage. Especially in the absence of neocortical abilities that might seek to restrain the more extreme feelings engendered in a perilous situation, there would be nothing whatsoever to restrain the angry responses of an animal in that state sans a neocortex.

An enraged animal acting out its extreme vexation is a far more formidable opponent than is one merely experiencing anger internally. That creature can safely be ignored, whether it is a tiny mouse or an elephant. Primitive emotions, in this case, are the stimulus, and a creature's emotional reaction is the intended response.

When evolution adapts an emotion, it is through a trial-and-error process. Through this method, the necessary outcome will dictate what kind of response will need to be displayed in a given situation. This, in turn, will determine the exact flavor of emotion that will need to be created.

I fully realize that this is a very anti-intuitive and even radical concept for our minds to entertain. It is my personal opinion that this is perhaps why there have not been more compelling theories regarding how and why emotions originated. It seems as if a sheer quantity of theories have substituted for taking the effort to reason this through from the perspective of the creatures who first evolved them. We naturally know that we have emotions, but we see the feelings aspect of the emotion as being the primary consideration as if the reaction that the emotion motivates in the creature is somehow secondary. That is, however, not at all the case. In fact, it is the other way around.

Let me give an example illustrating my point. Let's say that a primitive ancient reptilian ancestor of ours is, by nature, a timid and inoffensive beast. Its equable nature, though, results in it being bullied away from the best feeding areas by creatures that it could easily vanquish in combat, but are aggressive enough to bully our ancestor to get their way. As it's quite timid, however, it allows itself to be driven away to lesser-quality feeding grounds. As a result, its species of like-minded creatures are underfed, malnourished, and on their way to extinction.

Let's assume that this reptile has a very embryonic feelings brain that is capable of employing emotions, but has not yet evolved an entire assemblage of them. In the case of our timid reptilian species, and over a very protracted time frame, an emotion is created through mutation and adaptation which makes the creature angry when another creature tries to harass or annoy it. The aggressor creature now discovers that its bluff has been called, and these creatures are no longer timid. Rather, they will bite you if you vex them, and it has a chunk missing from its butt to prove it! By evolving this one single emotion, our reptilian ancestor's life has been totally altered.

What has happened here? The important thing that has occurred is that now a creature pushed to the edge of extinction because of its inherent timidity has learned to employ an emotionally-induced *reactive aggression*[142] by means of a completely unconscious series of adaptations. Over a long time, through numerous small changes, the animal evolves an emotion of anger. Like all emotions, it naturally arises when a certain circumstance occurs to trigger it, creating a very simple reality understandable by even incredibly primitive organisms. Aggress against me, and I will bite, scratch, and trample you; so be nice. What matters from an evolutionary point of view is that our reptilian ancestor finds a way to survive the dilemma posed by its own (formerly) timid disposition.

> "First, reactive aggression is the ultimate behavioral expression of anger and thus we can begin to understand anger by understanding reactive aggression. Second, neural systems implicated in reactive aggression (amygdala, hypothalamus, and periaqueductal gray; the basic threat system) are critically implicated in anger." *(Blair, James. National Institute of Mental Health, Bethesda, Maryland. Wiley Interdiscip Rev Cogn Sci. 2012 Jan-Feb; 3(1): 65–74. doi: 10.1002/wcs.154. Citation #142)*

This quite elegant solution to our reptilian ancestor's dilemma is provided by the *relatively* simple evolution of an emotion of anger within an already existing emotional structure. In the same way, every emotion in the creature's repertoire would develop similarly for similar reasons. It is no more complex than that. I find it is often the case that the simplest answer is usually the correct one. The more I study matters pertaining to evolutionary adaptations, the more I see that they usually seem to occur in the simplest, most straightforward, and often, most elegant way. I always look for that when considering such matters, as simplicity and elegance are often the imprimaturs of what usually turns out to be the most plausible answer or solution to a problem of this nature.

Our reptilian ancestor had very crude emotions because it was very intellectually limited. It developed the emotions that were necessary to sustain its life, so it could survive to eventually evolve greater capabilities. It would also have developed specific emotions that would pertain to the particular problems it would experience in its environment. A specific problem, concern, or dilemma would precede the development of a specific emotion. The emotion itself would evolve as *the solution* to the problem, concern, or dilemma.

Emotions are secondary to the emotional reactions they create. These reactions are the predictable consequences of the feelings contained within the emotion. The anger the reptile felt was a programmed reaction designed to ensure that a certain retaliatory reaction could repeatedly be counted on to occur dependably.

Although a creature often does not want to be predictable, predictability can become a great strength in the right circumstances. As a rule, *unpredictability is good for an individual creature* but very *bad for an entire species*. The aggressor creature that discovered to its dismay that the formerly timid reptile was no longer timid learned a lesson, but it wouldn't have been a very good lesson if, the next time it bullied the timid reptile, it succeeded in its shakedown. In this case, the timid reptile *needed* to predictably display anger and its frequent accomplice, aggression, or the emotion would be valueless.

One of the most valuable aspects of any emotion is that it is *predictable*. This is critical when you're a primitive creature living hundreds of millions of years ago, although it's still true for reptiles and mammals worldwide to this very day. Predictability of expression is a hallmark of a good and effective emotion. Through the expression

204

triggered by its emotional reaction of anger, the timid reptile was no longer timid, and the aggressor creature came to realize that it would invariably suffer similarly if it made the reptile angry again.

As emotions resist change, they would continue to provide dependable, non-variable reactions and the responses that would follow. This was an especially important characteristic in the case of a primitive creature, as nuance and subtlety were lost on both them and their contemporaries. Note: May I ask that you keep what I just said about how *emotions are designed to resist change* in the back of your mind until Chapter 11 when I will be referencing this characteristic of emotions in greater depth.

What a tremendously powerful and positive survival benefit a simple emotion can create. As a consequence of the evolution of this crude emotion, the species has become more aggressive and now has better feeding grounds. As a result of this, its population dramatically increases, and its descendants thrive to speciate even more advanced creatures such as mammals. Those mammals will now inherit not only anger and all of the other reptilian feelings, but even more interesting sorts of emotions better suited to the needs of mammals, and custom-tailored to their lifestyles.

What does this story teach us? A creature could weigh 10 tons, but without an emotion by which to benefit from this bulk, and in the absence of reason to guide it, it could not effectively use its massive size to its benefit. Through the evolution of a single emotion, however, it could suddenly convert into a complete terror. In this case, as in all cases, emotions are innate calls to action, as well as triggers that inspire and instigate actions.

An emotion begins with a feeling. The feeling stimulates the entire mind and body of the creature, which becomes aroused, excited, and motivated by the emotion. If the creature feels it is necessary or to its advantage, it is now primed to take aggressive or even physical action in service to the exhortations of that emotion. In this way, emotions were introduced to the world, not as constructions by which to bring feelings to otherwise affectively *flat* creatures but to save them from becoming extinct. That is more than a slight distinction: it is a matter of life or death.

The main point at which emotions of a *new* type and variety became necessary to ensure survival was when mammals speciated from reptiles. Primarily, this was because of child-rearing considerations. Emotions such as love, tenderness, and nurturing helped them to better care for the young, and were critically essential for the continued survival of these new types of creatures that the world had never seen before. This mammalian series of adaptations created most or even all of the emotions that still live on in all mammals, including humans.

One might enquire as to why I believe we highly-evolved humans don't have some kind of higher and far grander emotions reflective of our elevated opinions of ourselves? What for? I would reply. In my opinion, the time for developing emotions in all mammals is, in the main, over. We have retained our prior emotions and still have the capability to adapt them if that is needed. We can also create relatively subtle variations so that they may better serve the cause of survival if and when our environment changes in some unforeseen way. We must realize, though, that emotions are quite limited in terms of what they do. Emotions are inherently primitive, and they produce highly effective but otherwise equally primitive responses and reactions.

We mammals now have a highly developed neocortex that is inherently far more advanced and capable than the sorts of crude neuronal circuitry from which our latest tranche of emotions arose at the dawn of mammals. We shouldn't expect to evolve more emotions, because we don't need them. In fact, I think it is both fair and rational to suggest that we should not in any way desire more, given that they are intensely problematic in their current form. I believe the ones we already possess can be quite troublesome enough by themselves, without the need for others to further confuse and befuddle our reasoning mind; which, if it could speak, would no doubt make a passionate plea for mercy against any such notions.

To my way of thinking, emotions are not things *initially* designed for any purpose greater than that which I earlier specified. They cause a creature to react in certain ways in certain situations in a predictable, outwardly directed, and motivating manner. Predictability is a feature that we expect to find in a reptile, but then, so are basic emotions.

Most of these reptilian emotions, it is true, are aggressively oriented. Some reptilian emotions, however, such as those associated with social aspects, cooperation, and procreation can be seen as quite positive, in the full meaning of the term. Emotions are simply whatever the circumstances that gave rise to them required them to be when they were created. In the fullness of time, they can adapt in nature, complexity, and capability. If you don't first evolve the basic emotions necessary to help ensure your survival, though, there won't be any "later on."

The reason that emotions evolved in reptiles and mammals was to provide innate standardized reactions, as well as powerful motivation by which an animal would be spurred on to do certain things, and/or complete certain tasks. They were like uber-instincts. These tasks were determined, though, by the specific ways that a certain species tend to react.

On another level, though, individual creature's precise reactions would have included an inevitably individual and unique way of *displaying* the intent contained within the emotion as they experienced it, thus necessarily adding a certain amount of variation in the expression of a given emotion.

Let's remember that no two things that have ever existed in this world have been exactly alike. All animals are both like unto others of their kind, while simultaneously being unique. It isn't only humans who have uniquely memorable personalities, after all, despite what the word suggests. If you're not sure that you agree with me, simply own two dogs, and you will very soon.

Emotions are always intentionally motivating in their effect on a creature. We have to remember that, before we had evolved the neocortical reasoning mind, we had to have another method by which to inspire creatures to take action to do all of the various things that are necessary for a life form to survive, thrive, and avoid extinction. Creatures had to be able to defend themselves and their territories, their food supply, as well as their young. The thing is, we humans have forgotten that, because we evolved a cerebral cortex with very high reasoning abilities, and have become spoiled and pampered by the high level of civilization made possible by the social organization reason makes possible.

Like emotions, our reasoning brains also provide motivation. The difference is that emotional motivation arises spontaneously; whereas our intellectual motivation arises as a result of reasoning out why we *need* to do certain things. The motivational origins of both proceed from different neural structures, and the process by which each is evoked is also completely different. What they both have in common, however, is that they are both intrinsic, highly motivating features in humans

Emotions (as we have discussed) strongly inform and influence our reason. They can even affect our reason in numerous ways to cause us to sympathize with the emotion's stance on an issue. An example of this often arises when someone says or does something to offend us, and we have an instantaneous emotional reaction. Our blood pressure rises precipitously, adrenalin pumps into our bloodstream, our heart rate increases, and our body prepares to fight. Simultaneously, the emotion in question sends a direct and unambiguous message to our reasoning brain that this person must now suffer for their impudence. In so doing, the emotion shows its expertise in co-opting not only our entire bodies to their cause but poses a rhetorical question (or, at least, a similar emotionally analogous presentation) to our reasoning faculties that seek to inveigle and entice reason to show solidarity with it.

Emotions are tricky in this way, no doubt due to their hundreds of millions of years of adaptations within our minds. Emotions can be like a friend who gets us into a fight and then offers to hold our coat. They are cunning entities, these emotions, and we are usually right to suspect their good intentions at certain times, such as in this example.

They first initiate a reaction and then do their very best to motivate both our bodies and minds to respond at all levels, including the reasoning level. *Oh, we think, this person is being mean to me, and my emotions are being supportive! I totally agree with my emotions in this case, therefore, as they seem to have the right of it!* Of course you are in accord with them! They are you! Now, however, they're going to recede into the background, so that they can better hold your coat, now that they have motivated you into a battle of *their* own devising.

Wait a minute, you later think as you are getting stitched up at the ER, *isn't my reasoning mind supposed to be smarter than my emotions?* Welcome to the world, fellow traveler. Perhaps the day will come in which humans do evolve new emotions, but I'll make an offer to anyone out there right now: you can have my new emotions as soon as they become available. I'm all set.

Early mammals developed new emotions because they were necessary to protect their young. Unlike reptiles, who could just lay their eggs and walk away, many mammals would dedicate literally years of their already short lives to their progeny. Child-raising required an entirely different additional set of emotions than are required by reptiles.

Just try to interact with a reptile in such a way as to bring out their whimsical or loving side, and be prepared to be disappointed if you can't. That is for the very simple reason that they never evolved these emotions because they weren't necessary to ensure reptilian survival. When you try to bring out the whimsical or loving side of most mammals, however, you will immediately see that they have both of these capabilities in abundance, and in many mammals, they are very highly developed.

I have read the results of several MRI studies indicating that dogs react almost equally positively to food and the presence of their beloved owners[170], and the same areas of their brains activate as do humans when seeing images of those we love. To suggest that our dogs love us as much as food is especially surprising, as they really love that kibble. It is touching.

In a feelings brain, the thing that feels so deeply, the spur to prepare the body and mind for action, and that which makes a decision that motivates action *is* the emotion. The emotion, when it decides it is appropriate and/or necessary, motivates the creature, body and mind, to perform the tasks it is commanded to by the emotional system. The action that is taken is not necessarily wise, well-conceived, or even effective, as emotional reactions are often clumsy. When you have no other neurological entities at your disposal, however, it is all you have, and all you will ever have.

I fully realize that it must seem that I am looking at this matter in a backward fashion by putting the importance of a display ahead of the emotion that precipitates it. In fact, that is exactly what I am doing. In my opinion, the very act of attempting to fathom the mystery of emotions is so inherently counter-intuitive that one needs to look at it in a way that may seem to, in a manner of speaking, put the cart before the horse.

It is natural for us, with our advanced reasoning abilities, to intellectualize the emotional process into something more than it truly was initially intended to be. It is the most apparent thing for us to do, for that is how we perceive our own emotions; but that which is apparent is not always real. We would have to totally disengage ourselves from our reasoning aspect to actually experience how a crude feelings brain would operate sans intellect.

Our minds won't allow us to do that, of course, but we can imagine it, and imagination is a function at which our reasoning minds excel. All of these early creatures, including the more advanced reptiles and the less advanced mammals, operated under the dictates and guidance of their emotions, which were the primary determinants of most of their actions. Their entire conscious experience must necessarily have been a melange of various emotional impulses competing to be heard and acted upon, combined with numerous extant instincts, reflexes, and responses. It all sounds quite exhausting, and it often undoubtedly was, we can be sure.

In those extreme moments when our emotions overwhelm the usual dominance of our reason, though, we get a glimpse of what life must've been like when our distant ancestors were nearly completely controlled by the tyranny of their feelings-based brains. As we can all recall when such things have occurred within us, powerful emotional reactions invariably cause an extremely stressful situation to occur. This is also nearly always an extremely *uncomfortable* situation most of us are anxious to not repeat, and most people will usually go far out of their way to avoid the underlying circumstances that gave rise to such things in the first place.

We have all experienced times such as these when our emotional brain does take over and starts making decisions. Is there any doubt at such times as to which aspect of our mind is in control? No, it is generally a quite definite thing. It is only after the greatest part of the emergency has passed that our somewhat disoriented reason can reassert control.

Laden with uncompromising feelings and determined to turn its feelings into action in a very direct, no-nonsense sort of way, it acts! It does this so precipitously that our poor intellect needs time to simply catch up before even realizing what has just happened. Let's not forget that it does this for the express reason that this ancient assemblage of interconnected structures is still both incredibly powerful and useful, and its continued presence is all the proof that is needed to confirm this fact.

When one stops to consider that it is only the most critically essential reactions that created specific emotions necessary to trigger them, it makes you realize that evolutionary adaptations didn't seem to accept that a large number of emotions were necessarily a desirable thing, either. The fact that we never evolved a huge panoply of them suggests that they were viewed as being problematic (from an evolutionary perspective) even back then.

If you accept that the feelings brain was emotionally directed, then it follows that the emotions that it created would be inherently motivating in such a way as to cause a generalized reaction throughout the entire animal. Has there ever been an emotion that was not motivating? This sort of reaction is far more valuable to the creature than that of, by comparison, a crude instinctive display, with its many inherent and dynamic limitations. The entire creature would become imbued with the strong feelings generated, and it would mentally, physically, and bio-chemically begin to prepare itself for what might occur. What remains the most important aspect of this entire sequence? It is the invariably powerful reaction to the emotional motivation by the entire animal's body and mind.

The entire point of an emotion is to create or promote a situation in which an animal is likely to react in a certain predictable way. Very often, in actual practice, several emotions would often be present, each of them in different states of stimulation. An emotion does not exist with an absolute numerical intensity value, as it is an analog with a theoretically infinite number of values. If a single emotion has an infinite number of possible values of intensity, then several combined emotions would have a combined product of several times infinity. I'm not a mathematician, but I am guessing that that would add up to a *lot* of possible emotional states. It's very simple to create a unique emotional state, though, so let's build one for, let's say, an Hylonomus. You take a pinch of curiosity, add a touch of territoriality, swirl in two measures of rage, and voila! You just created a unique emotional state!

It is the extreme variability of possible emotional states which adds a degree of unpredictability to all emotional situations. As we've discussed in prior chapters, it can sometimes be very detrimental to any creature's future prospects to be highly predictable. The bodies and minds of most creatures evolve means and methods to avoid the predictability trap. To clarify, an *individual animal* can come to harm if other animals figure out how its predictable behavior can be used against it, but *species predictability* is actually a great strength.

Emotions gain in power as they become ever more predictable. This is for the simple reason that species become known for, and associated with, their predictable emotional reactions so that other creatures can know what they can get away with, and not get away with in their interactions with them. I would prefer to not be the gazelle who thinks to himself: *I know most leopards are vicious killing machines intent on the destruction of all gazelles, but I somehow think this particular leopard over on the rock just wants someone to talk to.* You go and have that talk, Mr. Gazelle. I'll hold your coat.

We have to realize that animals would need to maintain certain fairly well-defined interactions with their environment and other creatures in their environment for numerous purposes. The mammals that were rapidly spreading throughout the world (as much as plate tectonics and ice ages allowed) benefited from the specific emotions they developed. Those emotions would be reflective of their needs not only as members of a given species but as creatures having to survive in a particular environment. Very often, that is how sub-species developed.

215

Each species generally knew what to expect from other species, and each other species knew what to expect from them. This ensured a more predictable environment for all. If all of a creature's competitors were running about expressing themselves emotionally in wildly random and variable ways, the only beneficiary would be chaos. Some situations within this havoc might prove to be positive in such an inconsistent scenario; while others might involve fights to the death over seemingly inconsequential matters, both within and outside a species.

A creature would just never know, and that is equally bad for everyone, as they would have no predictable frame of reference for their inevitable interactions with other creatures. Emotions provide the requisite predictability by which reptilian and mammalian species could find a certain degree of order in the world. The fact that a specific reaction would be expected (though not certain) would predictably inform other creatures of its own, and other species, to know what to expect. That would provide a universal benefit for all.

People tend to first consider an emotion in and of itself, and only then speculate what effects that emotion might engender in a creature. In my opinion, and as I've been hammering on, this is exactly the wrong way to look at this. Consider that it is the overall reaction engendered by a given emotion that is important. The creature is going to become *extinct* if it isn't emotionally informed as to how to react in commonly occurring circumstances. This is literally a matter of life and death. We might not realize this now, but our ancient ancestors certainly did. Then again, we can afford to be more blasé about it, because it isn't our lives that are in imminent peril.

If an antagonist behaves aggressively, which is more important? Is it more important that an animal is emotionally reacting to several separate complex feelings, each of different intensity? Or is it more important that those feelings motivate the animal to take action in the most effective way it can, in accordance with its emotional directives?

That is a simple choice, as the former reflects a dilemma in Existentialism, while the latter reflects an existential dilemma in which the poor animal may become someone else's lunch! That is a pretty huge difference. Armed with the constant prodding and ongoing motivation at which emotions excel, though, most creatures were in good hands, at least until smarter creatures arose. Enter the hominids.

Emotions are both simple and complex, but I think the intent of natural selection, in this case, was pretty clear. Natural selection saw to it that these initially crudely constructed emotions motivated creatures to do virtually all of the tasks that would be required for them to survive, flourish, and pass on their genetic code to the next generation. It is always the same answer forever.

If a new type of critical task arose, a new emotion might need to evolve. It had to have been the actual circumstances that certain species experienced that would've been the greatest determinants of precisely what emotional qualities would be needed to most appropriately motivate them to do that which was required. As time passed, new and different emotions would be needed, especially in the case of mammals.

Through numerous adaptations, the requisite emotions would evolve to fulfill all critical purposes. The early mammals evolved many emotions that were absent in reptiles because mammals' needs were so different, particularly in how they took care of their young. As most newly-born mammalian offspring are fairly helpless in the absence of a great deal of care by the parents, the new *mammalian* emotions were specifically created to address this dire need. They must have evolved in a great hurry under huge adaptational pressures that we cannot fathom.

A creature such as this, unlike a reptile such as described above, has need of many new emotions promoting such feelings as persistence, parental caring, dedication to one that is helpless, love, courage in the face of adversity, and even emotional combinations like those that comprise "metaneeds" such as goodness, order, unity, and others propounded by Abraham Maslow in his "Hierarchy of Needs Theory[143]."

Human emotions all arise from the original reptilian emotions, combined with the novel early mammalian emotions that were added on top, later in deep time. All emotions came to us at these times, I believe, and it is doubtful that we'll need any new emotions in the future. Emotions being problematic, why would we want more?

We can't even understand the emotions we already have. Even love, which we humans can't stop singing about and writing odes to, will forever remain a thing we can only experience, but never truly understand. That is because its roots extend far into the eternally unconscious realm from which all emotions spring. They aren't meant to be understood, and they won't be.

All of the emotions I enumerated above and more still remain in every fiber of our beings as mammals. We humans know exactly how strong these emotions are, and we can surmise that they were probably extremely powerful in early mammals, also. When a child is in danger, an otherwise meek parent can convert into a deadly adversary in the blink of an eye. Most parents in such a situation, desperate as it might be, mammal or human, will willingly sacrifice their lives in an attempt to safeguard their offspring. I know of nothing more powerful than a feeling that is so strong as to make a creature forfeit its life to uphold the tenets which that emotion embodies.

Our emotions run through our being like a deep, twisting river moving silently along while containing great power. Emotions tend to not *generally* make a fuss unless provoked. It is for this reason that the wisest among us excel at avoiding the sorts of provocations that cause others to feel the need to make their own emotional expressions. In cultural terminology, this is called being diplomatic.

I realize that I have made extra clear in my theory that we must first focus on the objective of the emotion prior to even considering the emotion itself. That is because the key to understanding all emotion is in the consideration of the motivation that emotion produces in the creature to result in a positive survival benefit justifying its continued existence.

It is possible that in the long period between early reptiles and modern humans, our ancestors might have shed emotions that were disfavored by circumstances. Emotions can be adaptationally disfavored in the same way that unhelpful instincts can be, if it becomes necessary. The monumental emotional adaptations undertaken by our reptilian and mammalian ancestors while fighting the day-to-day battle for survival still remains an amazing and even inspirational story on many levels.

One's heart should go out to these creatures that faced the perils of their primitive world, fought for those they cared about, and ultimately perished and were forgotten. If they hadn't been who they were, though, we would never have obtained the opportunity to show the world who *we* are, and can become. So thank you, brave and stalwart creatures of all species who fought the odds and each other for basic survival. If you had not persisted with such heart and determination, we would not be here to recall and honor your persistence, courage, fortitude, and indomitable spirit. Rest in peace. We who are your descendants thank you.

BECOMING HUMAN
A New Perspective on the Origins of the Human Mind
Chapter 11

Emotions and Predictability

*Let's not forget that the little emotions are the great
captains of our lives and we obey them without realizing it.*
-Vincent Van Gogh, 1889-

In the last chapter, I was discussing how emotions
are so critically important to basic creatures such as reptiles
and early mammals because they are naturally resistant to
change. At that point in the chapter, unwilling to get driven
off-topic, I said that I would be taking up this issue in the
next chapter. Well, here it is. As emotions were each
individually adapted into what was then the feelings brain,
it became obvious that they could only be useful to an
entire species over a long period of time if they
were *incredibly highly resistant to change*. I believe that
the reason for this has to do as much with other species as it
does with the creatures of that species.

Every species has what could be considered a
generalized personality type distinct from that of all other
species. Some species have a quite tranquil personality,
such as a lemur. Others, such as a tiger, are anything but
tranquil. Of course, the sort of personality which is
reflective of the particular emotions that a species has

evolved depends upon (as we considered at length in chapter 10) the actual types of motivation and motivational goals that the emotion evolved to serve. Consider our docile reptile, and why and how he evolved an anger emotion, and what the result was.

Having gone to all that trouble to evolve the anger emotion to rescue its species from extinction, this reptilian species had a vested interest in the effects of this emotion not being diluted or lessened over the succeeding generations. What would be the point of developing an unstable emotion? There would be no lasting value unless an emotion was incredibly resistant to change or alteration of any kind.

Emotional predictability informs individuals within the species what they can generally expect from other members of their species. Even more importantly, however, emotional predictability is an absolute essential for survival with creatures outside of one's species. Every species needs to know what to expect from every other species, or it won't know what it can and can't get away with in terms of its own behavior and actions.

The predictability of emotions, then, is one of their most powerful features (but it is also its least obvious attribute to the human mind). This is not surprising when you consider that an angry emotional display is what catches your attention. What with all the screaming and biting and trampling and suchlike that comes as a result of violent anger occurring, it is easy to miss the predictability angle until you dig deeper.

It is impossible to believe that evolutionary adaptation could somehow conceive that evolved emotions must inherently be resistant to change, or they would otherwise be lacking in consistent value to creatures in the long term. That is a reasoning argument, and evolution does not reason. The answer to this question, therefore, is not to be found within the realm of reason. Now, though, let's consider the nature of a feelings-based brain. Let us ask ourselves: is a feelings brain a group of structures that are themselves conducive to change? The answer to that question instantly comes back as an unambiguous no.

This kind of brain is only going to ever change through laborious evolutionary adaptations resulting from pressures within the environment that would force change. Feelings-based brains resist change for a reason. It appears that this basic brain has been incredibly consistent and stable over millions of years[126].

You would anticipate that a thinking brain would be able to *turn on a dime*, as the saying goes. You would anticipate that it would be nimble and that its inherent power of neuronal perfection would endow it with flexibility. Indeed, the thinking brain demonstrates its nimbleness every day, and nearly every moment of our waking lives.

The thinking brain is naturally awash in a sea of constantly and dynamically changing events to which it must adapt moment-to-moment. Consider our own human minds. Their greatest strength is their ability to make great leaps of intuition and intellect to completely restate or restructure a concept on the fly. What proves the great nimbleness of our reason greater than its capacity to make huge extrapolations? The extrapolative power of the human mind proves it to be a structure of incredibly flexible design. The thinking brain is designed and wired for power and change. That is its great gift, aside from its pure computing power.

Now, by comparison, let us consider the feelings brain as it would have existed in reptiles 250 million years ago, when its neocortex was, at best, miniscule[168]. If I were to think of several words to describe it, I would use words like basic, non-logical, emotionally-driven, dense, and crude. Believe it or not, I am actually very fond of my emotional system, and I do not mean to untowardly castigate it for its obvious inadequacies.

The emotional system of all creatures from reptiles to humans is intentionally designed to be basic. Its very crude nature is actually its strength. The basic feelings brain such as existed in ancient reptiles is fundamentally little changed in 200 million years. It has greatly altered, of course, in mammals.

This crude brain thus demonstrates its incredible resistance to change, as are the emotions that evolved within it. So, while we now understand why it resists change due to its inherent crudeness of design coupled with a positive survival benefit to be accrued by not changing, why are emotions so resistant to alteration? Let us consider what would happen if there wasn't this natural ability of emotions to obstruct all change. At first glance, it occurred to me that perhaps adaptations would tend to naturally put a creature back on the proper emotional path from which it had strayed.

The problem with this is that if all members of a given species were losing and then regaining emotions through adaptations, then there would still be a *slow but inexorable process* by which the species would vary in their emotional responses. This would have the direct effect of causing every member of the species to behave differently than every other member of the species. That could have the direst of consequences!

Over time, such differences would inevitably continue, and variation of behavior would increase, causing a continually greater *drift* of all emotions. Does this seem to happen in life? Are creatures fairly dependable in their temperaments and dispositions? Do species seem to generally behave as one would expect a given species to behave? Or are individual representatives of all species radically different? Are there Cape Buffalo that are laid-back and languid? Are there pandas that are just waiting to leap upon you from their bamboo grove with deadly intent? Have you ever encountered a homicidal mole? Have you ever encountered a wolverine that *wasn't* homicidal?

Excepting all animals that have been artificially selected for certain traits by humans, it would seem to most people that species-specific behaviors as determined by emotional responses remain fixed and predictable within certain bounds. Keeping in mind that the creature is also behaving based upon their neocortical abilities as well as their experiences; they yet produce an incredibly predictable species response, in the main.

This says to me in no uncertain terms that there is something else that is occurring in the core of the emotional systems of all reptiles and mammals, including humans. This is the only way that I can conceive that *all* of these creatures are so uniform in their responses within a species, especially. The possibility that this is first *drifting* from an emotional norm, and then being corrected to its starting point through further adaptation does *not* explain the way it remains so consistent.

Emotional consistency of this nature over very long periods of time equals immutability, does it not? We can't know the temperament of a creature from deep time, but humans have experienced other animals and recorded their impressions for many thousands of years, and they seem quite predictable (although, of course, we don't have any written records going back a long time, as writing is a relatively new invention. If ancient Egyptians were paddling around on docile Nile crocodiles like they were surfboards, though, I think they would have inscribed it in stone in the same way as the Minoan bull riders recorded their experiences (or written it on papyrus, at least). They certainly would have made note of it, at any rate.

Emotions are the linchpins of species predictability in all reptiles and mammals. In the case of our timid reptile, we examined why the anger emotion that it evolved to successfully rescue its species from extinction was resistant to change. Any change would ever-increasingly result in large variable individual reactions on the part of every other member of the species. This could be expected to further drift as generations continued until eventually; there would be no consistency of behavior or disposition in any member of the species. At that point, it would have lost all value to benefit both the individual as well as the species.

The only way to prevent this consistency drift would be by building in safeguards to ensure that it didn't happen. Perhaps, when the first emotions appeared, they did not have this quality of permanence. In such an instance, then, there would be no long-term benefit to be garnered for the unlucky species with this *limited-time-only* emotion. That being the case, adaptational pressures would mindlessly keep trying to correct this defect in future models until they got it right. In the absence of safeguards within either the emotion or the feelings-based brain that housed the emotions, there would be little benefit in developing an emotion that would change, when its primary benefit is obtained by being immutable.

It is entirely obvious and virtually inescapable that a helpful emotion to a reptile or early mammal would require that it be inherently fixed and unchanging in both the nature of its feeling, as well as in its response. Let us not forget that the entire purpose of an emotion is to ensure a standard top-to-bottom feelings reaction to a given stimulus that can *always be counted on* to deliver in a well-defined, highly specific way. Furthermore, if that consistency is *not always provided*, it has no value. Given that all such creatures are dependent upon the reactions engendered by their emotions, their entire range of actions is instantly imperiled by a lack of consistency.

If we as humans are reacting oddly emotionally, it is of little consequence. If a reptile from 250 million years ago was reacting oddly emotionally, however, it would affect their entire reaction to other creatures, including predators and competitors. In such a situation, one would have to question the entire value of a feelings-based brain, if it were so easily diverted from its hardwired course. It would be similar to a reasoning brain losing its power to reason. It would instantly lose all value. I believe that there must be specific neuronal circuitry shared by both reptiles and mammals that safeguard against any capacity to drift from the original intent of any emotion, except over eons.

While there is no way to know exactly what the emotional affect of a creature from hundreds of millions of years ago might have been, we do know that the emotions they did have needed to be extremely consistent because they regulated and motivated the animal's reactions. Once again, it is easy to fall into the human trap of equating emotions with feelings, when as we have said, emotions evolved to motivate specific reactions within a creature.

The actual feeling that inspires the reaction is only directly important insofar as it is responsible for that action dependably occurring. The same predictability that benefits an entire species, however, would be catastrophic to an individual animal in that species, as *individual animals need to be unpredictable* in the same way that *species need to be predictable*. Let's use an example to illustrate this point.

When a rabbit is running away from a fox, it runs in a seemingly haphazard manner, ducking and diving this way and that as it attempts to evade the predator. Why does the rabbit perform this strange irregular running pattern? It is to be *unpredictable*. If the rabbit ran in a perfectly straight line, perhaps it could outrun its pursuer by dint of pure speed. What if the pursuer was quicker, though? The rabbit cannot assume that it can outrun its pursuer, so it instead relies on unpredictability as an ally.

It is somewhat confusing, but true, that while species benefit from predictability based upon their own immutable and unchanging emotions, individual creatures within a species nevertheless benefit greatly from the unpredictability of behavior that makes them harder targets upon which to predate. In this case, not knowing what to expect from a creature is a benefit to that creature.

At the same time, conversely, it is predictability that provides a very strong survival benefit for an entire species. Predictability of response on a species level informs animals both within and outside the species what to expect from a given species. Let me provide an example of the benefits of predictability in order to elucidate the true circumstances of almost every creature in the wild order.

A pack of hyenas were drinking down at the water hole while anticipating the arrival of some prey animals that were hopefully also planning to get a drink. Instead of a delectable troop of small and easily digested mammals, however, a pride of lions shows up. What will the hyenas do now? They will turn their tiny tails without another thought, and get out of there fast. Why would they do this?

The hyenas would not wait for the lions because they know perfectly well the predictable reaction that the lions will have upon seeing them. Lions and hyenas have an innate hatred for each other that is well-documented. In this case, the reputation of the lions for fierce aggressiveness precedes them. The hyenas have no doubt as to how the lions will react to their presence, and they have no intention to be around to witness an inevitable bloodbath, with them as the designated bathers.

Does it help the hyenas that the lions are a species that is predictable in their reactions? Yes, as it assists them to know what to expect from the lions. Does it help the lions that they are predictable in their reactions? Yes, as it informs competitors and others that may wish to take advantage of their good nature to realize that *lions don't have a good nature*.

If it wasn't clear to another species that lions were not to be trifled with, then they would trifle with them. This certainly wouldn't help the species that is provoking the lions, but it also doesn't help the lion. In such a case, the lion would have to repetitively prove to other creatures that it was a dangerous opponent.

By being species predictable, the lion is not required to prove that it is a ruthless and savage predator, for the simple reason that *all* lions are ruthless and savage predators, and all other creatures are keenly aware of this fact. The odd animals that might not have gotten the 'Vicious Lion' memo will be missed, but they will serve as a graphic reminder to the others, while providing an appropriately cautionary tale.

As soon as a creature sees a lion, then, they know it's time to leave right now. This helps both creatures in numerous ways. One creature gets to live, and the lion doesn't have to prove to every other creature it comes across that it can make a meal of it, when all the lion might really want to do is munch on a far more tender ibex. The needs of both species are thereby served through the one simple and incontrovertible fact that the true nature of the lion is that it is a vicious predator.

Of course, the same factor is in play with all mammals, whatever their species personalities might be. The hard way to find out that badgers are incredibly ferocious and foul-tempered beasts would be by attempting to take their dinner away from them just as they sit down to sup. The easy way would be to see a badger and realize that this is not a creature whose dinner you should mess with, unless you would like to be dessert.

BECOMING HUMAN
Chapter 12

Summarization of Theories

"Life is nothing until it is lived; but it is yours to make sense of, and the value of it is nothing else but the sense that you choose."
-Jean-Paul Sartre-

  This chapter is a summarization and condensation of all of the main theories contained in "Becoming Human." I term the entire interrelated group of theories contained herein "dual aspect theory" for simplicity, as a good descriptive term, and as a convenient collective term under which these separate beliefs, theories, and postulates can seek shelter. Each theory presented can stand alone, but they also directly relate to each other.

  The central premise is that humans have a conscious mind with two distinct aspects present; reason and feelings. The distant ancestors of humans developed this way over two hundred million years ago, and evolution intends for us to continue to have this dual aspect of mind for good reason. Our minds will continue to operate like this, but whether we accept it is up to us. To fight against the demands of our emotions is sometimes necessary, but is often an exercise in futility.

In this book, we have encountered many new theories that have afforded a truly unique and novel way to view the nature of human nature. We began by examining the deep time history of the species in our direct lineage from Archaea to Homo sapiens. What a fascinating history we have! I find it so surprising that such complexity can arise from such simplicity. In its own unique way, there is great beauty in this.

From single-cell organisms over 4 billion years ago, constantly greater complexity was created to conform to the specific conditions that prevailed in all periods and epochs of the history of Earth. Single-celled creatures became multi-celled creatures. Marine vertebrates evolved amphibians. Amphibians evolved reptiles, and reptiles evolved mammals.

Around 600 million years ago, after billions of years of evolutionary pressure, the neuron first appeared, and life on earth was forever changed. In short order, neurons went to work to fulfill a desperate need for creatures to feel sensations, and to be able to turn those sensations into actions and interactions within their environment. Neurons were soon fulfilling all sorts of duties for innumerable creatures.

Entire new senses were developed to better inform creatures of both positive and negative elements in their environment. Neurons connected all of the senses, and other crude neuronal structures evolved to provide basic direction to increasingly complex animals. Neural nets composed of loops of neurons provided sensation and awareness of the various areas of their body, and groups of neurons agglomerated in central areas, usually near the sensory apparatus in the head.

Although there are still creatures on earth that have only neural nets, such as the hydra, most creatures went on to develop actual brains. The first brains were quite crude constructions composed of various limbic structures that had evolved as standalone components to perform certain tasks. Over a very long period, they interconnected with other similar structures to form what is termed a feelings-based brain.

This sort of brain is characterized by relatively unsophisticated structures. The brain that reptiles possessed was primarily composed of three-layer neuronal structures such as the hippocampus and hypothalamus. Even for a neuron, developing the extraordinary capability of abstract intelligence was a tremendously difficult endeavor. It took many millions of years to give rise to a six-layer neuronal structure using highly evolved neurons to create the neocortex. This was originally evolved in fish and was passed on as a nascent neuronal structure to amphibians, and then reptiles. At first, the neocortex was unimpressive, even after it first appeared in mammals.

It has to be assumed that if it had any authority at all, it would have been minimal; presumably advisory. Over time, it grew to become stronger than the feelings brain. This brain, due to its crude neuronal construction, as well as the relatively ancient types of neurons employed in its development, was not capable of any sort of thought.

Thought requires the ability to create abstractions. The feelings brain was far too primitive to do that then, and still is. This brain did not think. This brain felt. To feel something, you need to have emotions. Emotions do not, however, help you to think. The connection between something that feels and something that thinks is inherently tenuous, at best.

It happened over unknown millions of years, but Mother Nature had to try to bring this evolutionary odd couple to an understanding, each with the other so that they could arrive at a working arrangement. In the thought-free manner in which adaptations occur, what choice did she have? Here were two neuronal structures operating in completely different ways using totally unlike methods, but if they could somehow be trained to work in harness, they could be extremely helpful to the success of a species.

Mother Nature didn't have any other option. Both components of mind were already there in the same head. It isn't as if evolution could order a more appropriate neural structure online if these didn't work out. Reptiles had already proven they could survive on a feelings-based brain nearly exclusively. For mammals, though, this was the only chance they had, or would ever have to establish themselves as a new type of animal. An animal such as the world had never before seen; one who bore its young alive, and was mentally capable of literally nursing them through their formative years, while teaching them most of what they needed to know along the way.

The feeling brain worked in a way that is somewhat difficult for people with human emotions to understand. We humans regard an emotion based upon the feelings it generates. This, however, has little to do with the reason for which they first evolved. Their purpose then was actually the same purpose emotions have now, but humans have forgotten that purpose, to their detriment.

Our experience of them has been ineluctably altered through the influence of our human mind. In their initial form in mammals, however, the emotional brain still ruled supreme. If a creature required a dependably powerful, invariable response to assist them in their quest for survival, then they would evolve a specific emotion that would elicit this exact response when it was needed.

It wouldn't just create a desire to perform a thoughtless response similar to an instinct. Rather, an emotion would create a tremendous urge to *do* something. Very often, in creatures possessing such a brain, most of these overwhelmingly powerful motivational urges would be aggressive, but theoretically, any emotion that was truly necessary for a creature's survival could be generated by a feelings-based brain. It could create any kind of emotion, but it has to be sufficiently important to cause myriad adaptations to occur before it became a reality.

If any of those adaptations prove to have negative consequences of virtually any type, though, it could well spell the death of the creature involved, which would then not be able to breed and pass on its genetic characteristics to the next generation. That is a high bar for success, but a long fall that will result from failure. The world of 200 million years ago was a terribly primal and incessantly violent place. It is normal, then, that the emotions that were evolved would comport with this reality. To allow the creature to survive in the tough neighborhood which, back then, encompassed the entire world, it was necessary to first evolve emotions that would oppose this primitive state of existence.

Under the influence of an emotion and lacking the reason by which to mitigate its effect, a creature would be immediately overcome by this irresistible urge. Because of the emotion's motivational power gained through its dominant feelings brain, it would use this might to inspire the entire creature to comply with the feelings that it was generating throughout the organism.

A creature under the sway of emotion was capable of instantly reacting in a huge variety of ways. This was made possible by the potential combination of other emotions also being created by a given situation, and those emotions were all capable of enormous possible levels of vexation. That's a virtually infinite number of possible emotional states that were created by the simple evocation of only several feelings.

This provided flexibility of approach to virtually any possible problem or dilemma the creature was likely to encounter. In a neocortically-based brain, this would be generally analogous to several separate thoughts coming together to form a greater thought. If that's not a good analogy, it is because these two separate ways by which brains can operate are so incredibly different that it's very hard to make tight analogies.

A creature in the thrall of strong emotion was fully ready and highly motivated to do virtually anything it was directed to do by its feelings-based brain. It was more a matter of the sorts of things that feelings might demand its owner to do. What they would ask would be based on the specific emotions that it had evolved to better interact with its environment, but do them the creature would, even if it killed it (and it often did).

The evolution of a six-layer neocortex from the three-layer cortex that already existed in reptiles allowed the mammals to have the potential to overcome the tyranny of the feelings-based brain if they could survive long enough for it to develop. Until then, they were on shaky ground (unrelated, in this case, to the massive volcanic and seismic activity underway).

The interconnections between limbic structures that had already been established within the emotional brain would have been conserved, but greatly improved over time. An interconnection would also exist between them and the neocortex, and these connections could be assumed to most likely contain both neurons from the emotional brain and the more capable neocortical neurons. The new interconnection was probably only as sophisticated as the neocortex was at any given time. They were evolving together, and a change in one would be likely to trigger commensurate changes in the other, in order to keep up.

Some would have us believe that the neocortex appeared fully formed in early mammals, but this is incorrect in several ways. Ultimately, it has been demonstrated that this did not happen and that the neocortex was small and simple in early mammals. Presumably, the time frame by which it substantially improved occurred over millions of years. It was, therefore, only long after early mammals had speciated from reptiles that their neocortex substantially grew in authority within what was still a feelings-based brain, assisted minimally by a cortex and neocortex. It was undoubtedly millions of years before the neocortex actually assumed much responsibility as a reasoning component.

I often wonder about present-day mammals? How much of their mind is under emotional authority, and how much is under the authority of reason? We humans may never know, but certainly, both qualities are apparent in abundance. My (totally subjective) impression is that most mammals seem to have a decidedly dominant emotional aspect, based on my own observations. Perhaps there is greater internal serenity to be found in achieving this mammalian compromise between reason and feelings? If so, we humans kissed serenity goodbye a long time ago when we embarked on becoming the smartest, but arguably, the most un-serene creatures on the planet.

It was in the millennia after speciating from reptiles that early mammals would have been under truly desperate pressure to evolve new emotions that were in concert with their radically new responsibilities, given that its young were born alive in a very dependent form. With mammalian young, it could take years between when one was born and when they became fully mature. This required an entire new assemblage of emotions that were radically different from that of a reptile.

Reptiles were amniota. As such, their parental responsibilities were generally minimal. Usually, they would be confined to procreation and the subsequent laying of eggs. In most cases, there would've been little to no parenting needed, as most newborn reptiles come out of the egg fairly ready to go it alone. Not so for the mammals, however, who needed to be doted upon.

When one considers how humans, and by extension, most mammals, react with tenderness, love, and long-suffering tolerance toward their progeny, it is obvious that the emotions that the mammals would have had to evolve in a quick hurry would've been nearly diametrically opposed to the sort of aggressive and pugnacious emotions of the reptiles.

Nevertheless, those aggressive emotions had served reptiles extremely well. The mammals, therefore, simply continued to use them and had little choice but to use them, as they already existed in their repertoire. How could they not have used them, anyway, insofar as they had been born with them? The world as it existed then would've required a constant show of aggression as much for an early mammal as it would've for a reptile.

The new mammalian emotions, therefore, would have been added to the already existing stock of reptilian emotions. If you consider reptiles and mammals as they now exist, there is still a huge difference in affect between the two based upon these entirely different emotions, as well as the brains from which they are derived. Reptiles have very small palliums compared to the neocortex of mammals. The pallium is the part of the brain of reptiles, birds, and some other types of creatures that is roughly analogous, and serves the same purpose as the neocortex in mammals. Although reptiles have never seen fit to develop high intelligence, birds with similar pallial construction to that of reptiles have added large numbers of neurons to their brains to become highly intelligent, often more intelligent than some mammals.

In the case of birds, their development of highly capable, neuron-intensive pallial structures is an example of convergent evolution resulting in analogous forms. It underlies a deep understanding on the part of Mother Nature that creatures need intelligence to function at their best. The more intelligent a species is, the higher the level of functioning of which it is capable. While a feelings brain can suffice for a crude creature, they will stay crude as long as that's all they have with which to work.

Feelings, unlike thoughts, have distinct limits. After a certain point, how would it help a creature to be more emotionally driven? Would it get so upset that it would make bad choices, like tangling with a more deadly creature than it was? I think it's pretty obvious that it could enrage itself right into another animal's belly. In this respect, emotional brains have definite limits. Their one redeeming characteristic? While crude, they were simple and easy to construct, and they were the only game in town. As such, they were the Model T's of the Triassic, and everybody wanted one.

Reason, on the other hand, is as unlimited as the bounds of abstract intelligence and imagination. There is no corresponding hazard to an animal becoming too intelligent in the same way that it can become dangerously overly emotional. One can always become smarter without it turning into a liability. Or can they?

The time of greatest danger for the early mammals was undoubtedly after they first speciated from reptiles. They lacked the requisite intelligence and capability that they would develop in time. The reason for the greatest danger, though, was that they initially did not have a full repertoire of necessary mammalian emotions by which to ensure that their young received appropriate care. If they could not make this happen, extinction awaited. This was something they had to get right on the first try, so we can only imagine the incredible adaptational pressures which must've been applied to ensure that they succeeded.

What would have been the first likely distinctly *mammalian* emotion? In my personal estimation, it was, without a doubt, *love*. When you love someone, especially your offspring, there is nothing that you won't do to protect them. In the absence of any other helpful emotions, love will cause any mammalian parent to find a way to come through for their babies, or die trying. Undoubtedly, many did die, but enough of their progeny survived to inherit the earth. Only love, among all emotions, is strong enough to make up for all the very real deficits that the early mammals possessed. Only love is strong enough to prevail in such impossible circumstances as they faced. Only love.

It is fascinating to speculate on how early mammals managed to both develop their neocortex to its fuller potential while simultaneously evolving mammalian-appropriate emotions. The difficulty of achieving both of these incredibly critical adaptations boggles the mind. The best thing that they could develop relatively quickly toward the goal of buying time for their nascent mammalian emotions to fully develop would've been enhanced reasoning ability.

While it might've taken quite a long time for the countless mutations necessary to develop a suite of appropriate mammalian emotions, they already had an embryonic neocortex. It stands to reason that it would take

242

a lot less time to develop a more capable neocortical capability than it would to evolve a large number of new emotions.

To develop a more effective neocortex would only require more neurons. Lots and lots of neurons could relatively quickly help early mammals survive by increasing their general intelligence so that they could improvise where necessary in their childrearing while allowing them to teach other important skills to their likewise more intelligent offspring. The period between when they first speciated with only their reptilian capabilities, and when their mammalian emotions would have been perfected would have certainly taken millions of years to accomplish, but they didn't have millions of years.

Something dramatic and highly effective had to arise in only a fraction of that time if mammals were to survive the interstice between when they began to bear their young alive and helpless and the millions of years later when their full mammalian emotions would be online. Under what was probably the greatest evolutionary pressure that any species has ever undergone before or since, the neocortex would have been spurred on to develop within a very truncated period. Either that occurred, or mammals would become yet another one of evolution's failed projects. Evolution would not, of course, have cared a whit, but it would have made our lives problematic, as we would not be alive, and would have never lived.

It was in this period, I believe, that a dual aspect of mind between the feelings-based brain and the early neocortex would have begun to emerge apace of the neocortical development. If the neocortex could not adequately communicate with the emotional brain, it could not be of help in saving the early mammals. In later years, more advanced mammals would continue to develop protocols to create ever improved capacities by which to interface between their neocortex and their feelings brain. The neocortex had amazingly capable construction and highly evolved neurons which could be used to create a very competent interconnection area with the emotional brain to further enhance their ability to communicate.

In dual aspect theory, the area which arose in humans within the interconnection is termed "the interface." Within the interconnection and the interface, neuronal circuitry from each component combined and intergrew. Our brains remain that way to this day. This afforded the crude feelings brain the *borrowed* wit to be able to meaningfully interact with the neocortex. It also allowed the neocortex to understand the fundamentally simple nature of not only this brain but the products of this brain; the emotions.

The interface that resulted from this interconnection had been created and adapted as the only part of the emotional system that can directly communicate with the conscious mind and the reasoning aspect of the neocortex. Even this feature of the emotional system remains unable to communicate except by use of feelings. The neocortex, though, had also evolved a reciprocal capability to directly and consciously be in contact with this aspect of the emotional system through the interface between these two totally dissimilar systems.

The neocortex was under enormous adaptational pressure to increase its ability to understand the symbolic meanings behind the emotions, let us remember, so that it could be of greater assistance. The emotions, on the other hand, would never be able to comprehend the abstractions of the reasoning aspect. The first few million years would probably have been replete with bad communications and unfortunate results, one can imagine. The infant mortality rate must have been exorbitant, but somehow, early mammals survived.

Given that this interconnection between these two aspects of mind was first formed over 200 million years ago, however, I think they have learned to communicate quite well. Allowing 20 million years between when mammals were first speciated from reptiles and when they had finally developed a proper interface, though, still allows us 200 million years in which to have established harmony between the two.

Has harmony been achieved? No. Isn't it likely, then, that insofar as evolutionary forces have eschewed harmony for all this deep time, that what they truly desire and intend is a *deficit* of harmony? That would be discord, would it not? Isn't that the secret of these dual aspects? That evolutionary forces see benefits to be obtained through a variable, dynamic tension between the feelings and the reason? Whether or not that was Mother Nature's intent, that remains humanity's reality.

As the feelings brain was attempting to develop the rudimentary emotions necessary to ensure mammalian existence, the neocortex, likewise, was feverishly attempting to improve its own capacity and abilities. In all of this process, however, these two vastly different neurological systems worked out a way by which their relative strengths could be combined to create an entirely new sort of brain; a brain that was simultaneously based in both feeling and thinking. This was a thing that the world had never seen! This was a monumental evolutionary accomplishment of the highest order! A brain that was initially under the control of feeling, but came to ultimately be controlled by a reasoning aspect.

Since that time, all mammals have evolved with these two capabilities simultaneously in evidence. In most mammals except humans, it appears that the feelings-based brain still holds sway, with the neocortex being able to assert itself to ensure the greatest benefit from its reasoning abilities. At the same time, the pure strength and motivation of emotions provides the primary power that most mammals use to assert themselves in their environment. Perhaps other mammals have found a greater balance between their dual aspects of mind than have humans? They could scarcely have less.

Let us consider the sort of lives that most mammals live in the wild order in terms of their two aspects of mind. The first thing that we have to think about is how difficult the natural order can be. In the words of Thomas Hobbes, life in the natural order is "solitary, poor, nasty, brutish, and short." (1651. Hobbes, Thomas. *"Leviathan, or the Matter, Forme, and Power of a Commonwealth, Ecclesiasticall and Civil." Citation #172)*

What Hobbes said in 1651 remains as true today as it was then, for *both* humans and animals. We humans, kept safe by our systems of laws and punishments, don't have to interact with the world on a Hobbesian basis because of the complex social systems we've invented. It is natural for us to extend our situation as humans to include other creatures, but we still know perfectly well that the true situation of all undomesticated mammals *is* the wild order.

Evolutionary forces, mindlessly and unthinkingly, have had to take the brutal order of the wild into account as certain adaptations occurred. As I observe the multitudes of wild creatures that live around my own country home adjacent to a wilderness area, I have far more than ample opportunities to see how this world beyond my windows operates. It can be quite chilling.

Whenever I consider the balance between reason and feelings in a creature trying to survive in this natural world, I am immediately struck by how critical their emotional aspect is in causing them to physically fight for that which they need to survive. For the most part, they do this in a relatively incessant and continuously vicious manner. If a creature is unwilling to demonstrate unrelenting violence, they will not survive. If it wasn't someone from their own species that would do them in, it would be a creature from another species. Either way, it would work out badly for them.

Aren't all *wild* mammals caught by such circumstances? While it is good to have at least enough intelligence to be able to reason through otherwise bad emotional decisions as well as to be able to out-wit competitors, there could actually be disadvantages in a wild creature that was too smart. Especially if being smarter would give less relative authority to the feelings, which really needs to be the primary authority for survival.

Feelings, let us recall, are responsible for the *fire in the belly* of a wild creature (as well as people). Feelings react virtually instantly, and that is sometimes their most important characteristic. I was raised on a farm, and I have lived in the country nearly all of my life in close proximity to wild animals and nature. When an animal survives the perpetual, incredibly common near-death experience that characterizes almost every day of their lives, it is rare that their survival has been predicated on a reasoning decision that they have made. Quite to the contrary. Their amazing ability to get themselves out of tight places with little forewarning are virtually always tied to their feelings ability. This is because the feelings ability occurs so quickly, as opposed to the reasoning ability which has to be thought through. While a very highly intelligent mammal might still be formulating his strategy, he would probably be doing so from the belly of a hawk.

As we know, one of the primary characteristics of all feelings is that they occur incredibly rapidly. Much of it has to do with the relatively simple construction of limbic structures, but much of it also has to do with the way that emotions initially evolved to provide immediate responses. This was because things happen so rapidly in the wild order. Most predators specialize in rapidity, and are designed to give scant warning.

Over the course of my lifetime, I have witnessed hundreds (if not thousands) of such incidents. I've seen cornered chipmunks frontally assault cats. I've seen frenzied cats leap into the air to attack swooping hawks. I once saw a desperate raccoon beat up a pig, and more! What did all of these creatures have in common? They all managed to stay alive by following the *outrageous* dictates of their emotions, not their reason. The word that would have depicted their situation if they had instead used their reason rather than their emotions would have been *lunch*.

If other mammals (besides humans) have indeed retained a feelings advantage over their reasoning abilities, we should consider that it is the environment in which they live that necessitates it. When the hawk swoops and the cat strikes, it is no time to be wasting your time thinking. If you do waste your time thinking, you will be dead. Feeling and reacting are what you do when you don't have time to think.

In such circumstances as these which I've observed, it seems obvious to me why animal's emotions appear to be stronger than their reason. It is because it is necessary for survival. It is because if reason was any stronger, it would be more apt to interfere with completely essential emotional decisions. Unlike humans, though, this would invariably result in disaster.

If you are a non-human mammal, then, you will use your reason all the time to assist your emotions, but you don't necessarily want to be smarter, if it results in your demise. Like all mammals, you want to act and react however wildly and frantically as is necessary to get you out of tight spots unencumbered by the complications of surplus reason. That is why the emotional aspect is now, and will remain, dominant over the reasoning aspect as long as there *is* a wild order. The mammals will continue to exist as they have as long as life still remains on earth, with their dominant emotional aspect keeping them ever alert and alive, assisted by their reason.

These points represent an implication of dual aspect theory to mammals *other* than humans, but what of humans? In the case of mammals, we saw that increasing the size of their neocortex would have almost inevitably worked against them. Presumably, this is why these animals have not, like humans, become increasingly intelligent.

We humans seem to believe that an ever-increasing level of intelligence is the natural path of evolution, but it definitely is not. We humans just blithely assume nearly everything that puts us at the center of all discussions in our humanocentric existences. Our view of the world is invariably anthropomorphic. In our heart of hearts, the world begins and ends with us. Humans, though, not other mammals, are the recent (and still ongoing) experiment.

Mammals have been around in the same general form for over 200 million years, let's remember. Humans, on the other hand, have only existed as Homo sapiens for about 300 thousand years. That means that mammals have existed approximately 666 times *longer* than have humans. Just think about that difference, and realize how much we're *not* at the center!

Many of the other human species such as Homo habilis were around for over a million years, more than three times our run, so far. The species that spawned us, Homo heidelbergensis, were also around for about twice as long as us. How were they as caretakers of this world? We can be fairly certain that they were at least roughly at our general intelligence level, so it isn't like it is only we who have taken part in this experiment. Actually, both of these other human species seem to have left the world pretty much as they found it, even though they were in it for far longer than we have been.

Homo sapiens, on the other hand, partially through our innate cleverness which we've used to create highly sophisticated social orders, have literally brought the world to the brink of destruction. We've created a runaway climate crisis, and created an ever-growing stockpile of nuclear weapons that poses an ongoing existential threat to all life on this planet.

So, I ask you, dear reader: how do you think we're doing so far? How well has this perfect brain of ours perfected our world? If Mother Nature was capable of thought, what do you suppose she would think of us? It would be my guess that she would be mulling over thoughts to the effect of: *what the hell was I thinking?*

It is presumably only in humans of Genus Homo that the neocortex grew to assume executive authority as the primary aspect of a new reasoning brain. The emotional brain was essentially demoted to an *emotional system* (Ouch! Hopefully, at least it got a gold watch). In the human mind, the reasoning aspect of the conscious mind is nominally in control. This unique mind of ours, nevertheless, has made great allowances to ensure that the concerns of the eternally irrational emotional system can still exert a very large influence on our life. We all know that, of course (too well, sometimes).

Because there has been over 200 million years in which to simply disfavor and thereby ensure the removal of the emotional system, it is absolutely and unquestionably the case that evolution has decided that humans actually benefit from this unique mind. As we have had millions of years of highly intelligent human species to test this theory of disfavoring emotions, they've had more than ample time to vanish, but they haven't.

It does seem as we have, possibly through the intent of adaptational forces, reduced what we believe to be the power of the emotional system to a more minor player in our minds than is truly the case. Imagining ourselves to be the paragon and epitome of informed reason, we have favored the reason, while attempting to reduce the power and impact of our emotions to that of an incidental factor. We do this at our own hazard. It doesn't matter the import that we *ascribe* to the emotional aspect of our mind. What is more salient is the importance that it actually *has* in our lives.

It is easy to be dismissive of many things in our existence, but dismissiveness has consequences. If it causes one to doubt the relative importance of an emotional reaction in a given instance, that person may be setting themselves up for a rude awakening when the emotions refuse to be so easily and summarily dismissed. What one believes to be true becomes irrelevant when that which *is* true makes its desires manifest.

Emotional prerogatives must sometimes be repressed for many reasons. This is an unavoidable and invariably painful circumstance for anyone who has had to make that determination. Exercising one's will against a blindly emotional impulse can be a necessity at times, as emotions are irrational. But it can be very difficult and sometimes even painful. We need to develop a much better understanding and appreciation of the true nature of the interactions that occur between these two aspects.

This chapter may admittedly seem a bit redundant, as it is a summary. I would rather, though, be redundant than vague. I have noticed that when a particular subject is exposited from several viewpoints, it can add an additional dimensional quality than is otherwise the case. My purpose in taking a different tack in some situations is to add context in which the concept under consideration hopefully achieves a more fulsome understanding.

Primarily, because virtually all of my theories are radical (in the true sense of the word), there aren't many common referents with other theories of which people are more familiar. I *can't* relate it to another similar theory, as there *are* no similar theories. This isn't because I'm *attempting* to develop radical theories; it is because this just happens to be where my research has led me.

In this entire book, the hardest part, naturally, has been to formulate these novel theories. I believe, however, that they are well-supported by the actual deep time history not only of our species, but also; of the other myriad species that have collectively made us who we are over 4 billion years. In some ways, it was like trying to solve a series of interrelated mysteries. It does get complicated.

If I were to present my conclusions in a more simplified fashion just to make them easier to understand, though, it would be doing a disservice to everyone reading this book. I have chosen not to do that as a matter of respect for the reader. At the same time, I would be the first to say that if dual aspect theory does not at least somewhat discombobulate you, then nothing will. I fear that this may well be one of its legacies. It is what it is, because we are who we are.

I have distilled all of the primary dual aspect theories which I have enunciated in greater detail throughout the book in this chapter. I hope that by doing so, it will clearly demonstrate that they are all quite consistent, each to the other. For most people, though (including many folks with whom I have shared this book already), the feedback that I have received has been supportive of this approach for the reason that some of the theories that I've expounded in this book can, otherwise, easily give one a headache.

I believe this is because our conscious mind seems to have a sort of built-in aversion to fully understanding emotions. I believe that our mind has evolved to unwittingly assist the emotional system to maintain a low profile *most* of the time. I think it does this because it has evolved in human beings to be less obvious. It's as if it wants to stay relevant, but under the radar whenever possible. It's for a very good reason, when you think about it.

When a situation requires it to come to the fore, we give it far more credence than would be the case if it were always harrying and harping at us in such a way as to give us reason to revile it as a nuisance. If it was doing that, it would be far easier to discount when it did rear up, as it would have become the "boy who cried wolf." If that were to occur, it would lose significant power to affect outcomes, and that would place it at a disadvantage in comparison to the reason.

When you think about it in this way, it would be illogical and counter-productive for it *not* to present itself in this manner. By sinking out of sight in the normal course of events, when it does arise from the diluvial swamp of our unconscious mind to make its demands known, we tend to give it greater credence than would otherwise be the case.

It is to the emotional system's benefit to maintain this low profile, but I can't help but believe that it also benefits the reasoning mind. If we were incessantly aware of the constant and often, completely irrational emotional input into virtually every decision we make, it would be distracting, at the very least. At the worst, it would not be so very dissimilar from the sense of mental fragmentation characteristic of schizophrenia. What we do know, however, is that evolutionary adaptations have created us this way for their own reasons, and evolution's reasons are not necessarily ours. Rather, they are wholly separate and unique from their product, which just happens to be us.

BECOMING HUMAN
Chapter 13

The Deep Time Component

As humans, we often tend to romanticize our roots. This book doesn't do that. I'm trying to accurately portray events that actually occurred, events as real as any you or I have ever been through. Extraordinarily traumatic incidents are not uniquely human. Without wishing to recapitulate the theories enumerated in this book, I will point out some specific instances that occurred in deep time that helped me formulate these theories. Hopefully, they will provide a bit more context to my conclusions.

The utterly unique geological circumstances that began in the Triassic period approximately 250 million years ago put extreme pressure on all the animals of the Earth. Unlike today, however, there were not temperature-regulating creatures like mammals and birds that were capable of dealing with the cold that resulted. Cynodonts speciated mammals, but cynodonts weren't mammals. Cynodonts evolved from therapsids. Therapsids had some mammalian characteristics, but cynodonts had more. Cynodonts became well-established and highly successful about 260 million years ago, and that would've put them squarely in the Permian period, when the entire world had become severely glaciated.

It is at this time that warm-bloodedness first appears. The cynodonts were the last link between reptiles and mammals. It would appear that all of the mammalian type characteristics had already been in gradual development in both therapsids and cynodonts. In this respect, we can see it as a series of minor adaptations occurring over a protracted time of 40 or 50 million years. That is the period of time between when cynodonts and then mammals first appeared. This is in the time frame between about 260 to 220 million years ago.

Visualize a species' evolution similarly to a city's evolution, as they both have many commonalities. Both tend to change slowly, and by millions of (relatively) tiny increments, as required by constantly changing circumstances. Over time, though, these tiny changes add up, and something unique is created as a consequence. As any new development occurs, the entire creature or city has to accommodate that change. This evolutionary process is incredibly gradual because it has to be incredibly gradual to work. So it was with the reptilian speciation of mammals. In the fullness of time, the paleontological record will better demonstrate this. Until then, however, we will continue to only get "snapshots" of what actually transpired, and these "snapshots" will continue to not give us the full picture. We must remain patient.

It was a slow development toward what was an obvious goal of evolving warm-blooded creatures. Beyond that, there were many helpful adaptations for the cold that mammals possessed, but reptiles did not. Fur, for example, was a huge adaptation for mammals and materially assisted them to maintain that warm blood on cold days, which was every day for millions and millions of years.

If we assume that the cold times would've killed most of their competition combined with their newly adapted warm-bloodedness, this combination must have given them a surcease from what would otherwise be a huge infant mortality rate. Especially given that their parental emotions were not in place and they had an undersized neocortex, it would seem that they would require a special time in evolutionary history when they wouldn't be under otherwise relentless pressure from competitors. What an incredible story it will provide when humans finally understand what transpired! At the same time that the reptiles would've been at a huge disadvantage, the mammals were suddenly advantaged. Being that the two would have been competitors, this would have also assisted the mammals at this critical point...to the detriment of the reptiles.

At the end of the Permian came the Triassic, as we delineated in Chapter 1. This period was incredibly tumultuous on a worldwide geological basis. Coming out of the icebox of the Permian, the temperature rose to such an extent that 95% of marine creatures went extinct, and 90% of terrestrial creatures went extinct. It is referred to as "The Great Dying" for good reason.

It was the formation of Pangaea that caused the temperature to rise. In this situation, the cynodonts got yet another break. The same ability to regulate their body temperature which helped them to survive the Permian now helped them survive the high temperatures of the Triassic. In time, things settled down, but many of the competing species had been eradicated. If there was ever a time in which mammals could arise without a great deal of competition, this was it. I believe that they availed themselves of this unique opportunity to do just that.

As we know that cynodonts speciated mammals, we are ahead of the game compared to many other paleontological quandaries. We now know, at least, the succession of species, and that is a tremendous advantage. It is also far more credible to look at a cynodont, the successor species, and seeing in it a mammal than it is to look at a typical reptile and try to imagine it becoming a mammal. The latter is difficult to visualize on many levels.

It is a matter of the paleontological record needing to be completed to give us a better reconstruction of exactly what did happen at this time. I have many questions of my own. It is always a joy to find new answers presented as new research is conducted. This is an ongoing story. The important thing is to take the facts and conclusions that new research provides, and apply them sensibly. This is one of those things that sounds simple in theory but can be quite complex in practice.

The thing that I find even more fascinating than the initial mammalian speciation from reptiles is how mammals developed their own unique set of emotions in their predominately feelings-based brains by which to convert them into good parents. This is almost a "which came first, the chicken or the egg" question.

If paleomammals had live-born progeny but didn't know how to care for them, they would've been in trouble. If, on the other hand, they had developed a complete set of mammalian emotions, but were still laying eggs, that would be equally problematic. This remains an incredible untold story at this point. We can only hope that paleontology will persist in its efforts to answer this fascinating question. Obviously, though, this process took many millions of years from commencement to completion, undoubtedly replete with many dashed hopes and dead ends.

In the meantime, though, there is still much that has been determined, and it has been adequate to allow me to write this book with a fair amount of confidence that I am using the most up-to-date information available. It is in the nature of such things that, in time, yet more information will refine such determinations, and that is a good thing. A function of good science is that it is flexible and always amenable to updated information as it becomes available.

Just this week, a new species of human was identified in China. We live in an age of discovery. We never know where the next insight will come from, any more than we know when the next extremely rare brain fossil of the appropriate vintage will appear. The more this occurs, however, the more cooperation between the social and physical sciences in this area should develop. They both very much need each other at this point, if we are to perfect our understanding of this critical period.

Morganucodontids were the only line of small shrew-like creatures to survive the extreme climate upheavals which occurred from the Permian to the Triassic, and thus became the common ancestors of all mammals. Nocturnal insectivores, they were experts at keeping their heads down. This was a tremendous advantage, especially in the times in which they evolved. Tucked in their hollow trees or dens during such a prolonged cold spell, it is a lot easier to imagine how they might've made the incredible adaptational leaps that would be required to produce a mammal from a reptile. Nevertheless, we do know that it happened, and we have the evidence in stone…literally.

The question then becomes: what happened with our brains? What initially began as an attempt to radically adapt to a cold environment over millions of years caused far greater differences to ensue than could've been foreseen at the time. Certainly, the brain in reptiles did not become incredibly highly evolved in the way that it did in mammals, so high intelligence itself wasn't a necessarily inevitable development.

We must remember that, at that time, the early mammals were in the process of evolving many emotions in their feelings brains to survive, in addition to their already existing reptilian emotions. It would seem to me that this would be an optimal time to develop a better reasoning ability. Given that they were now responsible for infant mammals, they would need all of their faculties as well as any new emotions they could produce to keep their infant mortality rate less than 99%. Perhaps it was 99% for several million years? Perhaps that's what it took. We may never know. Once the emotions were in place over a period of millions of years, they would've been much better parents, and presumably, that would've been reflected in their infant mortality rate; which would probably now be approaching a more sustainable rate.

While some of the greatest theories ever derived, such as Existentialism or Psychoanalysis are entirely abstract, a theory about how the human mind evolved could benefit most by actual facts proving precisely what occurred at certain specific times long ago. Although much is known about many of these periods, there is still much that remains obscure. Because we did develop in a specific way at a specific time, our understanding of ourselves needs to comport with these facts.

My theories as presented here differ from that of many others, as I have said, in that they are based on the established deep time history of life on earth, and the numerous discoveries that provide strong factual proof leading to the development of our species. All of my theories that appear here are predicated on well-established facts. They are not pure abstractions floating out in space, untethered to objective reality. Rather, they are an outgrowth of the facts as they have been established by innumerable researchers to date across numerous disciplines. The facts determined all of my theories. The theories, on the other hand, were entirely determined by me.

While one may not agree with my conclusions or theories, I believe that we should all be in general agreement as to the facts. In matters involving deep time such as this, we must refer to the best factual information of which we can be in possession before we make our conclusions. In this case, the facts seem to be quite well affirmed, if not universally agreed upon.

I would like to briefly relate the deep time record of how we evolved. Reptiles speciated from amphibians and were thereby bequeathed with numerous amphibian characteristics. They were also able to do things that amphibians could not do, such as remain out of the water and lay their eggs on dry land. Because of this historical development, they quickly spread over the earth.

Because of extremely violent plate tectonics, a dire situation arose which killed off most of the animal life on earth. This placed extreme pressure on reptiles, especially insofar as their resistance to the cold of the ongoing global winter was quite limited. As a result, extraordinarily severe evolutionary pressures caused mammals to speciate from them through numerous transitional species with mammalian characteristics, such as the therapsids and cynodonts.

Mammals are warm-blooded, and the planet had turned into an icebox. A warm-blooded creature had a far better survival advantage than did one that was not. In a way, mammals were custom-made to thrive in this environment in which others were perishing.

As every parent knows, the more intelligence one can bring to bear in child-rearing, the better the child is likely to do. This in itself provides a reason for tremendous adaptational pressure to evolve an ever-improving reasoning mind from the neocortex. The fossil record is quite clear in expressing that that is what happened, and over succeeding millions of years, the neocortex became ever more capable.

To me, the question is not what we can learn by basing our beliefs on established facts about our past. Rather, it is how can we make conclusions without basing them on such facts? Are we to simply disregard what has been established to have actually happened in deep time? Should we discount the life's work of thousands of brilliant researchers, simply because their discoveries present an inconvenient truth? That isn't the human way. We are not creatures that flinch from the truth, even if it is hard to accept, or upsets established and venerated beliefs from the past. It might take us a while, but we will come to terms with our deep time history, however difficult it may be to do so. To paraphrase Winston Churchill, *humans are creatures that always do the right thing (after first trying everything else).*

BECOMING HUMAN
Chapter 14

New Perspectives

*"The truth is a snare: you cannot have it, without being
caught. You cannot have the truth in such a way that you
catch it, but only in such a way that it catches you."*
-Soren Kierkegaard-

What is the advantage of a new perspective on an
old subject? That is a question which could fairly be asked
of "Becoming Human." When you study any social science,
you are presented with a series of schools of thought. For
the most part, these are extremely well thought out,
articulate, and sensible ways by which certain essential
theories together form the tenets and central structure of the
beliefs of that particular school.

My primary interest, though, was to better
understand how a unique mammal, for very cryptic and
convoluted reasons, became this creature known as Homo
sapiens. Prior to writing this book, I'd been fascinated by
this topic all my life, and have been researching this area
for years as I formed my theories. Approaching what I saw
to be a very broad interdisciplinary topic, I was fortunate to
be able to direct much of my education in furtherance of
my interests. At some point in time, I felt the need to cut
loose my moorings, not from any particular school of

thought, but from all schools and their frequently constraining influence.

As I mentioned in the introduction, I metaphorically worked my way across the map to its very edge, and just kept on going. As I think anyone who has read this book would have to agree, terra incognita and I are well-acquainted. I'm quite comfortable here, and I'm not sure I could find my way back if I wanted to (and I don't).

When you consider dual aspect theory, including all of its related theories in "Becoming Human," I think it's important to first consider if it's a practical way of looking at the nature of human nature. To my way of thinking, the facts that underlie my theories are quite well established, as well as being well-referenced and agreed upon by eminent experts in their respective fields. I'm not a paleontologist, for example, but I've read the works of a couple hundred of them, and I think I've got the gist of it.

That is not to say that they all in agreement, because they certainly aren't. For the most part, though, there is broad agreement and general consensus on the facts. Like all facts, though, they are subject to periodic revision as appropriate. I could not have known many of the facts I have presented in this book without the amazing work of field paleontologists, as well as many other gifted researchers.

Humans have a brain full of various structures and components, and that brain creates many things, including a conscious mind. The brain is NOT the mind, but the brain does create the mind, one could say. On occasion, some physical researchers whose works I have read seem to have difficulty distinguishing between the two, and make incorrect assumptions about the mind, treating it as if it is a physical structure. If one is a researcher in the physical sciences who wants to expound about the mind, that isn't a bad thing, but they should at least qualify their terms to distinguish their meaning from a standard 'dualist' understanding to which many (or most) people subscribe.

I believe that in dual aspect theory, it is in the interactions between the reasoning aspect and the emotional aspect that our true nature is to be found. As well, we can gain insight into how we reach many of the conclusions that we do, why we feel the ways we do, and perhaps even learn how to resolve some of the conflicts that will inevitably occur within these two aspects. It may really be a matter of whether a person wants to experience the internal conflicts that will occur between their reason and feelings, and not understand them; or if they would prefer to experience the interaction between these two aspects and understand them. One could then state the obvious follow-up question: what is the value of understanding?

To that, I would answer that it is always a personal choice. Many people might be perfectly happy to not have a deep understanding of the interactions within their conscious mind between these two aspects. Some people might even find it disconcerting to consider such a thing in the first place. To them I would simply say: *you may want to avoid these theories if they make you uncomfortable.*

Another personal choice, however, might be oriented toward learning more about oneself. I think that there would've been nothing as helpful to me as a young psychology student than having the quite radical perspective which dual aspect theory affords. If a person wants to consider a new outlook about how their mind works, then this might be for them. If a person wants to better understand the true nature of human nature, then this might provide the sort of insights to assist them on their journey of discovery. It begins and ends as a personal choice. This approach provides, at the very least, another perspective by which to view human beings. As such, it is a good and positive thing.

The question could fairly be asked: do our dual aspects inevitably result in conflict in our minds? The eternal answer is always going to be yes. My theories only elucidate the conflict, though, they certainly don't cause it. You can blame Mother Nature for that one. Would it be better to not know? Would it be better to not formulate theories such as this to confound us? No, as neither of these possibilities are the human way. We humans are an odd mix of curiosity, drive, and determination. That's why we always and forever need to know the truth of any matter, whether we like the answer or not. This is one of our strengths as a species. This is why, for humans, "Truth, crushed to earth, shall rise again," in the immortal words of William Cullen Bryant.

My intent is to help others better understand how and why this odd evolutionary arrangement was custom-designed for our minds in the deep past. In my humble opinion, it is better to know than not to know the truth of any matter, including this one. People should, I believe, first consider the implications of these theories. Then, if it is an individual's choice, take from it what they will.

Your emotional system, naturally, doesn't care if you understand this or not. It is not going to change its modus operandi based on your reason's level of personal enlightenment. It will continue to perform its critical work in the same irrational, sometimes aggravating, and completely essential way it always does. It will work with reason when it desires, and it will conflict with reason when it must, as it always has, and always will. It will eternally resist change, at its core, and we have discussed the essential adaptational importance of this quality in all emotions.

It is only the reasoning aspect that is capable of comprehending implications and can formulate strategies by which to lessen the more hurtful effects of a rampaging emotional system. It is only our reason that can intercede on its own behalf, and often, in its own best interests to better interface with its feelings aspect. We are not trapped by our emotion's irrational whim of iron, as we can use our reason to improve our interactions. Reason is the epitome of flexibility, and emotion is the epitome of inflexibility. When you realize this, your life may change for the better.

To live is to experience conflict. No organism has ever existed bereft of conflict, from the most simple to the most complex of creatures. Humans just happen to be the most complex. We employ our unparalleled reasoning abilities to look out upon what appears to be an infinite universe in wonderment, and we find it a marvel to behold. Then, we apply our reason even more and discover that there *are* limits to this cosmos of ours, and we make accurate maps *of the universe* that prove it. We discern the rules by which it operates, codify them, and call it "physics."

We use our reasoning abilities to undertake a subjective study of our minds, and we collectively term what we discover "psychology," my area of study. We look inside our minds in psychology, for the most part, rather than outward toward the cosmos. The search to understand and discover, though, is the same process in both sciences. It is only the objectives that differ. This inner search, primarily transpiring on the subjective, rather than the objective level makes it inherently more difficult to comprehend, in my opinion. There is a genuine irony in the way our powerful intellects transformed the *infinite* universe into one that is finite and bounded, while simultaneously revealing that the *finite* reach of our minds is actually boundless. Human beings are paradoxes with arms and legs is my conclusion on this issue.

This is not only the human situation. This is the situation of all mammals. This is how we mammals have been wired for millions of years. In nearly all of our fellow mammals, though, their neocortical growth ceased at a level in which their brains, while extremely capable of employing reason to help them survive, were still very limited, in relation to their emotional systems.

Except for primates, whales, elephants, and a few other species, other mammals have only a tiny fraction of a human's brain neurons. At the same time, their reason generally appears to be primarily following the directives of their emotional systems, in the main. Or so it appears. We humans have no idea what any other species of mammal is thinking, feeling, or experiencing, and we never will.

All we have, then, is observation, and it certainly *appears* as if their emotional system continues to run the show, by and large. Yet, they still have far more highly developed reasoning capabilities than early mammals. Consider this: if our neocortical growth stopped as it has in nearly all other mammals, we would not have the intellectual ability to understand that we remain in the thrall of our emotional system. We could not even formulate the concerns and insights I am sharing, and no one would be able to comprehend them if I could.

All mammals, of course, have the same dual aspects in their minds that we humans do. They just don't know it, as they lack the reasoning capacity for such insights. How can I be so sure that they remain unaware of their dual aspects of mind? If it isn't immediately obvious to us humans, I think it's fair to state with relative certainty that possums and wombats also remain unenlightened in this regard. Or perhaps, they know something we don't?

While I may comment on the number of brain neurons a given mammal possesses as being indicative of their intelligence level (which it is), you'll notice that I don't ever comment about how that affects their state of mind. That is because no one has any idea at all what the subjective experience of being such a creature might be...none at all. We all have to guard against making unwarranted extrapolations in subjective areas in which we cannot possibly have any meaningful insight whatsoever.

Our two aspects have desired outcomes that frequently differ, and this creates alternatives, and sometimes, conflict. How is a person even going to make a decision, though, unless they have considered alternatives?

As differences are implied in the very existence of alternatives, it follows that there will necessarily be conflict between them. Let us consider that one outcome in a given situation is desired by the reason, and another outcome is desired by the feelings. Alternatives represent two different possible paths to take, of which only one can ultimately be chosen. That is what makes conflict within our minds inevitable. That is not ever going to change, nor should we want it to change. If we could change that, we would no longer be human.

The thing that might change as a result of study in the area of dual aspect theory is that one might gain a better understanding of these inevitable internal conflicts, as well as what impels our species to be so prone to conflict in general. One of my goals is to help people to better understand those internal conflicts that exist, and will occur at times. One does not have to try to understand something to have a happy or more complete existence. Most people don't know how their computer works, and yet, they can operate it perfectly adequately.

Although understanding never equates directly with a happy existence, some of us are curious by nature. Many of us want to understand our world, our species, and ourselves better. Virtually all of the philosophies and human sciences were created for this express purpose, and have existed for this reason for thousands of years. Ever since people first made cuneiform writings in clay and fired them in the Sumerian sun, human beings have been trying to understand the various elements of their existence. Sometimes we succeed, and sometimes we fail, but the persistent character of humanity demands that we forever quest for understanding of ourselves and the world in which we live.

When one reads in this book about the many ways in which our feelings can befuddle and complicate our existences, it can make one wonder if they are worth all the trouble they inevitably produce in our lives. It is true, and I would have to acknowledge that emotions are a two-edged sword in every human's existence. But just try to imagine how sterile and bland our lives would be without them.

In mammals, emotions are necessary to ensure the very survival of the creatures possessing them. They are now as essential as they have always been since mammals first arose, and humans are mammals. When we consider the reasons that emotions evolved, it had nothing to do with adding joie de vivre to an ancient mammal's life, but as an absolute necessity to ensure their survival. For all mammals, let us remember, emotions are there to act as spurs to action, motivating energies, and a powerful force that makes creatures interact with their environments to stave off extinction.

In humans, however, while emotions still perform not entirely dissimilar responsibilities, their actual effects have been somewhat muted by the constraining influence of our far stronger reasoning aspect. While it is true that we have evolved to have a far stronger reasoning than feelings aspect, that is still a very recent development. The species Homo sapiens has only existed for about 300,000 years, which is the blink of an eye, in the great scheme of things.

Although emotions do complicate our lives, they add far more than they take from us. Even as our mind's subordinate aspect, they yet remain incredibly powerful, dynamic entities. They provide us the capacity to love, to hate, to feel deeply, and so much more. Our reptilian-era emotions allowed our distant ancestors to survive in their various embodiments for hundreds of millions of years, and our mammalian emotions are equally responsible for the success that our distant ancestors achieved through making us passionate protectors not only of our young, but by extension, the aged, the infirm, and the helpless.

That is, of course, all in the past, but feelings are as important to us now as they were way back then. What they do is different, of course, but every bit as necessary as when they first evolved. They were critical for survival then, and they are critical for survival now. Whether or not we accept or acknowledge it, emotions are still enormously powerful in our own daily lives, as well as in our human world.

While it is essential to think, it is equally essential to feel. Sometimes, when our feelings become overstimulated, they can cause great difficulties in our lives. The same thing, however, could be said of our reasoning abilities. In a very real way, one aspect serves to restrain the other from establishing complete hegemony that would inevitably have a very deleterious effect in general.

We don't think about the importance of this balance in our day-to-day existence until we encounter someone who has a surfeit of one aspect over another. Such individuals stand out like sore thumbs in the human world. We are all known to others in our lives based upon our individual balance of these two aspects. Either aspect is capable of elevating us to incredible heights or lowering us to incredible depths.

Who among us, though, would volunteer to give up either aspect? I would suggest that it would be the rarest of individuals who would choose to be bereft of either. We have become this way as a result of literally millions of tiny adaptations to our very DNA. We should never wish to change this, but I believe that we will certainly benefit as a species when we better understand it.

Human history is replete with failures of human imagination to see that which is totally obvious. A good example of this is provided by an understanding of plate tectonics. When I was a high school student, we were taught that the continents were eternally fixed in place. We subsequently learned that a process called "plate tectonics" made the *seemingly* fixed continents float about like lily pads on a pond.

That was a completely radical theory. It also just happened to be totally and ineffably correct, and millions of geography books were quietly disposed of by red-faced pedagogues. When, like untold millions of other bemused students regarding a globe, we pointed out to the teacher that all the continents seemed to *fit* together like a puzzle, we were informed (as were you, if you are of my vintage) that that was just a "big coincidence."

Whenever I am astonished by the way some of the tenets of my theories that I have shared in this book have historically been overlooked, I think about plate tectonics, and I feel a lot better. I think I understand why it has been overlooked. If it is this easy for people to miss that which is right in front of them, it is understandably much more difficult for most people to see that which is *inside* of them.

The simple truth of the matter is that parts of our brains are incredibly ancient, going back many hundreds of millions of years. Let us recall that this marvel of a cerebral cortex began its development in the head of a fish. It is easy to disregard such facts. Some people might feel that it's not relevant to who we are as a species today, but they are as wrong as it is possible to be. In reality, this is completely and totally relevant now and will remain relevant into the future as long as human beings draw breath. If, as the saying goes, child is father to the man, then it follows that Hylonomus is father to the human. Rather than disparaging our humble origins, I think we should celebrate them. We are descended from creatures that all had a single dominant trait in common: they were survivors.

Some people seem to believe that we humans just appeared fully formed in our present guise, although I certainly respect it if a person has religious beliefs that inform their judgment in such matters. Faith is an important thing to some people, and I would never seek to undermine a person's beliefs. The facts as I present them in this book are amply cited, although subject to honest differences of opinion. Especially regarding the plethora of facts I bombarded you with in the first few chapters, these are based on the writings of innumerable researchers in many and diverse fields of study. If I am incorrect in terms of the facts that I have used to support my theories, then I have never been in better company.

I think we should be humble because we have a lot to be humble about. We should also be realistic. It is my experience that humility often immediately follows realism. What is real as it pertains to my theories in this book is that there was a time early in the development of mammals in which we had a brain primarily driven by feelings. In the fullness of time, we developed a uniquely powerful reasoning ability to complement, and eventually, supplant this feelings-based brain.

I have to accept the overwhelming evidence that this is what occurred, as I am not well versed in paleontology, neuroanatomy, and the numerous other fields of study on which I have based my theories. I must, therefore, rely on others who are experts in these respective fields. By examining the work of numerous authorities in each field, I was usually able to obtain a good sense of the preponderant opinion. I never expected to find total agreement, and I was not disappointed. Some things don't change over time, like emotions and the contentiousness of researchers.

In my mind, the various theories in this book appear to interlock almost seamlessly. It makes me feel like one who has discovered something that had previously been invisible. If so, it was always staring us right in the face, waiting to be noticed. Some things are so obvious that they can appear abstruse. I think that this is such a thing; remember plate tectonics. Simply because something *feels* right, of course, does not mean that it *is* right (things that feel wrong, on the other hand, are usually wrong).

As you are on the last section of the text, thank you for taking the time to read what I've been trying to explain. This book has been the venue I have employed to tell a fascinating story while elucidating some of my theories. This is important to me because I believe they are especially relevant at this time in human development. If I can help people to better understand themselves and others, I find that an entirely satisfactory outcome to the entire project. It is up to everyone to look at different beliefs and theories, and decide which they want to be their beliefs. It is pretty obvious that I have. If you haven't, good for you!

There is no absolute certainty in such matters as these. There is only *relative* certainty, and that will just have to do. One century's axioms become the next century's charming but otherwise ancient intellectual artifacts. It is good when this happens, though, as it is indicative of progress. If we can somehow just let this unlikely experiment continue for another 4.54 billion years, I think we might just get it right!

What I refer to as dual aspect theory (or DAT for short) can take on an enhanced import once one is aware of its numerous implications. I have intentionally refrained from discussing the many implications of my theories for the reason that this book is designed to present them for consideration on their own intrinsic merits, not on what their implications might be. That is another book.

Having said that, I would now like to completely reverse myself about refraining, and suggest that dual aspect theory does indeed have far-reaching implications. It can help us to better understand ourselves and others. It can help us to become better citizens of the world. It can encourage us to become more responsible guardians of a world that is becoming more imperiled by our thoughtless human actions every day, among other things, but I will say no more.

Before I leave implications behind, however, do you recall that in the introduction, I spoke about how my 14 year-old mind was not at all certain that human beings were rational, and that I'm still not sure? Based upon everything I've written in this book, I am now willing to share my conclusions...and the verdict is...

Humans are <u>not</u> rational creatures, and it is quite easy to demonstrate this as an inescapable implication of dual aspect theory. Although humans do have a rational aspect to their conscious minds, they also have an emotional aspect which is inherently irrational. How can a human be considered a rational creature when a significant aspect of their conscious mind (and a large component of their mental make up) is eternally irrational? The answer is that we can't be considered rational. We can sometimes, even frequently, behave in a *rational fashion*, but that's not the same as being rational.

Ever since mammals speciated from reptiles, the primary emotional component that originally served as a brain has been present in all mammalian brains. Humans are mammals, and that's why we have this emotional aspect. Let us remember that we have retained this aspect because myriad adaptations collectively decided that it was to our benefit to do so. In the timeframe in which they emerged, of course, they would have been essential to survival for the reasons that I've explained in other parts of the book. As our neocortex grew in power on its way to overtake the authority of the emotional brain, however, we still retained the feelings aspect as part of our new (primarily) reason-based minds. That is the answer.

This was an inescapably, obviously intentional decision on the part of evolutionary forces. With such a capable reasoning aspect to our minds, why would an

279

innately irrational emotional system still be present in such a powerful configuration as that in which it still exists? Evolution is perfectly capable of disfavoring any or all of our emotional components so that they would eventually disappear. If this happened, then we would have only our reasoning minds to make all of our decisions. By definition, then, we would become rational creatures.

What we are now, at the core of our true natures, are creatures possessing both a reasoning aspect which is dominant, but also; an emotional aspect which is secondary but still very powerful. In fact, humans are a blended rational/emotional creature that is completely unique, but we will always remain an odd assemblage that is partly rational and partly irrational, with our reason usually in the ascendant. That's us in a nutshell.

If humans were truly designed to be rational, then we would have a dominant neocortex and no emotions whatsoever. Over the years, our emotions would have been disfavored, and being maladaptive, would have disappeared. Consider this one implication of dual aspect theory as perhaps being very determinative of whom we really are as creatures. Here's your answer, 14 year-old me. It took me a while to get there, but you were right to have your doubts back then, even as I have been right to carry those doubts forward until now, although it is not a conclusion I gladly draw. It is what it is.

Implications like this and others of similar types will actually assist us to become more human, more realistic, and more aware of the full nature of human nature. Hopefully, it will also make us less prone to untowardly idealizing ourselves as paragons of perfection among all creatures of the earth. What we really should be spending our time doing is making such decisions as who we want to be when our species finally begins to grow up. We need to decide as individuals, as well as collectively. Maybe, we'll decide we don't want to be those who just take what they want for themselves without consideration of the needs of others. Maybe we'll decide we don't want to be those who've made war on others because we haven't understood ourselves. My hope is that the knowledge related through "Becoming Human" will help my fellow humans to grow, become, thrive, and succeed. I would like to leave you with some words that I try to live by, from one of humanity's wisest theorists and philosophers:

"I would address one general admonition to all; that they consider what are the true ends of knowledge, and that they seek it not either for pleasure of the mind, or for contention, or for superiority to others, or for profit, or fame, or power, or any of these inferior things; but for the benefit and use of life; and that they perfect and govern it in charity."

-Francis Bacon, 1620-
INSTAURATIO MAGNA

BECOMING HUMAN
A New Perspective on the Origins of the Human Mind

Epilogue

"Man is a strange animal. He generally cannot read the handwriting on the wall until his back is up against it."
-Adlai Stevenson-

I hope this book has helped you to broaden your perspective of your world, other human beings, and the other creatures with which we share this planet. Whether we like it or not, humans are the only guardians this planet has, even if we have been very poor guardians. I have tried to portray a factual story describing the evolution of animal life on earth, particularly as it pertains to our species, while presenting my theories in various chapters along the way.

The reason for this approach was to present my beliefs of what our species encountered as it developed, and how our experiences caused us to develop the way we have. In "Becoming Human," we have actively engaged with questioning the very nature of human nature. I have tried to present my beliefs and theories in a perspective reflective of the times in which they occurred, rather than retrospectively examining them from a present-day vantage point. The fact is that the present world is in no way similar to what life would have been like hundreds of millions of years ago, so we should be very careful not to make pronouncements as if it was.

If one looks at all sciences, it is easy to see that they are not always evolving toward perfection. There was a time not so long ago when phrenology was considered a legitimate science. Millions of people still consult with astrologers, and despite the best efforts of NASA, millions more still think the world is flat. Is this scientific or logical? Of course not, but nothing is pure in this world, and science is certainly no exception to this truth. Many things influence and shape the *truth* of any assertion or theory.

Most often, though, the best minds of our species dutifully employ their creative abilities in search of truth for the betterment of everyone. We should acknowledge the genius and perseverance of all whose gifts are employed in the quest to better understand this universe we all share. It is not my intent to disparage the work of others in any way. I feel that every scientist, theorist, and researcher of all types deserve not merely respect, but the thanks of all humankind for the wonderful blessings that their work has bestowed on us.

Scientific method over the centuries has taken us from the level of a benighted hominid from the African savanna to Mars and beyond. It is scientists, researchers, and theorists, not conquerors, who have elevated us to the position of masters of this planet. They have made us healthier, happier, and far better informed in all ways. The innumerable insights and accomplishments of science and all related endeavors have made this world a better place to live.

If I were to have precisely adhered to any particular school of psychological (or any other) thought exclusively, I could not have written this book. I certainly would not have begun the long eclectic examination of human sciences which has resulted in these unique and sometimes radical theories contained here. For some of us, there are few greater joys in life than making a discovery, and there are great discoveries still to be made in this area. They are all around us, waiting to be noticed. You just have to look.

I have thought for a long time that most theories regarding the nature of humans to which I'd been exposed just hadn't rung true. I don't necessarily desire to be a naysayer. Rather, it is because it genuinely disturbs me when the pieces of a puzzle don't fit, or the given answers don't add up. It disturbed me enough to cause me to embark on a pursuit of what I feel is a better answer than the one I was given.

For a number of years, I've immersed myself in numerous and disparate areas of study that have helped me to better understand the factors that have influenced our species to develop as it has. Even as my fascination with the innumerable theories regarding the human animal have edified me, they have also perplexed and puzzled me for their numerous inconsistencies and seeming inability to *truly* explain the essential nature of human beings. Somewhere along the line, I fear that our conceptualization of ourselves has drastically gone awry.

This book is my way of attempting to explain what I understand to be the true nature of human nature. I deeply desire to decipher why our species developed the way it did, and tends to think and feel as it does. This book

284

contains many of my explanations and conclusions. I believe that they form a meaningful, albeit radical, group of interrelated theories that provide a coherent additional understanding to other more conventional theories and explanations. I've always found that a new perspective on any subject is a helpful thing.

Most people (myself included) don't want to be told what to think. They want to be presented with possible ways in which to understand their world, so that they may choose that which they believe. I was fascinated with this subject area initially because I have never felt that anyone had adequately addressed these issues in a convincing fashion. That really bothered me, as it was an area that I felt needed greater exploration, explanation, and understanding.

When something exists outside of the purview of an existing school of thought, it becomes necessary to create a new system of reckoning to properly evaluate it. Isaac Newton[148], for instance, felt compelled to develop calculus to explain the movement of celestial bodies, and not as some perverse torture to be inflicted on 17th to 21st Century physics students (as is customarily believed). Newton was unable to obtain satisfactory answers to the questions he was posing and therefore sought to create a new framework by which to better understand that which he was studying.

That is exactly what I am trying to achieve in this book. I have created a new perspective and framework by which to better understand people (and other nicer mammals). It is difficult to create a new outlook that only *slightly* differs from a widely accepted understanding. It is even harder to create a novel framework by which to better

285

understand a concept that hasn't even been identified! Increasingly, as my inquiries proceeded, I found that my ideas and conclusions had ever-fewer connections to traditional schools of thought.

After having unsuccessfully spent years trying to get my ideas to fit into someone else's system, I eventually found myself (by necessity) having to create my own. What has resulted is this interrelated group that I collectively term dual aspect theory. I gave it this term for the reason that my belief in the dual aspects of the conscious mind are at the heart of every theory in "Becoming Human." It is the common thread that binds them all together.

While my theories provide a different perspective than others, that is not to say that there aren't many other perspectives that also have merit. Looking at ourselves in numerous ways and with different perspectives is a well-established approach in the history of psychology, and such an approach has obtained many positive benefits over the years. I believe that my model actually complements most other theories. For the most part, DAT is not antithetical to anything. It is simply different than anything. In my mind's eye, I see it as a segment or formative element in a diverse foundational structure of cross-disciplinary understanding. Time will determine such things, though, not mere mortals.

We need to know who we are as humans. If we don't know who we are, then we will continue to fumble around in our uncertainty, ever grasping for bits of truth. These bits that we collect, though, won't necessarily coalesce into greater knowledge or insight of our true nature on their own. The only thing that would accomplish that (so I had concluded when I began this project) would be a very broadly-encompassing fact-based theory taking into account the actual deep time history of how we developed from our predecessors.

I was surprised by what happened when I did that. The succession of neural structures, especially, pointed the way to the greater story, and elements started to come into focus over a period of time. This approach of employing deep time to determine how organisms actually developed based on the fossil, paleontological, and archaeological record has not been used enough in this general area of inquiry, in my opinion. In this book, I have detailed some of the reasons why I believe this has occurred. Whatever the reasons, however, this is a golden age of discoveries about our ancient past, and it is mistaken to not take advantage of it. Why speculate when you can know?

The important thing is that we now take all that we know about ourselves as a species, and apply it to solve our many problems. If we don't know who we are, then we cannot become who we wish to be. It is only by having true knowledge of ourselves that we can build a solid foundation for our future. My belief, as you are aware, is that the nature of human nature is that we are creatures whose conscious mind has two aspects, reason and feelings. When one considers human beings in terms of this, things can change in a positive way.

I hope people enjoy reading "Becoming Human" as much as I have enjoyed creating it. Human beings will continually learn more about their true nature by a combination of paleontological discoveries, new theoretical understandings of the subjective processes of the mind, a better understanding of our origins in deep time, and the work of other researchers from numerous disciplines. My approach has been to consider all these areas together simultaneously, and the results that I have obtained by this have answered my queries.

I end where I began; full of questions. The ones I now have, though, are more specific and focused than those with which I began. I started with a desire to better understand the nature of human nature, and I feel that I have achieved my goal. I have shared what I have learned on both a factual and theoretical level under the collective term of dual aspect theory. I will continue my work in this and related areas, so please visit online at **www.josephcollier.org** for new developments, and to view my book in various formats. Thank you for taking the time to allow me to share "Becoming Human" with you. I hope it is of benefit to you in your life.

In the evolution of humans, we have become distinct from all other creatures through the extreme development of our reason. It is the *gift of all gifts* to our species. It does not merely add to our capabilities; reason creates a door to the very cosmos. We have only to open it and enter. Our destiny awaits us on the other side.

Joseph Collier, Sr.
Morrisville, Vermont

BECOMING HUMAN
A New Perspective on the Origins of the Human Mind

Bibliography

1. Hazen, R. M. How Old is Earth, and How Do We Know? *Evo Edu Outreach* 3, 198–205 (2010). https://doi.org/10.1007/s12052-010-0226-0

2. Gomes, R., Levison, H., Tsiganis, K. *et al.* Origin of the cataclysmic Late Heavy Bombardment period of the terrestrial planets. *Nature* 435**,** 466–469 (2005). https://doi.org/10.1038/nature03676

3. Service, Robert F. How an ancient cataclysm may have jump-started life on Earth. *Chemistry,* (2019)https://doi:10.1126/science.aaw6068.

4. Brock, T. D., Madigan, M. T., Martinko, J. M. & Parker, J. 1994. *Biology of Microorganisms*, 7th ed. (New Jersey: Prentice Hall).

5. C. R. Woese & G. E. Fox, 1977. Phylogenetic structure of the prokaryotic domain: The primary kingdoms. Proc. Natl. Acad. Sci. USA 74: 5088-5090.

6. Harbison, G., Matsumoto, Richard, Robison, George I.**,** Bruce, H.**,** (2001). *Lampocteis cruentiventer* gen. nov.,

sp. nov.: A new mesopelagic lobate ctenophore, representing the type of a new family (Class Tentaculata, Order Lobata, Family Lampoctenidae, fam. nov.). *Bulletin of Marine Science*, 68: 299-311

7.   Kennedy, B. R. C., Cantwell, K., Sowers, D., Quattrini, A. M., Cheadle, M. J., McKenna, L. (2015) EX1502L3 Expedition Report—Océano Profundo 2015: Exploring Puerto Rico's Seamounts, Trenches, and Troughs. Office of Ocean Exploration and Research, Office of Ocean and Atmospheric Research, NOAA, Silver Spring, MD 20910. OER Expedition Report 2015-02-03, 93 p. doi:10.7289/V5NG4NM8

8.   Erwin, D. H., Laflamme, M., Tweedt, S. M., Sperling, E. A., Pisani, D., Peterson, K. J. 2011The Cambrian Conundrum: Early Divergence and Later Ecological Success in the Early History of Animals. *Science* 334, 1091–1097. (doi:10.1126/science.1206375)

9.   He, S., Grasis, J. A., Nicotra, M. L. *et al.* Cnidofest 2018: The Future is Bright for Cnidarian Research. *EvoDevo* 10, 20 (2019). https://doi.org/10.1186/s13227-019-0134-5

10. Nielsen, Michael A. "Neural Networks and Deep Learning", Determination Press, Dec 26, 2019

11. Hammond, Constance. Cellular and Molecular Neurophysiology (Fourth Edition), Pages 3-23,Chapter 1 Neurons, 2015, Academic Press, ISBN 9780123970329

12. Paterson, John R., Edgecombe, Gregory D., and Lee, Michael S. Y. PNAS March 5, 2019 116 (10) 4394-4399; first published February 19, 2019

13. Stanley, P. 2017. What have we Learned from Glycosyl Transferase Knockouts in Mice? *J Mol Biol* 428: 3166–3182.

14. Han, Jian *et al*. Meiofaunal Deuterostomes from the Basal Cambrian of Shaanxi (China). *Nature*, published online January 30, 2017; doi: 10.1038/nature21072

15. Donoghue, P. C. J., Purnell, M. A. The Evolutionary Emergence of Vertebrates From Among Their Spineless Relatives. *Evo Edu Outreach* **2,** 204–212 (2009). https://doi.org/10.1007/s12052-009-0134-3

16. Vaškaninová, Valéria, Chen, Donglei, Tafforeau, Paul, Johanson, Zerina, Ekrt, Boris, Blom, Henning, Ahlberg, Per Erik. Marginal Dentition and Multiple Dermal Jawbones as the Ancestral Condition of Jawed Vertebrates. *Science*, 2020 DOI: 10.1126/science.aaz9431

17. Froebich, Nadia. *Nature* 574, 494-495 (2019) doi.org/10.1038/d41586-019-03107-0

18. Shubin, N. H., Daeschler, E. B., Jenkins, F. A. Jr. *(2006) The Pectoral Fin of Tiktaalik Roseae and the Origin of the Tetrapod Limb. Nature 440(7085):764–771.*

19. Dawson, J. (1891). IV. Note on Hylonomus Lyelli, with Photographic Reproduction of Skeleton. *Geological Magazine, 8*(6), 258-259. doi:10.1017/S0016756800188788

20. Lungmus, Jacqueline K., Angielczyk, Kenneth D. *Proceedings of the National Academy of Sciences* Apr 2019, 116 (14) 6903-6907; DOI: 10.1073/pnas.1802543116

21. Florides, G. A., Wrobel, L. C., Kalogirou, S. A., Tassou, S. A. A Thermal Model for Reptiles and Pelycosaurs, *Journal of Thermal Biology*, Volume 24, Issue 1, 1999, Pages 1-13, ISSN 0306-4565,

22. Blob, R. (2001). Evolution of Hindlimb Posture in Nonmammalian Therapsids: Biomechanical Tests of Paleontological Hypotheses. *Paleobiology, 27*(1), 14-38. doi:10.1666/0094-8373(2001)0272.0.CO;2

23. Ruta, Marcello, Botha-Brink, Jennifer, Mitchell, Stephen A., and Michael J. Benton. The Royal Society Publishing, Published:22 October,2013 doi.org/10.1098/rspb.2013.1865

24. Brown, Caleb M., Greenwood, David R., Kalyniuk, Jessica E., Braman, Dennis R., Henderson, Donald M. Published:03 June 2020https://doi.org/10.1098/rsos.200305

25. Bowring, S. A.; Erwin, D. H.; Jin, Y. G.; Martin, M. W.; Davidek, K.; Wang, W. 1998: U/Pb Zircon

Geochronology and Tempo of the End-Permian Mass Extinction. *Science* 280: 1039-1045.

26. Benton, Michael J. 2018. Hyperthermal-driven Mass Extinctions: Killing Models During the Permian–Triassic Mass Extinction. Phil. Trans. R. Soc. A.3762017007620170076

27. University of Leeds. (2020, June 11). New Insight into the Great Dying. *ScienceDaily*. Retrieved May 25, 2021 from.www.sciencedaily.com/releases/2020/06/2006111145 27.htm

28. McIntyre, Sarah R. N., .and Chopra, Aditya. 2017. Global Biogeography Since Pangaea. *Proc. R. Soc.* B.2842017071620170716

29. Clemens, W. (1970). Mesozoic Mammalian Evolution. *Annual Review of Ecology and Systematics, 1*, 357-390. Retrieved May 26, 2021, from http://www.jstor.org/stable/2096778

30. Rakic, P., Evolution of the Neocortex: a Perspective from Developmental Biology. *Nat Rev Neurosci* **10,** 724–735 (2009). https://doi.org/10.1038/nrn2719

31. Davydov, V., Wardlaw, B. R., Gradstein, F. M., Edited by Felix M. Gradstein, Universitetet i Oslo, Ogg, James G., Purdue University, Indiana, Smith, Alan G., University of Cambridge Publisher: Cambridge University

Press DOI: https://doi.org/10.1017/CBO97
80511536045.016 pp 222-248

32. Montiel, J. F., & Aboitiz, F. (2015). Pallial Patterning and the Origin of the Isocortex. *Frontiers in Neuroscience*, 9, 377. https://doi.org/10.3389/fnins.2015.00377

33. Mehta, Arpan R., Mehta, Puja R., Anderson, Stephen P., MacKinnon, Barbara L. H., Compston, Alastair. Etymology and the Neuron(e), *Brain*, Volume 143, Issue 1, January 2020, Pages 374–379, https://doi.org/10.1093/brain/awz367

34. Andirkó, Alejandro, Boeckx, Cedric. Derived Homo sapiens cis-eQTL Regulation: Implications for Brain Evolution. bioRxiv 771816; doi: https://doi.org/10.1101/771816

35. Silcox, M., Gunnell, G., & Bloch, J. (2020). Cranial Anatomy of Microsyops Annectens (Microsyopidae, Euarchonta, Mammalia) from the Middle Eocene of Northwestern Wyoming. *Journal of Paleontology, 94*(5), 979-1006. doi:10.1017/jpa.2020.24

36. Begun, D. (2001). African and Eurasian Miocene Hominoids and the Origins of the Hominidae. Bonis, L., Koufos, G., & Andrews, P. (Eds.), *Hominoid Evolution and Climatic Change in Europe: Phylogeny of the Neogene Hominoid Primates of Eurasia* (pp. 231-253). Cambridge: Cambridge University Press. doi:10.1017/CBO9780511600449.010

37. Yaxley, K., & Foley, R. (2019). Reconstructing the Ancestral Phenotypes of Great Apes and Humans (Homininae) Using Subspecies-level Phylogenies. *Biological Journal of the Linnean Society*, 128 (4), 1021-1038. https://doi.org/10.1093/biolinnean/blz140

38. Böhme, Madelaine, et al. A new Miocene Ape and Locomotion in the Ancestor of Great Apes and Humans, *Nature* (2019). DOI: 10.1038/s41586-019-1731-0

39. Helm Welker, Barbara, The History of Our Tribe. © 2017 Barbara Helm Welker. ISBN: 978-1-942341-40-6 ebook, 978-1-942341-41-3 print

40. Kimbel, William H., Villmoare, Brian. From Australopithecus to Homo: the Transition that Wasn't. Phil. *Trans. R. Soc.* 2016 B3712015024820150248 http://doi.org/10.1098/rstb.2015.0248

41. Leakey, M. G., Spoor, F., Brown, F. H., Gathogo, P. N., Kiarie, C., Leakey, L.N., McDougall, I., 2001. New Hominin Genus from Eastern Africa Shows Diverse Middle Pliocene Lineages. *Nature* 410, 433-440.

42, Herries, A.I.R., el al., "Contemporaneity of Australopithecus, Paranthropus, and Early Homo erectus in S. Africa," *Science* (2020). science.sciencemag.org/cgi/doi.1126/science.aaw7293

43. Stringer, Christopher. (2012). The Status of Homo heidelbergensis (Schoetensack 1908). *Evolutionary Anthropology*. 21. 101-7. 10.1002/evan.21311.

44. Tattersall, I., & Schwartz, J. H. (1999). Hominids and Hybrids: the Place of Neanderthals in Human Evolution. *Proceedings of the National Academy of Sciences of the United States of America*, *96*(13), 7117–7119. https://doi.org/10.1073/pnas.96.13.7117

45. Bennett, E. A., Crevecoeur, I., Viola, B., Derevianko, A. P., Shunkov, M. V., Grange, T., Maureille, B., & Geigl, E. M. (2019). Morphology of the Denisovan Phalanx Closer to Modern Humans than to Neanderthals. *Science Advances*, *5*(9), eaaw3950. https://doi.org/10.1126/sciadv.aaw3950

46. Détroit, F. et al., "A New Species of *Homo* from the Late Pleistocene of the Philippines," *Nature*, doi:10.1038/s41586-019-1067-9, 2019.

47. Bailey, S. E., Brophy, J. K., Moggi-Cecchi, J., Delezene, L. K. The Deciduous Dentition of Homo naledi: A Comparative Study. *J Hum Evol.* 2019 Nov;136:102655. doi: 10.1016/j.jhevol.2019.102655. Epub 2019 Sep 20. PMID: 31546194.

48. Curnoe, Darren, Manzi, Giorgio. 2011/05/04. Before the Emergence of Homo sapiens. 582678. https://doi.org/10.4061/2011/582678

10.4061/2011/582678. *International Journal of Evolutionary Biology*

49. Hublin, J. *et al*. *Nature* 546, 289–292 (2017).

50. Callaway, Ewen, *Nature* 592, 339 (2021). April 2021doi: https://doi.org/10.1038/d41586-021-00916-0

51. Collinge, John. Human Prion Diseases and Bovine Spongiform Encephalopathy (BSE), *Human Molecular Genetics*, Volume 6, Issue 10, September 1997, Pages 1699–1705, https://doi.org/10.1093/hmg/6.10.1699

52. Janvier, Philippe. 1997. Vertebrata. Animals with Backbones. Version 01 January 1997. http://tolweb.org/*Vertebrata*/14829/1997.01.01 *in* The Tree of Life Web Project, http://tolweb.org/

53. Naumann, R. K., Ondracek, J. M., Reiter, S., Shein-Idelson, M., Tosches, M. A., Yamawaki, T. M., & Laurent, G. (2015). The Reptilian Brain. *Current Biology : CB*, *25*(8), R317–R321. https://doi.org/10.1016/j.cub.2015.02.049

54. Moriyama, Yuuta, Koshiba-Takeuchi, Kazuko. Significance of Whole-genome Duplications on the Emergence of Evolutionary Novelties, *Briefings in Functional Genomics*, Volume 17, Issue 5, September 2018, Pages 329–338, https://doi.org/10.1093/bfgp/ely007

55. Lanciego, J. L., Luquin, N., & Obeso, J. A. (2012). Functional Neuroanatomy of the Basal Ganglia. *Cold Spring Harbor Perspectives in Medicine*, *2*(12), a009621. https://doi.org/10.1101/cshperspect.a009621

56. Hunt, S. P., Webster, K. E. The Projection of the Retina upon the Optic Tectum of the Pigeon. *J Comp Neurol.* 1975 Aug 15;162(4):433-45. doi: 10.1002/cne.901620403. PMID: 1150928.

57. Baxter, Mark G., Croxson, Paula L. Amygdala and Emotional Faces. *Proceedings of the National Academy of Sciences*. Dec 2012, 109 (52) 21180-21181; DOI: 10.1073/pnas.1219167110

58. Rajmohan, V., & Mohandas, E. (2007). The Limbic System. *Indian Journal of Psychiatry*, *49*(2), 132–139. https://doi.org/10.4103/0019-5545.33264

59. Roxo, M. R., Franceschini, P. R., Zubaran, C., Kleber, F. D., & Sander, J. W. (2011). The Limbic System Conception and its Historical Evolution. *The Scientific World Journal*, *11*, 2428–2441. https://doi.org/10.1100/2011/157150

60, Tessmar-Raible, K., Raible, F., Christodoulou, F., Guy, K., Rembold, M., Hausen, H. and Arendt, D. *Evolution of the Vertebrate Hypothalamus: An ancient Set of Sensory–Neurosecretory Cell Types in the Annelid and Vertebrate Brain, Cell*, 29 June 2007

61. Reiter, S., Liaw, H. P., Yamawaki, T. M., Naumann R. K., Laurent, G. Brain Behav *Evol* 2017;90:41-52 https://doi.org/10.1159/000478693

62. Baizer, J. S. (2014). Unique Features of the Human Brainstem and Cerebellum. *Frontiers in Human Neuroscience*, 8,202.https://doi.org/10.3389/fnhum.2014.00

63. Dutta, Sanchari Sinha. (2021, May 24). Limbic System and Behavior. *News-Medical*. Retrieved on May 26, 2021 from https://www.news-medical.net/health/Limbic-System-and-Behavior.aspx.

64. Rajmohan, V., & Mohandas, E. (2007). The Limbic System. *Indian Journal of Psychiatry*, 49(2), 132–139. https://doi.org/10.4103/0019-5545.33264

65. Goel, Vinod, Shuren, Jeffrey, Sheesley, Laura, Grafman, Jordan. Asymmetrical Involvement of Frontal Lobes in Social Reasoning, *Brain*, Volume 127, Issue 4, April 2004, Pages 783–790, https://doi.org/10.1093/brain/awh086

66. White, T., Cullen, K., Rohrer, L. M., Karatekin, C., Luciana, M., Schmidt, M., Hongwanishkul, D., Kumra, S., Charles Schulz, S., & Lim, K. O. (2008). Limbic Structures and Networks in Children and Adolescents with Schizophrenia. *Schizophrenia Bulletin*, 34(1), 18–29. https://doi.org/10.1093/schbul/sbm110

67. Baylee, Porter A., Thomas, Mueller. The Zebrafish Amygdaloid Complex Functional Ground Plan, Molecular Delineation, and Everted Topology. *Frontiers in Neuroscience*. VOLUME 14, 2020. DOI=10.3389/fnins.2020.00608. ISSN=1662-453X

68. Schiller, F. (1992). Paul Broca: Explorer of the Brain. New York, NY: Oxford University Press.

69. Smaers, J. B., Rothman, R. S., Hudson, D. R., Balanoff, A. M., Beatty, B., Dechmann, D. K. N., de Vries, D., Dunn, J. C., Fleagle, J. G., Gilbert, C. C., Goswami, A., Iwaniuk, A. N., Jungers, W. L., Kerney, M., Ksepka, D. T., Manger, P. R., Mongle, C. S., Rohlf, F. J., Smith, N. A., Soligo, C., Weisbecker, V., Safi K. The Evolution of Mammalian Brain Size. *Science Advances.* 28 Apr 2021 : eabe2101

70. Muthukrishna, M., Doebeli, M., Chudek, M., & Henrich, J. (2018). The Cultural Brain Hypothesis: How Culture Drives Brain Expansion, Sociality, and Life History. *PLoS Computational Biology*, *14*(11), e1006504. https://doi.org/10.1371/journal.pcbi.1006504

71. Herculano-Houzel, Suzana. The Not Extraordinary Human Brain. *Proceedings of the National Academy of Sciences* Jun 2012, 109 (Supplement 1) 10661-10668; DOI: 10.1073/pnas.1201895109

72. Rosales, Carlos, Uribe-Querol, Eileen. "Phagocytosis: A Fundamental Process in Immunity", *BioMed Research International*, vol. 2017, Article ID 9042851, 18 pages, 2017. https://doi.org/10.1155/2017/9042851

73. Berg, J. M., Tymoczko, J. L., Strye, L. Each Organ Has a Unique Metabolic Profile. 2002. *Biochemistry, 5th Edition.* Section 30.2, New York: W H Freeman; https://www.ncbi.nlm.nih.gov/books/NBK22436/

74. Weilgart, L., Whitehead, H., Payne, K., A Colossal Convergence. *American Scientist*, Vol. 84, May-June, 1996, pp. 278-287.

75. Faber, D. S., & Pereda, A. E. Two Forms of Electrical Transmission Between Neurons. *Frontiers in molecular neuroscience*, *11*, 427. (2018). https://doi.org/10.3389/fnmol.2018.00427

76. Stanford University Medical Center. (2010, November 17). Stunning Details of Brain Connections Revealed. *ScienceDaily*. May 24, 2021 from www.sciencedaily.com/releases/2010/11/10117121803.htm

77. Guy-Evans, O. (2021, Feb 21). *Neurotransmitters: types, function and examples*. Simply Psychology. https://www.simplypsychology.org/neurotransmitter.html

78. Lambert, J. E. (2012) Primates in Communities: The Ecology of Competitive, Predatory, Parasitic, and

Mutualistic Interactions Between Primates and Other Species. *Nature Education Knowledge* 3(10):85

79. Anand, K. S., & Dhikav, V. (2012). Hippocampus in Health and Disease: An Overview. *Annals of Indian Academy of Neurology*, *15*(4), 239–246. https://doi.org/10.4103/0972-2327.104323

80. Kirkland, Tabitha, Turowski,Vincent Y., Man, Cunningham, William A. Positive Emotion and the Brain, The Neuroscience of Happiness DOI:10.1093/acprof:oso/9780199926725.003.0007

81. West, H., Capellini, I. Male Care and Life History Traits in Mammals. *Nat Commun* **7,** 11854 (2016). https://doi.org/10.1038/ncomms11854

82. Adolphs, R. (2013). The Biology of Fear. *Current Biology : CB*, *23*(2), R79–R93. https://doi.org/10.1016/j.cub.2012.11.055

83. A Common Developmental Plan for Neocortical Gene-expressing Neurons in the Pallium of the Domestic Chicken Gallus Domesticus and the Chinese Softshell Turtle Pelodiscus sinensis. *ResearchGate.* https://www.researchgate.net/figure/Comparison-of-pallial-structures-among-three-amniotes-The-pallial-subdivisions-of-the_fig1_261957318 [accessed 26 May, 2021]

84. Roth, G. (2015). Convergent Evolution of Complex Brains and High Intelligence. *Philosophical Transactions*

of the Royal Society of London. Series B, Biological Sciences, 370(1684), 20150049. https://doi.org/10.1098/rstb.2015.0049

85. Cosmides, L., Tooby, J. Beyond Intuition and Instinct Blindness: Toward an Evolutionarily Rigorous Cognitive Science. *Cognition.* 1994 Apr-Jun; 50(1-3):41-77. doi: 10.1016/0010-0277(94)90020-5. PMID: 8039372.

86. Dixon, L. M., Duncan, I. J. H. & Mason, G.. What's in a Peck? Using Fixed Action Pattern Morphology to Identify the Motivational Basis of Abnormal Feather-pecking Behaviour. University of Guelph, Ontario (Received 7 December 2007; initial acceptance 2 February 2008; final acceptance 12 May 2008; published online 2 July 2008; MS. number: A07-20015R)

87. Bergman, Jerry, Ph.D. 2014. Jean-Henri Fabre: Anti-Evolutionist French Scientist. *Acts & Facts.* 43 (7).

88. de Bivort, B. L., van Swinderen, B. Evidence for Selective Attention in the Insect Brain. *Curr Opin Insect Sci.* 2016 Jun;15:9-15. doi: 10.1016/j.cois.2016.02.007. Epub 2016 Feb 22. PMID: 27436727.

89. Titchener, E. B. (1921). Wilhelm Wundt. *The American Journal of Psychology, 32,* 161–178. https://doi.org/10.2307/1413739

90. Picower Institute at MIT. (2020, November 30). Cortex over reflex: Study Traces Circuits where Executive Control Overcomes Instinct. *ScienceDaily*. Retrieved May 25, 2021 www.sciencedaily.com/releases/2020/11/20113013517.htm

91. Stanley, W. C., & Jaynes, J. (1949). The Function of the Frontal Cortex. *Psychological Review, 56*(1), 18–32. https://doi.org/10.1037/h0062790

92. Coelho, C. M., Suttiwan, P., Faiz, A. M., Ferreira-Santos, F., & Zsido, A. N. (2019). Are Humans Prepared to Detect, Fear, and Avoid Snakes? The Mismatch Between Laboratory and Ecological Evidence. *Frontiers in Psychology*, 10, 2094. https://doi.org/10.3389/fpsyg.2019.02094

93. Enquist, M., & Ghirlanda, S. (2005). Fundamentals of Neural Network Models. *Neural Networks and Animal Behavior* (pp. 31-66). Princeton University Press. Retrieved May 26, 2021, from http://www.jstor.org/stable/j.ctt5hhpg8.5

94. Gravitz, L. Animal Behaviour: Nested instincts. *Nature* 521, S60–S61 (2015). https://doi.org/10.1038/521S60a

95. Damasio, A. (2000). *The Feeling of what Happens: Body and Emotion in the Making of Consciousness*. New York, NY: Mariner Books.

96. Wigginton, A. J., Cooper, R. L., Fryman-Gripshover, E. M. and Birge, W. J. 2010. Effects of Cadmium and Body

Mass on two Anti-predator Behaviors of Five Species of Crayfish. *Int. J. Zool. Res*., 6: 92-104.

97. Walkowski, A. D., Munakomi, S. Monosynaptic Reflex. [Updated 2021 Feb 8]. *StatPearls* [Internet]. Treasure Island (FL): StatPearls Publishing; 2021 Jan-. Available from: https://www.ncbi.nlm.nih.gov/books/NBK541028/

98. Chance, P. (2007). The Ultimate Challenge: Prove B. F. Skinner Wrong. *The Behavior Analyst*, *30*(2), 153–160. https://doi.org/10.1007/BF03392152

99. Heidbreder, E. (1939). William McDougall and Social Psychology. *The Journal of Abnormal and Social Psychology, 34*(2), 150–160. https://doi.org/10.1037/h0056726

100. Lorenz, Konrad. NobelPrize.org. Nobel Media AB 2021. Tue. 25 May 2021. <https://www.nobelprize.org/prizes/medicine/1973/lorenz/facts/>

101. Fahrbach, Susan E., Van Nest, Byron N., Synapsin-based Approaches to Brain Plasticity in Adult Social Insects, *Current Opinion in Insect Science*,Volume 18, 2016, Pages 27-34,ISSN 2214-5745, https://doi.org/10.1016/j.cois.2016.08.009

102. Renard, Emmanuelle. Origin of the Neuro-sensory System: New and expected insights from sponges.

September 2009. *Integrative Zoology* 4(3):294-308. DOI:10.1111/j.1749-4877.2009.00167.x

103. Herculano-Houzel, Suzana. The Not Extraordinary Human Brain. *Proceedings of the National Academy of Sciences* Jun 2012, 109 (Supplement 1) 10661-10668; DOI: 10.1073/pnas.1201895109

104. Thau, L, Reddy, V, Singh, P. Anatomy, Central Nervous System. [Updated 2021 May 8]. In: StatPearls [Internet]. Treasure Island (FL): StatPearls Publishing; 2021Jan.https://www.ncbi.nlm.nih.gov/books/NBK542179/

105. Wright, Anthony, Ph.D., Department of Neurobiology and Anatomy, McGovern Medical School, Contents © 1997-Present - McGovern Medical School at UTHealth Department of Neurobiology and Anatomy nba.webmaster@uth.tmc.edu Revised 10 Oct 2020

106. Hutching, Gerard. 'Dolphins - Ancient Dolphins – the Fossil Record', Te Ara - the Encyclopedia of New Zealand, http://www.TeAra.govt.nz/en/diagram/4690/pakicetus-whale-and-dolphin-ancestor (accessed 26 May 2021)

107. Walls, E. A., Berkson, J., Smith, S. A. (2002). The Horseshoe Crab, Limulus polyphemus: 200 million years of existence, 100 years of study. Reviews in Fisheries Science, 10(1).

108. Maslow, A. (1954). Motivation and Personality. New York: Harper & Row.Herzberg, F. (1966). Work and the Nature of Man. Cleveland: World Publishing Co.

109. Zalasiewicz, Jan, Williams, Mark, Haywood, Alan, Ellis, Michael. (2011) The Anthropocene: a new epoch of geological time? *Phil. Trans. R. Soc*. A.369835–841http://doi.org/10.1098/rsta.2010.0339

110. Hou Z, Li S. Tethyan changes shaped aquatic diversification. Biol Rev Camb Philos Soc. 2018 May;93(2):874-896. doi: 10.1111/brv.12376. Epub 2017 Oct 12. PMID: 29024366.

111. Pessoa, L. (2017). A Network Model of the Emotional Brain. *Trends in cognitive sciences*, *21*(5), 357–371. https://doi.org/10.1016/j.tics.2017.03.002

112. Stancher, G., Sovrano, V. A., & Vallortigara, G. (2018). Motor Asymmetries in Fishes, Amphibians, and Reptiles. In G. S. Forrester, W. D. Hopkins, K. Hudry, & A. Lindell (Eds.), *Progress in brain research: Vol. 238. Cerebral lateralization and cognition: Evolutionary and developmental investigations of behavioral biases* (p. 33–56). Elsevier Academic Press. https://doi.org/10.1016/bs.pbr.2018.06.002

113. Briggs, F. (2010). Organizing Principles of Cortical Layer 6. *Frontiers in Neural Circuits*, *4*, 3. https://doi.org/10.3389/neuro.04.003.2010

114. Arnsten, F. T., Stress Signalling Pathways That Impair Prefrontal Cortex Structure and Function.amy Nature reviews *Neuroscience,* vol. 10, pages 410–422; june 2009.

115. Liqun, Luo y, *as published in* Think Tank: Forty Scientists Explore the Biological Roots of Human Experience, April, 2018. edited by David J. Linden, and *published by Yale University Press.*

116. MacLean, Paul D. 1952. "Some Psychiatric Implications of Physiological Studies on Frontotemporal Portion of Limbic System (Visceral Brain)." *Electroencephalography and Clinical Neurophysiology* 4 (4): 407-418.

117. Morelli, N., Rota, E., Immovilli, P., Spallazzi, M., Colombi, D., Guidetti, D., & Michieletti, E. (2020). The Hidden Face of Fear in the COVID-19 Era: The Amygdala Hijack. *European neurology*, *83*(2), 220–221. https://doi.org/10.1159/000508297

118. Stringer, C. (2016). The Origin and Evolution of Homo sapiens. *Philosophical Transactions of the Royal Society of London. Series B, Biological sciences*, *371*(1698), 20150237. https://doi.org/10.1098/rstb.2015.0237

119. University of Zurich. (2021, April 8). Modern human brain originated in Africa around 1.7 million years ago. *ScienceDaily*. Retrieved May 25, 2021 from www.sciencedaily.com/release/2021/04/21048153650.htm

120. Roxo, M. R., Franceschini, P. R., Zubaran, C., Kleber, F. D., & Sander, J. W. (2011). The Limbic System Conception and its Historical Evolution. *TheScientificWorldJournal*, *11*, 2428–2441. https://doi.org/10.1100/2011/157150

121. Lambert, H., Carder, G., & D'Cruze, N. (2019). Given the Cold Shoulder: A Review of the Scientific Literature for Evidence of Reptile Sentience. *Animals : an open access journal from MDPI*, *9*(10), 821. https://doi.org/10.3390/ANI9100821

122. Freud, Sigmund, "Mental Functioning," in A General Selection From the Works of Sigmund Freud, edited by John Rickman (Garden City, 1957, 38-45)

123. Hall, Calvin S. and Lindzey, Gardner. (1998), "Theories of Personality," John Wiley and Sons Inc, New York.

124. Baxter, Mark G., Croxson, Paula L. *Proceedings of the National Academy of Sciences* Dec 2012, 109 (52) 21180-21181; DOI: 10.1073/pnas.1219167110

125. Ebel, R., Müller, J., Ramm, T. *et al.* First Evidence of Convergent Lifestyle Signal in Reptile Skull Roof Microanatomy. *BMC Biol* 18, 185 (2020). https://doi.org/10.1186/s12915-020-00908-y

126. Naumann, R. K., Ondracek, J. M., Reiter, S., Shein-Idelson, M., Tosches, M. A., Yamawaki, T. M., & Laurent, G. (2015). The reptilian Brain. *Current Biology : CB*, *25*(8), R317–R321. https://doi.org/10.1016/j.cub.2015.02.049

127. Leitch, Duncan, Catania, Kenneth. Brain Mass and Cranial Nerve Size in Shrews and Moles. 10.1038/srep06241 *Scientific Reports*. 2014/09/01

128. *Howe, James R.,* Human and Reptile Brains aren't so Different After All*, Neuroscience and Genetics,* UC San Diego, August 20, 2018.

129. Jarvis, E. D. (2009) Evolution of the Pallium in Birds and Reptiles. In: Binder, M. D., Hirokawa, N., Windhorst, U. (eds). *Encyclopedia of Neuroscience*. Springer, Berlin, Heidelberg. https://doi.org/10.1007/978-3-540-29678-2_3165

130. SØRENSEN, BODIL, WEBER, ANDROY E. *The Journal of Experimental Biology198*, 953–959 (1995) Printed in Great Britain ©The Company of Biologists Limited 1995.

131. Jung, C. G. *Memories, Dreams, Reflections.* Rev. ed. Edited by Aniela Jaffé. New York: Vintage Books, 1989.

132. Sigmund Freud Biography Updated:Mar 4, 2020 Original:Apr 27, 2017. The Biography.com websitehttps://www.biography.com/scholar/sigmund-freud

133. Naumann, R. K., Ondracek, J. M., Reiter, S., Shein-Idelson, M., Tosches, M. A., Yamawaki, T. M., & Laurent, G. (2015). The Reptilian Brain. *Current Biology : CB*, *25*(8), R317–R321. https://doi.org/10.1016/j.cub.2015.02.049

134. Howe, James R., Human and Reptile Brains aren't so Different After All, 2018. *Neuroscience and Genetics*, UC San Diego.

135. Hagmann, Patric, Cammoun, Leila, Gigandet, Xavier, Meuli, Reto, Honey, Christopher J., Wedeen, Van J, Sporns, Olaf. Mapping the Structural Core of Human Cerebral Cortex. Published: July 1, 2008. https://doi.org/10.1371/journal.pbio.0060159

136. Hawkins, Jeff. *HYPOTHESIS AND THEORY article Neural Circuits*, 30 March 2016 | https://doi.org/10.3389/fncir.2016.00023

137. Kragel, Philip A., Knodt, Annchen R., Hariri, Ahmad R., LaBar, Kevin S. Decoding Spontaneous Emotional States in the Human Brain. Published: September 14, 2016. https://doi.org/10.1371/journal.pbio.2000106

138. Schultheiss, O. C., Pang, J. S., Torges, C. M., Wirth, M. M., Treynor, W,. Derry, D. Perceived Facial Expressions of Emotion as Motivational Incentives: Evidence from a Differential Implicit Learning Paradigm. *Emotion.* 2005 Mar;5(1):41-54. doi: 10.1037/1528-3542.5.1.41. PMID: 15755218.

139. Bernard, L. C., Mills, M., Swenson, L., Walsh, R. P. An Evolutionary Theory of Human Motivation. Genet Soc Gen Psychol Monogr. 2005 May;131(2):129-84. doi: 10.3200/MONO.131.2.129-184. PMID: 16779946.

140. LeDoux, Joseph E., Brown, Richard. Emotions as Higher-order States of Consciousness *Proceedings of the National Academy of Sciences* Mar 2017, 114 (10) E2016-E2025; DOI: 10.1073/pnas.1619316114

141. Emslie, Steven D., McKenzie, Ashley, Patterson, William P._ 2018 The Rise and Fall of an Ancient Adélie Penguin 'Supercolony' at Cape Adare, Antarctica. *R. Soc.* open sci.5172032172032http://doi.org/10.1098/rsos.172032

142. Blair, James. National Institute of Mental Health, *Bethesda, Maryland.* Wiley Interdiscip Rev Cogn Sci. 2012 Jan-Feb; 3(1): 65–74. doi: 10.1002/wcs.154

143. Kenrick, D. T., Griskevicius, V., Neuberg, S. L., & Schaller, M. (2010). Renovating the Pyramid of Needs: Contemporary Extensions Built Upon Ancient Foundations. *Perspectives on psychological science : a Journal of the Association for Psychological Science*, 5(3), 292–314. https://doi.org/10.1177/1745691610369469

144. Edwards, Donald H*., Excitation and Habituation of Crayfish Escape, 2009. Journal of Experimental Biology 2009 212: 749-751; doi: 10.1242/jeb.021972)*

145. Gschwend, J., *1977. Disturbances of the Human Instinct Behavior in Hypothalamic Lesions* (author's translation). *Fortschr Neeurol Psychiatr Grenzgeb. Mar;45(3):187-93.*

146. Wilczynski, W. (2009) Evolution of the Brain in Amphibians. Hirokawa N., Windhorst U. (eds) Encyclopedia of Neuroscience. Springer, Berlin, Heidelberg. https://doi.org/10.1007/978-3-540-29678-2_3148

147. Tanghe, Koen B. 2019. On *The Origin of Species*: The Story of Darwin's Title Notes Rec.7383–100http://doi.org/10.1098/rsnr.2018.0015

148. Guicciardini, N. *Reading the Principia : the Debate on Newton's Mathematical Methods for Natural Philosophy from 1687 to 1736.* Cambridge University Press, 2003

149. Longrich, Nicholas R. 2020. *When did we become fully human? What fossils and DNA tell us about the evolution of modern intelligence.* The Conversation. Senior Lecturer in Evolutionary Biology and Paleontology, University of Bath

150. *Greenspan, S. I., Shanker, S. (2004). The First Idea: How symbols, language, and intelligence evolved from our early primate ancestors to modern humans. Cambridge, Mass.: Da Capo Press. ISBN 978-0-7382-0680-6.*

151. Shaffer J. (2016). Neuroplasticity and Clinical Practice: Building Brain Power for Health. *Frontiers in psychology*, 7, 1118. https://doi.org/10.3389/fpsyg.2016.01118

152. *Dunbar, R. I. M. (2014). "The Social Brain: Psychological Underpinnings and Implications for the Structure of Organizations". Current Directions in Psychological Science. 23 (2): 109–114. doi:10.1177/0963721413517118. S2CID 146463887*

153. Gilmore Edward C., Herrup, Karl. 1997. *Cortical development: Layers of complexity, Current Biology, Volume 7, Issue 4*, Pages R231-R234, ISSN 0960-9822, https://doi.org/10.1016/S0960-9822(06)00108-4.

154. Laurent, G., Fournier, J., Hemberger, M., et al. Cortical Evolution: Introduction to the Reptilian Cortex. 2016 May 3. In: Buzsáki G, Christen Y, editors. Micro-, Meso- and Macro-Dynamics of the Brain [Internet]. Cham (CH): Springer; 2016. Available from: https://www.ncbi.nlm.nih.gov/books/NBK435755/ doi: 10.1007/978-3-319-28802-4_2

155. Fogwe LA, Reddy V, Mesfin FB. Neuroanatomy, Hippocampus. [Updated 2021 Feb 15]. In: StatPearls [Internet]. Treasure Island (FL): StatPearls Publishing; 2021 Jan-. Available from: https://www.ncbi.nlm.nih.gov/books/NBK482171/

156. Tallinen, T., Chung, J., Rousseau, F. *et al.* On the growth and form of cortical convolutions. *Nature Phys* **12,** 588–593 (2016). https://doi.org/10.1038/nphys3632

157. Sherwood, C. C., Subiaul, F., & Zawidzki, T. W. (2008). A natural history of the human mind: tracing evolutionary changes in brain and cognition. *Journal of anatomy*, *212*(4), 426–454. https://doi.org/10.1111/j.1469-7580.2008.00868.x

158. Marcelo R. Roxo, Paulo R. Franceschini, Carlos Zubaran, Fabrício D. Kleber, Josemir W. Sander, "The Limbic System Conception and Its Historical Evolution", *The Scientific World Journal*, vol. 11, Article ID 157150, 14 pages, 2011. https://doi.org/10.1100/2011/157150

159. Feulner G. (2017). Formation of most of our coal brought Earth close to global glaciation. *Proceedings of the National Academy of Sciences of the United States of America*, *114*(43), 11333–11337. https://doi.org/10.1073/pnas.1712062114

160. Edmund T. Rolls, Limbic systems for emotion and for memory, but no single limbic system, *Cortex*, Volume 62, 2015, Pages 119-157, ISSN 0010-9452, https://doi.org/10.1016/j.cortex.2013.12.005.(https://www.sciencedirect.com/science/article/pii/S0010945213003110)

161. Kotarba J. A. (2014). Symbolic Interaction and Applied Social Research: A FOCUS ON

TRANSLATIONAL SCIENCE RESEARCH[1]. *Symbolic interaction*, *37*(3), 412–425.
https://doi.org/10.1002/symb.111

162. Strausfeld, Nicholas J.[1]Xiaoya Ma[23]. Fossils and the Evolution of the Arthropod Brain*Current Biology*, Volume 26, Issue 20, 24 October 2016, Pages R989-R1000
https://doi.org/10.1016/j.cub.2016.09.012

163. Westen, D. The superego: a revised developmental model. *J Am Acad Psychoanal.* 1986 Apr;14(2):181-202. doi: 10.1521/jaap.1986.14.2.181. PMID: 3700179.

164. McLeod, S. A. (2018, September 03). *Oedipal complex*. Simply Psychology.
https://www.simplypsychology.org/oedipal-complex.html

165. Stifani, Nicolas. (2014). Motor neurons and the generation of spinal motor neurons diversity. *Frontiers in Cellular Neuroscience*. URL=https://www.frontiersin.org/article/10.3389/fncel.2014.00293.
DOI=10.3389/fncel.2014.00293

166. Jon H. Kaas, The Origin and Evolution of Neocortex: From early mammals to modern humans, Editor: Hofman, Michel A. *Progress in Brain Research, Volume 250,* 2019, Pages 61-81, ISBN 9780444643179,
https://doi.org/10.1016/bs.pbr.2019.03.017.

167. Rakic P. (2009). Evolution of the Neocortex: a perspective from developmental biology. *Nature reviews.*

Neuroscience, *10*(10), 724–735. https://doi.org/10.1038/nrn2719

168. Robson, David. (September 2011) *New Scientist.* https://www.newscientist.com/article/mg21128311-800-a-brief-history-of-the-brain/#ixzz6x2zdkZwB

169. Diogo, Rui, Siomava, Natalia, Gitton, Yorick; Development of human limb muscles based on whole-mount immunostaining and the links between ontogeny and evolution. *Development* 15 October 2019; 146 (20): dev180349. doi: https://doi.org/10.1242/dev.180349

170. Cook, P. F., Prichard, A., Spivak, M., & Berns, G. S. (2016). Awake Canine fMRI Predicts Dogs' Preference for Praise Versus Food. *Social cognitive and affective neuroscience* PMID: 27521302

171. Naumann, R. K., Ondracek, J. M., Reiter, S., Shein-Idelson, M., Tosches, M. A., Yamawaki, T. M., & Laurent, G. (2015). The reptilian brain. *Current biology : CB*, *25*(8), R317–R321. https://doi.org/10.1016/j.cub.2015.02.049

172. Hobbes, Thomas. (1651). *"Leviathan, or the Matter, Forme, and Power of a Commonwealth, Ecclesiasticall and Civil.*

173. Montgomery, S. H., Mundy, N. I., & Barton, R. A. (2016). Brain evolution and development: *Proceedings. Biological sciences*, *283*(1838), 20160433. https://doi.org/10.1098/rspb.2016.043

BECOMING HUMAN

A New Perspective on the Origins of the Human Mind

Index

annelid, 36
Anolis evermanni, 143
antagonist, 69, 73, 79, 216
Antarctic, 188
Anthropocene, 74
anthropomorphize, 72
anti-intuitive, 201
ants, 68, 69
apex predator, 119, 179
aquatic, 34, 41, 54, 84
arboreal, 25, 59
Archaea, 14, 85, 86, 233
artifact, 278
asexually reproduced, 83
aspects of mind, 54, 97, 99, 100, 122, 140, 141, 147, 148,
        149, 150, 152, 154, 155, 156, 158, 170, 171, 176,
        177, 181, 185, 186, 187, 193, 245, 246, 286
Asia, 27, 28
Asia Minor, 28
atavistic, 21, 65
attributes, 30, 60, 135, 145, 147, 162
Australopithicus, 25, 26
autonomous, 36
avian, 59
avoidance, 78, 157
axons, 53

bacteria, 14
badger, 230, 231
basal ganglia, 34, 41, 92, 167
basal nuclei, 92

central nervous system, 15, 33, 35, 78

cerebellum, 41, 92,

cerebral, 15, 24, 38, 46, 49, 53, 113, 116

cerebral cortex, 15, 24, 38, 49, 52, 146, 172, 208, 275

Charles Darwin, 241

child, 10, 119, 145, 173, 184, 185, 190, 206, 210, 218, 243, 263, 276

chimpanzees, 25, 52, 170

China, 16, 26, 28, 260

choanocytes, 16

cilia, 15

cingulate cortex, 42

civilization, 208

class, 30, 36, 53, 62, 129, 196

classification, 30

Cnidarians, 15, 85

CNS, 15

comb jelly, 15, 26

command authority, 116, 179

communicate, 15, 84, 121, 135, 138, 140, 151, 170, 186, 244, 245

competitors, 25, 30, 31, 40, 87, 215, 227, 230, 247, 258

competition, 18, 33, 57, 59, 258, 259

complex, 12, 15, 19, 24, 28, 30, 43, 44, 51-57, 62, 65, 67, 69, 72, 75, 77-80, 88, 91, 110, 113, 129, 143, 164, 167, 168, 187, 203, 207, 217, 233, 246, 259, 269

conglomeration, 15, 86, 123

Conrad Lorenz, 80

conscience, 117, 118, 153, 176

Hylonomus, 18, 19, 35, 113, 134, 215, 277
hypothalamus, 35, 36, 42, 46, 56, 79, 92, 148, 204, 235
hypothesis, 12, 74, 201

immutability, 140, 141, 227
immutable, 32, 228, 229, 270
imprint, 80, 87
impulse, 61, 64, 68, 76, 84, 108, 109, 111-113, 122, 167, 170, 185, 197, 200, 213, 253
impulse control, 112
inborn behaviors, 82
incremental, 20, 21, 42
Indonesia, 27
infer, 71, 132
inference, 43, 71
inferiority, 55, 282
innate, 36, 61, 63, 71, 82, 100, 115, 140, 175, 177, 206, 208, 230, 252, 280
innate behaviors, 82
insectivorous, 18
instinct, 57, 61-84, 87-90, 112, 165, 167, 189-191, 200, 209, 213, 220, 237
instinctive, 110, 61-63, 65, 66, 68, 71, 73-75, 80, 81, 84, 88, 89, 111, 112, 190
instinctive behaviors, 72, 79
instinctive display, 70, 72, 76, 80, 81, 83, 197, 214
instinctive reaction, 70-73, 165
intellect, 46, 51, 52, 61, 63, 68, 95, 98, 104, 112, 116, 121, 122, 140, 147-149, 154, 156, 158, 166, 170, 175-180, 187, 213, 214, 224, 271

physiology, 107, 181

pigeon, 145

planaria, 84

plate tectonics, 216, 264, 276, 278

pogram, 31

pond snail, 75

pre-conscious, 135, 177

precursor, 16, 35, 55, 65, 94, 167, 169

predate, 154, 173, 230

predator, 63, 68, 69, 73, 119, 180, 228, 229, 231, 249

predictability, 73, 154, 205, 208, 215, 217, 223, 227, 229, 230

predictable, 62, 68, 69, 72, 73, 75, 205, 208, 215-217, 226, 227, 229-231

predictably, 89, 205, 217

prejudice, 72

primal, 64, 101, 237

primate, 25, 44, 55, 128, 168, 169, 271

primitive, 15, 18, 20, 41, 43, 52, 54, 61, 62, 67, 84, 87, 91, 95, 104, 110, 147, 167, 169, 198-207, 220, 235, 238

prions, 29

processed, 78, 93, 196

procreate, 42

procreation, 81, 208, 240

progenitors, 65

progeny, 35, 88, 93, 211, 241, 243, 260

programmed, 83, 205

protosomes, 16

psyche, 10, 186

psychology, 11, 48, 50, 80, 108, 268, 270, 271, 287

psychological, 61, 77, 158, 285

Urmetazoans, 15, 33

variability, 83, 215
variations, 30, 83, 207
vector, 63
vertebrate, 16, 33-36, 40, 41, 80, 92, 168, 234
vocalized speech, 25
volition, 137

warm-blooded, 21, 22, 143, 257, 258, 263
Western Asia, 27
William McDougall, 80
William Wundt, 63

zeitgeist, 167